Heath
Mathematics

Walter E. Rucker

Clyde A. Dilley

D. C. Heath and Company
Lexington, Massachusetts   Toronto

About the authors

Walter E. Rucker Former Specialist in Education with the Curriculum Laboratory of the University of Illinois, has taught mathematics in public schools and is a coauthor of successful mathematics programs for elementary and junior high schools.

Clyde A. Dilley Professor, University of Toledo, Toledo, Ohio, is teaching methods courses in elementary and secondary mathematics. He has taught mathematics in public schools and is a coauthor of successful mathematics programs for elementary and junior high schools.

Illustrations Marc Tolon Brown and Linda Bourke

Photography Jonathan Barkan: 128;, 129, 210, 211, 227, 234, 235, 280, 317/ Sharon Beals: 203, 273/ Fredrik D. Bodin: Cover, 1, 30, 31, 43, 88, 115, 221, 243, 244, 251/ Kevin Galvin: 19, 35/ E. Trina Lipton: 21/ John McMahon, FPG Inc: 56/ Julie O'Neil: 37, 90, 91, 114, 248, 295/ James Rigney: 314. 315/ Frank Siteman: 97/ Deidra Delano Stead: 2, 8, 10, 33, 52, 72, 73, 79. 98, 108, 112, 131, 135, 140, 141, 167, 170, 171, 177, 188, 189, 199. 243, 247, 254, 255, 264, 269, 284, 297, 301
All photographs of money Bookmakers, Inc.

Published simultaneously in Canada.

Printed in the United States of America.

International Standard Book Number: 0-669-01239-4

Contents

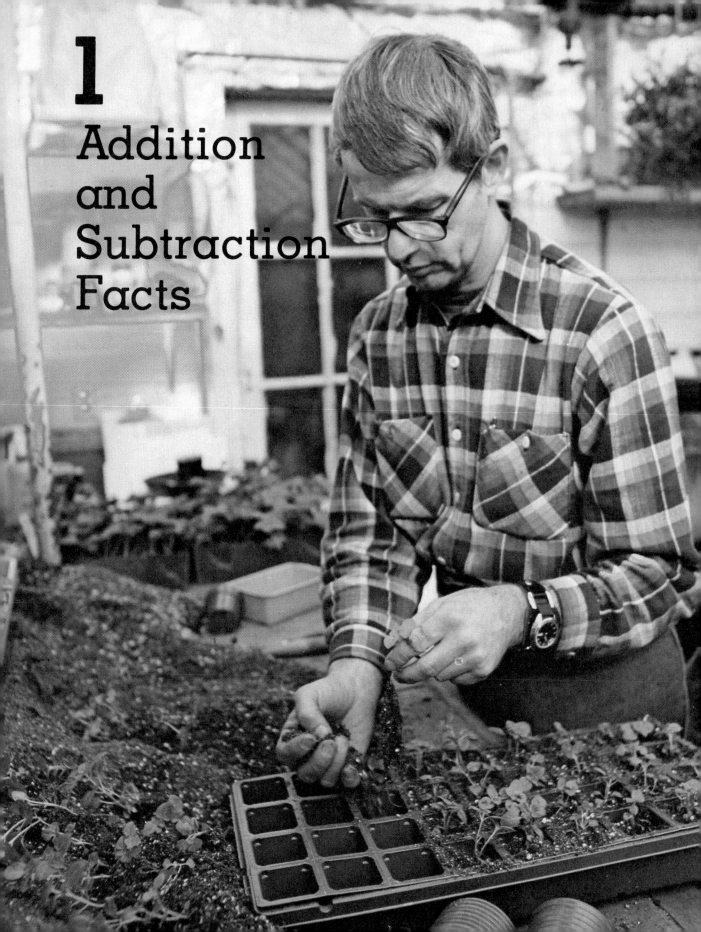

1
Addition and Subtraction Facts

Basic addition facts

The numbers you add are called **addends**.
The answer is called the **sum**.

EXERCISES
Add.

1. $\begin{array}{r} 2 \\ +6 \\ \hline \end{array}$	2. $\begin{array}{r} 9 \\ +3 \\ \hline \end{array}$
3. $\begin{array}{r} 4 \\ +5 \\ \hline \end{array}$	4. $\begin{array}{r} 3 \\ +6 \\ \hline \end{array}$
5. $\begin{array}{r} 5 \\ +6 \\ \hline \end{array}$	6. $\begin{array}{r} 4 \\ +3 \\ \hline \end{array}$
7. $\begin{array}{r} 7 \\ +3 \\ \hline \end{array}$	8. $\begin{array}{r} 5 \\ +2 \\ \hline \end{array}$
9. $\begin{array}{r} 3 \\ +5 \\ \hline \end{array}$	10. $\begin{array}{r} 5 \\ +5 \\ \hline \end{array}$
11. $\begin{array}{r} 1 \\ +9 \\ \hline \end{array}$	12. $\begin{array}{r} 4 \\ +4 \\ \hline \end{array}$

13. $\begin{array}{r} 6 \\ +4 \\ \hline \end{array}$	14. $\begin{array}{r} 6 \\ +2 \\ \hline \end{array}$	15. $\begin{array}{r} 2 \\ +8 \\ \hline \end{array}$	16. $\begin{array}{r} 7 \\ +2 \\ \hline \end{array}$	17. $\begin{array}{r} 3 \\ +7 \\ \hline \end{array}$	18. $\begin{array}{r} 6 \\ +6 \\ \hline \end{array}$
19. $\begin{array}{r} 7 \\ +9 \\ \hline \end{array}$	20. $\begin{array}{r} 4 \\ +8 \\ \hline \end{array}$	21. $\begin{array}{r} 8 \\ +6 \\ \hline \end{array}$	22. $\begin{array}{r} 8 \\ +8 \\ \hline \end{array}$	23. $\begin{array}{r} 5 \\ +8 \\ \hline \end{array}$	24. $\begin{array}{r} 6 \\ +9 \\ \hline \end{array}$
25. $\begin{array}{r} 5 \\ +6 \\ \hline \end{array}$	26. $\begin{array}{r} 3 \\ +8 \\ \hline \end{array}$	27. $\begin{array}{r} 7 \\ +6 \\ \hline \end{array}$	28. $\begin{array}{r} 7 \\ +8 \\ \hline \end{array}$	29. $\begin{array}{r} 9 \\ +4 \\ \hline \end{array}$	30. $\begin{array}{r} 9 \\ +8 \\ \hline \end{array}$

Remembering basic facts

31. 3 + 8　　32. 9 + 4

33. 6 + 8　　34. 6 + 5

35. 9 + 3　　36. 1 + 9

37. 9 + 5　　38. 4 + 6

39. 7 + 5　　40. 7 + 6

41. 4 + 4　　42. 9 + 6

43. 3 + 4　　44. 7 + 7

45. 9 + 9　　46. 4 + 8

47. 4 + 5　　48. 9 + 7

49. 7 + 2　　50. 6 + 6

51. 5 + 8　　52. 4 + 9

53. 3 + 3　　54. 4 + 7

55. 8 + 8　　56. 8 + 3

57. 9 + 8　　58. 5 + 6

59. 8 + 7　　60. 5 + 5

61. 6 + 9　　62. 3 + 7

63. 5 + 9　　64. 8 + 2

65. 8 + 9　　66. 7 + 8

67. Add the numbers in each row.

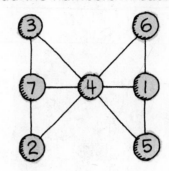

68. Arrange the balls so that the sum of the numbers in each row is 15.

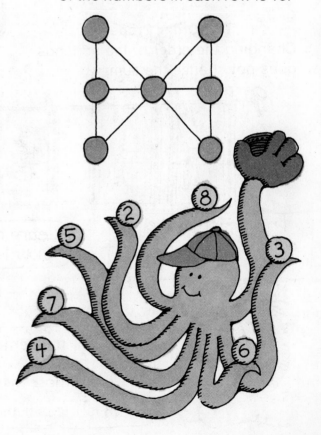

3

Remembering basic facts

These ideas help me remember the basic addition facts.

These are easy to remember.

The Adding 0 Property
The sum of a number and 0 is the same number.

The Order Property
Changing the order of the addends does not change the sum.

I never forget the "doubles" like
$$\begin{array}{r} 6 \\ +6 \\ \hline 12 \end{array} \quad \begin{array}{r} 9 \\ +9 \\ \hline 18 \end{array} \quad \begin{array}{r} 4 \\ +4 \\ \hline 8 \end{array}$$

Learn one fact. Know two facts.

They help me remember other facts.
7 + 6 is 1 more than 6 + 6.
9 + 8 is 1 less than 9 + 9.

SHORTCUT

SHORTCUT

4

EXERCISES
Find each sum.

1. 2
    +9

2. 5
    +7

3. 2
    +6

4. 3
    +8

5. 4
    +9

6. 6
    +8

7. 8
    +6

8. 4
    +8

9. 3
    +9

10. 5
    +8

11. 4
    +6

12. 7
    +9

13. 6
    +7

14. 5
    +9

15. 4
    +7

16. 8
    +9

17. 6
    +5

18. 7
    +8

19. 6
    +0

20. 0
    +8

21. 0
    +7

22. 4
    +0

23. 8
    +4

24. 3
    +7

25. 6
    +6

26. 4
    +4

27. 9
    +9

28. 8
    +8

29. 7
    +7

30. 5
    +5

31. **a.** 6 + 6
    b. 5 + 6
    c. 7 + 6

32. **a.** 8 + 8
    b. 9 + 8
    c. 7 + 8

33. **a.** 5 + 5
    b. 4 + 5
    c. 6 + 5

34. (3 + 5) + 6

35. 3 + (2 + 5)

36. 5 + (2 + 6)

Add these first.

37. (2 + 3) + 5

38. (2 + 6) + 5

39. **a.** (4 + 3) + 6
    b. 4 + (3 + 6)

40. **a.** (5 + 2) + 6
    b. 5 + (2 + 6)

41. **a.** (7 + 2) + 6
    b. 7 + (2 + 6)

42. **a.** (3 + 5) + 4
    b. 3 + (5 + 4)

43. **a.** (6 + 3) + 5
    b. 6 + (3 + 5)

44. **a.** (4 + 3) + 5
    b. 4 + (3 + 5)

5

More than two addends

GROUPING
PROPERTY

$(6+3)+2 =$
$6 + (3+2)$

Different Grouping,
Same Sum.

It is sometimes easier to add in a different order.

```
  6
  7
+ 4
────
 17
```

EXERCISES

Add. *Hint:* First look for a sum of ten.

1. 3 5 +7	**2.** 5 4 +6	**3.** 2 3 +8	**4.** 3 7 +5	**5.** 4 2 +6	**6.** 2 8 +4
7. 1 4 +9	**8.** 7 3 +6	**9.** 3 6 +4	**10.** 2 7 +8	**11.** 5 3 +5	**12.** 3 7 +3
13. 8 2 6 +1	**14.** 3 7 2 +6	**15.** 8 7 2 +1	**16.** 7 4 2 +3	**17.** 8 4 3 +2	**18.** 1 2 9 +3
19. 3 2 9 +5	**20.** 4 5 3 +3	**21.** 3 4 4 +2	**22.** 2 6 2 +3	**23.** 1 5 7 +2	**24.** 3 2 4 +5

6

25.	26.	27.	28.	29.	30.
5	6	6	9	6	8
1	2	4	2	7	1
9	8	4	1	3	2
8	4	3	3	4	4
+5	+1	+7	+8	+5	+7

31.	32.	33.	34.	35.	36.
4	5	2	3	3	5
3	5	8	3	5	5
7	5	6	7	9	6
8	1	9	4	7	5
+2	+9	+4	+4	+1	+5

37.	38.	39.	40.	41.	42.
3	8	7	5	6	5
4	5	3	5	4	3
7	1	5	2	7	5
6	5	2	1	5	7
+3	+2	+8	+9	+3	+6

These addends can be ordered in two ways.

How many ways can you order these addends?

43.

43. 5 7 3

44. 4 6 1 9

45. 3 8 2 6

7

Missing addends

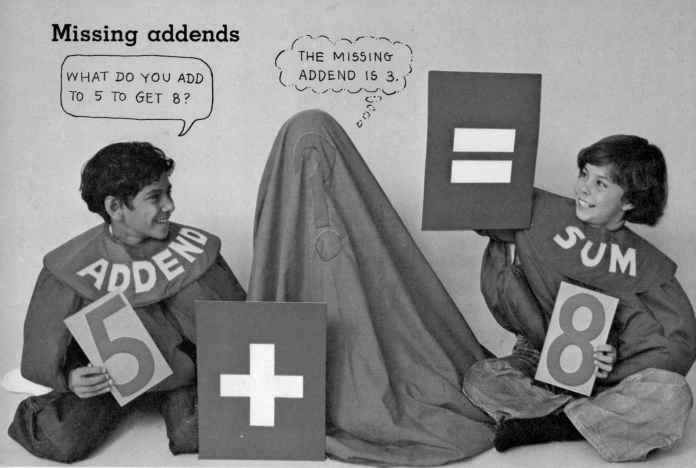

EXERCISES

Give each missing addend.

1. $3 + \underline{?} = 9$

2. $2 + \underline{?} = 4$

3. $3 + \underline{?} = 3$

4. $2 + \underline{?} = 10$

5. $3 + \underline{?} = 10$

6. $6 + \underline{?} = 9$

7. $0 + \underline{?} = 7$

8. $2 + \underline{?} = 9$

9. $2 + \underline{?} = 5$

10. $4 + \underline{?} = 10$

11. $5 + \underline{?} = 6$

12. $0 + \underline{?} = 6$

13. $3 + \underline{?} = 8$

14. $5 + \underline{?} = 9$

15. $1 + \underline{?} = 9$

16. $5 + \underline{?} = 7$

17. $2 + \underline{?} = 6$

18. $3 + \underline{?} = 10$

19. $2 + \underline{?} = 8$

20. $4 + \underline{?} = 8$

21. $1 + \underline{?} = 8$

22. $4 + \underline{?} = 6$

23. $7 + \underline{?} = 10$

24. $3 + \underline{?} = 6$

8

25. $5 + \underline{?} = 12$ **26.** $9 + \underline{?} = 12$ **27.** $4 + \underline{?} = 12$

28. $7 + \underline{?} = 14$ **29.** $6 + \underline{?} = 14$ **30.** $8 + \underline{?} = 15$

31. $7 + \underline{?} = 16$ **32.** $8 + \underline{?} = 13$ **33.** $5 + \underline{?} = 11$

34. $9 + \underline{?} = 13$ **35.** $7 + \underline{?} = 11$ **36.** $8 + \underline{?} = 17$

37. $9 + \underline{?} = 18$ **38.** $6 + \underline{?} = 15$ **39.** $8 + \underline{?} = 14$

40. $5 + \underline{?} = 13$ **41.** $7 + \underline{?} = 12$ **42.** $8 + \underline{?} = 16$

43. $\underline{?} + 9 = 16$ **44.** $\underline{?} + 9 = 14$ **45.** $\underline{?} + 6 = 13$

46. $\underline{?} + 7 = 15$ **47.** $\underline{?} + 9 = 15$ **48.** $\underline{?} + 9 = 17$

49. $\underline{?} + 6 = 12$ **50.** $\underline{?} + 3 = 11$ **51.** $\underline{?} + 8 = 12$

Who am I?

52. If you add me to 7, you get 16.

53. If you add me to 8, you get 8.

54. If you add me to myself, you get 16.

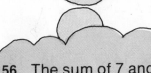

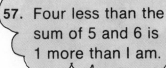

55. The sum of 6 and 9 is 2 more than I am.

56. The sum of 7 and 4 is 3 less than I am.

57. Four less than the sum of 5 and 6 is 1 more than I am.

Subtraction

The answer to a subtraction is called the **difference**.

EXERCISES
Subtract.

1.   6
   − 1
	2. 5
	   − 3

3.   9
   − 4
	4. 8
	   − 7

5.   6
   − 2
	6. 9
	   − 3

7. 10
   − 7
	8. 10
	   − 8

9.   5
   − 2
	10. 7
	   − 4

11.   9
   − 5
	12. 8
	   − 6

13. 12
− 6

14. 12
− 7

15. 14
− 7

16. 13
− 7

17. 15
− 8

18. 10
− 3

19. 9
− 5

20. 15
− 6

21. 18
− 9

22. 17
− 8

23. 14
− 8

24. 11
− 3

25. 12
− 4

26. 11
− 7

27. 13
− 9

28. 14
− 6

29. 12
− 9

30. 15
− 7

Give each difference.

31. 11 − 9   32. 12 − 6   33. 17 − 8

34. 13 − 4   35. 11 − 2   36. 14 − 7

37. 15 − 6   38. 13 − 6   39. 11 − 7

40. 11 − 6   41. 11 − 8   42. 12 − 7

43. 13 − 9   44. 11 − 5   45. 15 − 8

46. 12 − 4   47. 14 − 5   48. 11 − 3

49. 15 − 7   50. 12 − 5   51. 13 − 5

52. 12 − 9   53. 13 − 8   54. 16 − 8

55. 14 − 6   56. 18 − 9   57. 11 − 4

58. 17 − 8   59. 14 − 9   60. 16 − 9

61. 13 − 7   62. 16 − 7   63. 12 − 8

64. 15 − 9   65. 14 − 8   66. 17 − 9

67. 11 − 7   68. 12 − 4   69. 12 − 7

70. 14 − 7   71. 13 − 5   72. 16 − 8

Addition and subtraction

YOUR ATTENTION PLEASE

Do the work inside the grouping symbols first.

$(5 - 2) - 2 = 1$

$5 - (2 - 2) = 5$

EXERCISES
Compute.

1. $(5 + 3) + 2$ 2. $(6 - 3) - 1$ 3. $(8 + 2) - 5$

4. $(7 - 2) + 5$ 5. $(6 + 3) - 4$ 6. $(12 - 4) + 6$

7. $(15 - 6) - 4$ 8. $15 - (6 - 4)$ 9. $(14 - 8) + 6$

10. $(2 + 6) + 3$ 11. $2 + (6 + 3)$ 12. $(13 - 8) + 8$

Find the missing numbers.

13. $8 + 3 = 5 + \underline{?}$ 14. $6 + 8 = 7 + \underline{?}$ 15. $5 + 9 = 9 + \underline{?}$

16. $3 + \underline{?} = 6 + 5$ 17. $4 + \underline{?} = 5 + 8$ 18. $7 + \underline{?} = 8 + 8$

19. $13 - 9 = 7 - \underline{?}$ 20. $15 - 6 = 11 - \underline{?}$ 21. $14 - 8 = 9 - \underline{?}$

22. $8 - \underline{?} = 11 - 5$ 23. $10 - \underline{?} = 14 - 6$ 24. $17 - \underline{?} = 11 - 3$

25. $5 + 3 = 14 - \underline{?}$ 26. $13 - 6 = 3 + \underline{?}$ 27. $6 + 3 = 12 - \underline{?}$

28. $15 - \underline{?} = 4 + 5$ 29. $7 + \underline{?} = 12 - 3$ 30. $13 - \underline{?} = 4 + 4$

Skill Game

target **8** number

TEAM A

TEAM B

3 4 7

**Use only addition and subtraction.
Can you use the three numbers to
build the target number?**

1. target number **6** (8-4)+2

   8 2 4

2. target number **3**

   5 8 2

3. target number **5**

   7 4 6

4. target number **4**

   5 6 8

5. target number **8**

   4 6 0

6. target number **2**

   7 0 9

Play the game.

1. Prepare number cards for 0 through 9.
2. Choose a leader.
3. Divide the class into two teams, team A and team B.
4. Without looking, the leader picks a target-number card and 3 other cards.
5. If team A can build the target number using the other three numbers, it scores 1 point.
6. The leader chooses new cards, and the next team plays.
7. The first team to get 12 points wins the game.

Problem solving

The numerals have been covered. Follow the steps to tell whether you would add or subtract to solve the problem.

Step 1. Read the problem.

Step 2. What facts are given?

Step 3. What is the question?

Step 4. Add or subtract?

Tell what you would do to solve the problem.

1. Greg had ▇ ✎

   He broke ▇ ✎.

   How many did he have left?

2. Mrs. Allen carried ▇ 🪵

   Ruth carried ▇ 🪵.

   How many did they carry?

3. Jill dug up ▇ 🐛.

   Greg dug up ▇ 🐛.

   How many more did Jill dig up?

4. Jill caught ▇ 🐟.

   Greg caught ▇ 🐟.

   How many did they catch in all?

5. Mr. Allen baked ▇ 🍞.

   They ate ▇ 🍞.

   How many were left?

6. Mrs. Allen ate ▇ 🍞.

   Greg ate ▇ 🍞.

   How many more did Greg eat?

Solve.

7. Jill rowed 3 hours, and Greg rowed 2 hours. How many hours did they row in all?

8. Mrs. Allen saw 6 red squirrels and 8 gray squirrels. How many squirrels did she see in all?

9. Greg gathered 17 pieces of firewood, and Jill gathered 9. How many more pieces did Greg gather?

10. Mr. Allen took 13 fishhooks and lost 4 of them. How many did he have left?

✶11. Mr. Allen caught 16 fish and threw 7 back. Then he gave 3 fish away. How many fish did he have left?

✶12. Mrs. Allen had 8 eggs and bought 6 more. They ate 5 eggs for breakfast. How many were left?

Make up a story.

Number News

$8 + 4 = 12$

CHAPTER CHECKUP

Give each sum. [pages 2–5]

1. 5 +8	2. 9 +6	3. 7 +7	4. 3 +9	5. 9 +5	6. 6 +9
7. 4 +9	8. 8 +6	9. 8 +8	10. 4 +8	11. 5 +6	12. 9 +7
13. 9 +9	14. 4 +7	15. 6 +6	16. 8 +7	17. 6 +7	18. 6 +8

19. 5 + 9   20. 8 + 9   21. 6 + 9

22. 9 + 8   23. 7 + 8   24. 7 + 9

Give each difference. [pages 10–11]

25. 15 − 8	26. 11 − 8	27. 14 − 7	28. 13 − 8	29. 14 − 5	30. 16 − 8
31. 12 − 9	32. 16 − 7	33. 12 − 6	34. 17 − 9	35. 11 − 7	36. 15 − 6
37. 17 − 8	38. 12 − 8	39. 14 − 8	40. 13 − 6	41. 11 − 9	42. 13 − 9

43. 14 − 6   44. 18 − 9   45. 14 − 9

46. 15 − 9   47. 15 − 7   48. 16 − 9

Solve. [pages 14–15]

49. Randy had 9 baseball cards, and Sarah had 6. How many cards did they have together?

50. Beth had 16 baseball cards, and Jon had 7. How many more cards did Beth have than Jon?

Project

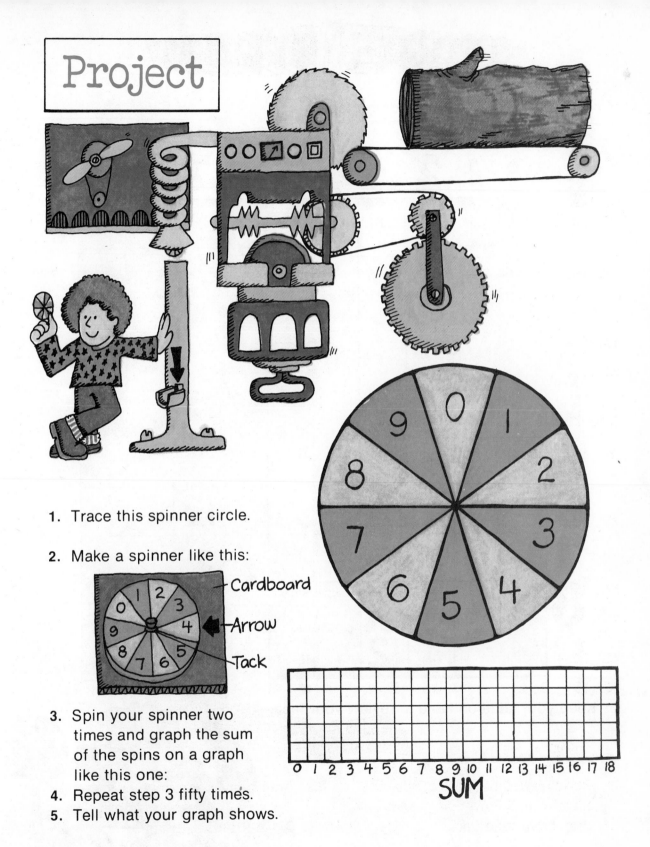

1. Trace this spinner circle.

2. Make a spinner like this:

   Cardboard
   Arrow
   Tack

3. Spin your spinner two times and graph the sum of the spins on a graph like this one:

4. Repeat step 3 fifty times.

5. Tell what your graph shows.

0 1 2 3 4 5 6 7 8 9 10 11 12 13 14 15 16 17 18
SUM

CHAPTER REVIEW

1. Copy and complete this addition table.

+	0	1	2	3	4	5	6	7	8	9
0	0									
1										
2										
3										
4				7						
5										
6								13		
7										
8										
9			12							

2. Keep your addition table to review your facts.

18

CHAPTER CHALLENGE

Copy and complete.
Add across. Add down.

1.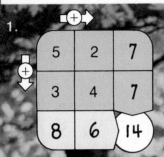

⊕→		
5	2	7
3	4	7
8	6	14

2.

⊕→		
3	?	7
?	2	8
?	?	?

Subtract across. Subtract down.

3.

⊖→		
15	6	?
8	2	?
?	?	?

4.

⊖→		
17	?	9
?	3	?
8	?	?

Add across. Subtract down.

5.

⊕→		
9	6	?
3	4	?
?	?	?

6.

⊕→		
9	8	?
3	5	?
?	?	?

7.

⊕→		
?	5	13
2	?	6
?	?	?

8.

⊕→		
7	?	9
?	?	?
4	?	5

Form W

13 a b c d
14 a b c d
15 a b c

33 a b c d
34 a b c d

a b c

13 a b c d
14 a b c d

c d

a b c

3 a b c d
4 a b c d

a b c

29 a b c d
30 a b c d
31 a b c d

MAJOR CHECKUP
Standardized Format

Choose the correct letter.

1. Complete.

$7 + 3 = \underline{?}$

a. 4
b. 10
c. 9
d. none of these

2. Complete.

$6 + \underline{?} = 9$

a. 3
b. 15
c. 16
d. none of these

3. Subtract.

16
− 7

a. 9
b. 7
c. 8
d. none of these

4. Add.

3
4
+6

a. 10
b. 12
c. 14
d. none of these

5. Add.

2
7
+8

a. 16
b. 17
c. 18
d. none of these

6. Subtract.

9
− 5

a. 5
b. 3
c. 4
d. none of these

7. Complete.

$9 + \underline{?} = 13$

a. 4
b. 3
c. 5
d. none of these

8. Complete.

$5 + \underline{?} = 6$

a. 11
b. 1
c. 12
d. none of these

9. Add.

$9 + 7$

a. 16
b. 15
c. 2
d. none of these

10. What is 3 more than 8?

a. 5
b. 12
c. 11
d. none of these

11. Subtract.

$12 - 7$

a. 6
b. 5
c. 9
d. none of these

12. Add.

$1 + 5 + 9$

a. 15
b. 17
c. 14
d. none of these

20

2
Place
Value

Hundreds

We use the digits 0, 1, 2, 3, 4, 5, 6, 7, 8, 9 in our place-value system to tell how many blocks.

583 ← Standard numeral

The 5 stands for 5 hundreds, or 500.

The 8 stands for 8 tens, or 80.

The 3 stands for 3 ones, or 3.

Hundreds	Tens	Ones
5	8	3

five hundred eighty-three

EXERCISES

How many blocks?

1.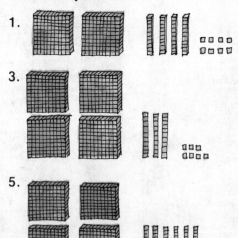

2.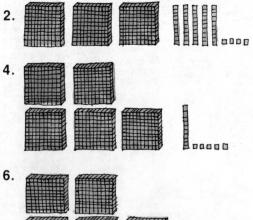

3.

4.

5.

6.

22

What does the red digit stand for?
Give two answers.

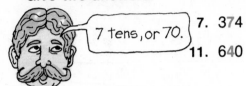
7 tens, or 70.

7. 3**7**4

8. 5**9**6

9. **7**08

10. 3**1**2

11. 6**4**0

12. 6**6**6

13. 6**6**6

14. **6**66

Give the standard numeral.

15. forty-three

16. one hundred twenty-four

17. three hundred thirty-eight

18. three hundred eight

19. six hundred twelve

20. eight hundred fifty-six

21. nine hundred seventy

22. four hundred twenty-two

23. five hundred fifty-five

24. two hundred thirteen

Write in words.

25. 400

26. 430

27. 436

28. 375

29. 621

30. 511

31. 819

32. 370

33. 506

34. 617

35. 720

36. 957

Give each score.

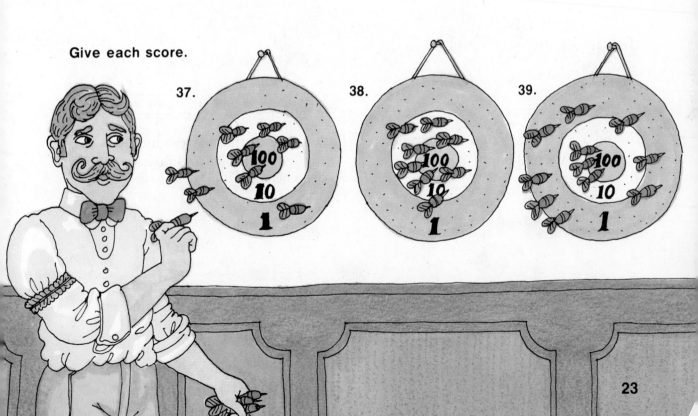

37.

38.

39.

Rounding

Here is how to round numbers to the nearest ten.

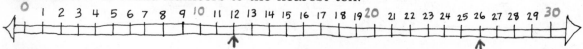

Round 12 to the nearest ten.
12 is between 10 and 20.
It is nearer 10.
So, round to 10.

Round 26 to the nearest ten.
26 is between 20 and 30.
It is nearer 30.
So, round to 30.

HOLD IT!

When the number is halfway between, round up.

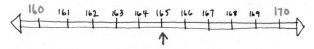

Round 165 to the nearest ten.
165 is halfway between 160 and 170.
So, round to 170.

Here is how to round numbers to the nearest hundred.

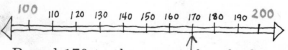

Round 170 to the nearest hundred.
170 is between 100 and 200.
It is nearer 200.
So, round to 200.

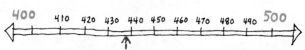

Round 438 to the nearest hundred.
438 is between 400 and 500.
It is nearer 400.
So, round to 400.

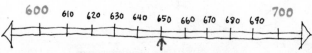

Round 650 to the nearest hundred.
650 is halfway between 600 and 700.
So, round to 700.

EXERCISES

Round to the nearest ten.

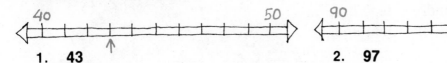

1. **43**

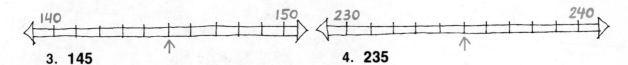

2. **97**

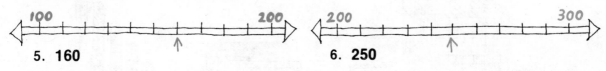

3. **145**

4. **235**

Round to the nearest hundred.

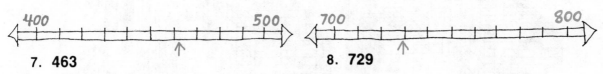

5. **160**

6. **250**

7. **463**

8. **729**

Round to the nearest ten.			Round to the nearest hundred.		
9. 8	10. 17	11. 31	18. 54	19. 176	20. 219
12. 40	13. 96	14. 105	21. 450	22. 501	23. 349
15. 238	16. 421	17. 995	24. 729	25. 851	26. 950

Keeping Skills Sharp

1. 3 +8	2. 5 +7	3. 7 +7	4. 4 +8	5. 9 +4	6. 5 +9
7. 9 +3	8. 8 +8	9. 7 +5	10. 9 +5	11. 8 +4	12. 7 +8
13. 9 +6	14. 6 +7	15. 6 +8	16. 9 +9	17. 8 +5	18. 7 +9
19. 8 +9	20. 3 +9	21. 6 +6	22. 8 +7	23. 4 +9	24. 5 +6

Thousands

When you put 10 hundreds together,
you get a large block of 1 thousand.

10 hundreds = 1 thousand = 1000

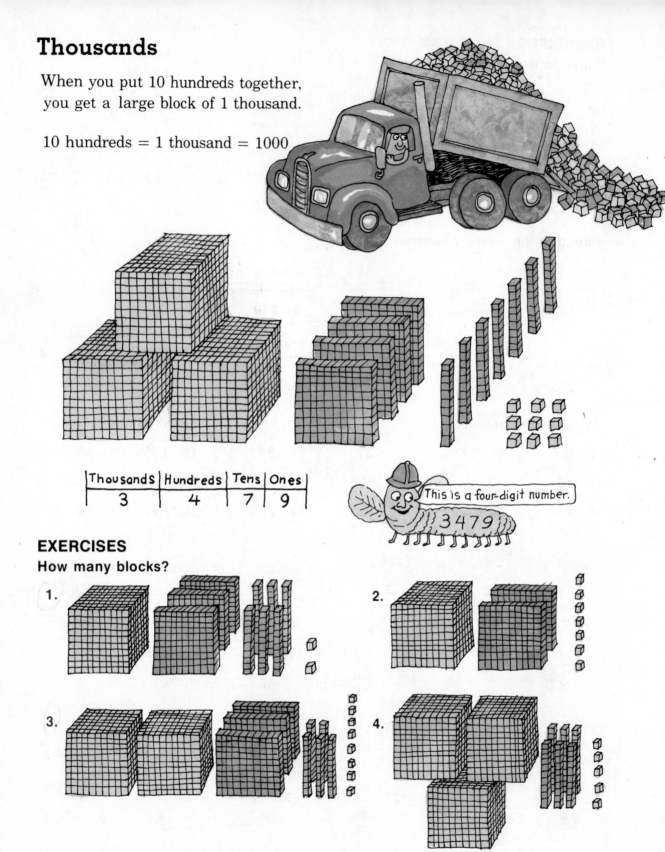

Thousands	Hundreds	Tens	Ones
3	4	7	9

This is a four-digit number.

3479

EXERCISES

How many blocks?

1.

2.

3.

4.

26

What does the red digit stand for?
Give two answers.

5. 3821   6. 5604   7. 9715   8. 7392

9. 8615   10. 2911   11. 8362   12. 9541

13. 2222   14. 2222   15. 2222   16. 2222

Build a numeral.

17. 4 in the **tens** place
6 in the **ones** place
7 in the **thousands** place
3 in the **hundreds** place

18. 2 in the **hundreds** place
5 in the **tens** place
9 in the **ones** place
4 in the **thousands** place

19. 6 in the **ones** place
1 in the **thousands** place
7 in the **tens** place
4 in the **hundreds** place

20. 2 in the **ones** place
5 in the **hundreds** place
3 in the **thousands** place
8 in the **tens** place

Give the standard numeral.

21. eight thousand five hundred fifty-four

22. six thousand two hundred ninety-three

23. five thousand four hundred eleven

24. two thousand six hundred twenty

25. four thousand five hundred seven

26. nine thousand thirty-five

Write in words.

27. 5000   28. 5300   29. 5380   30. 5386

31. 7802   32. 9051   33. 3012   34. 6009

Thousands

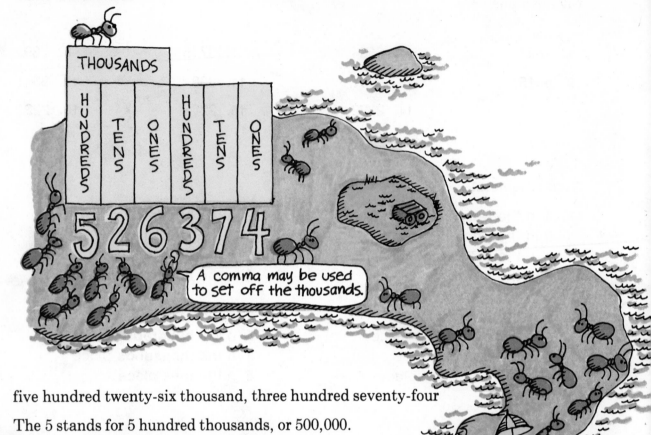

five hundred twenty-six thousand, three hundred seventy-four

The 5 stands for 5 hundred thousands, or 500,000.

The 2 stands for 2 ten thousands, or 20,000.

The 6 stands for 6 thousands, or 6000.

EXERCISES
Read each numeral.

1. 3217
2. 74,286
3. 539,160
4. 26,358
5. 473,519
6. 682,307
7. 85,620
8. 34,316
9. 52,086
10. 129,340
11. 610,725
12. 736,130
13. 405,274
14. 342,070
15. 250,300
16. 510,000
17. 946,003
18. 804,012
19. 606,600
20. 660,060
21. 600,606

Study this 6-digit numeral.

783,425

Give the digit that is in the

22. hundreds place.

23. tens place.

24. thousands place.

25. hundred thousands place.

26. ones place.

27. ten thousands place.

What does the red digit stand for?
Give two answers.

28. 16,753   29. 52,814   30. 96,360   31. 59,840

32. 444,444   33. 444,444   34. 444,444   35. 444,444

Give the standard numeral.

36. twenty-six thousand, four hundred sixty-two

37. five hundred seventy-two thousand, two hundred ten

38. six hundred forty thousand, one hundred twelve

39. nineteen thousand, sixty-one

Write in words.

40. 72,346   41. 59,307   42. 82,150   43. 65,040

44. 378,162   45. 829,460   46. 703,401   47. 800,075

Using numbers

Richard and Susan visited the Statue of Liberty. They learned many number facts about the Statue of Liberty.

Read each fact. Then write the standard numeral.

1. France gave the statue to the United States in eighteen hundred thirty-five.

2. It arrived in New York City in two hundred fourteen packing crates.

3. Workmen put the statue together in about three thousand seven hundred sixty days.

4. The statue weighs four hundred fifty thousand pounds.

5. The total cost was five hundred thousand dollars.

6. Richard and Susan climbed three hundred thirty-five steps to get to the head of the statue.

7. They counted thirty-six people in the head.

8. They had never seen such a large statue. The length of the index finger is ninety-six inches.

9. The length of the arm is one hundred ninety-seven inches.

10. The nose is as long as Susan is tall, fifty-four inches.

Keeping Skills Sharp

1. 12 – 8	2. 13 – 4
3. 14 – 7	4. 13 – 5
5. 13 – 9	6. 15 – 6
7. 15 – 9	8. 13 – 8
9. 11 – 2	10. 15 – 8
11. 17 – 8	12. 11 – 5
13. 11 – 9	14. 16 – 7
15. 14 – 8	16. 13 – 6
17. 14 – 5	18. 16 – 8

Comparing numbers

Notice that the symbol points out the smaller number.

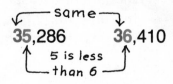

$52 <$ IS LESS THAN 54

38 IS GREATER THAN > 30

Here is how to compare 35,286 and 36,410.

Step 1. Compare the digits in the ten thousands place.

Step 2. Compare the digits in the thousands place.

same

35,286   36,410

5 is less than 6

So, $35,286 < 36,410$

EXAMPLE 2. Compare 652,834 and 652,095.

Start in the hundred thousands place and compare the digits.

652,834   652,095

8 is greater than 0

So, $652,834 > 652,095$

EXERCISES

Less than ($<$) or greater than ($>$)?

1. 59 ● 58

2. 829 ● 836

3. 743 ● 745

4. 7346 ● 7410

5. 5382 ● 5374

6. 9346 ● 8123

7. 53,742 ● 53,821

8. 69,385 ● 60,381

9. 42,478 ● 42,500

10. 274,369 ● 235,782

11. 763,510 ● 763,780

12. 593,261 ● 593,099

Give the number that is 1 hundred more.

13. 37,829

14. 53,421

15. 635,274

★16. 538,975

Give the number that is 10 thousand more.

17. 43,782

18. 53,176

19. 39,053

★20. 102,746

Which number is greatest?

1.

528613 813652 586213

2.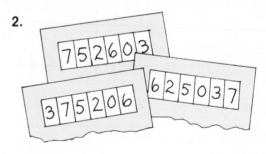

752603 625037 375206

Play the game.

1. Prepare ten cards, each with a different digit on it.

2. On a piece of paper, each player makes a table like this:

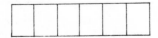

3. The game leader picks a card. Each player writes the digit in a square of the table.

4. Repeat step 3 until six digits have been picked.

5. The player who has built the greatest number is the winner.

Rounding

The Boston Garden can seat 15,314 people for basketball.

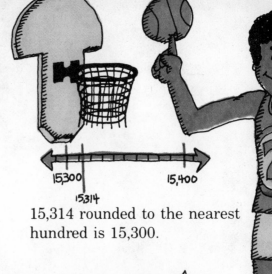

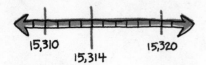

15,314 rounded to the nearest ten is 15,310.

15,314 rounded to the nearest hundred is 15,300.

15,314 rounded to the nearest thousand is 15,000.

Remember, when the number is halfway between, round up.

EXERCISES
Complete.

Basketball Arena	Seating Capacity	Rounded to nearest ten	Rounded to nearest hundred	Rounded to nearest thousand
Baltimore Civic Center	12,289	1.	2.	3.
Chicago Stadium	17,374	4.	5.	6.
Cow Palace, San Francisco	14,500	7.	8.	9.
Dallas Memorial Auditorium	8,088	10.	11.	12.
Kiel Auditorium, St. Louis	10,574	13.	14.	15.
Los Angeles Sports Arena	15,333	16.	17.	18.
Milwaukee Arena	10,746	19.	20.	21.
Nassau Coliseum, Hempstead, New York	15,367	22.	23.	24.
Sam Houston Coliseum, Houston	8,925	25.	26.	27.
Veterans Memorial Coliseum, Phoenix	12,535	28.	29.	30.

Millions

1000 thousands = 1 million = 1,000,000

Commas may be used to set off thousands and millions.

MILLIONS			THOUSANDS					
HUNDREDS	TENS	ONES	HUNDREDS	TENS	ONES	HUNDREDS	TENS	ONES
7	2	9	8	1	4	3	6	5

Seven hundred twenty-nine million, eight hundred fourteen thousand, three hundred sixty-five

To make it easier to read large numbers, start at the ones place and group the digits in threes.

729,814,365

EXERCISES
Read aloud.

1. 8,265,431

2. 9,058,162

3. 26,371,420

4. 58,296,095

5. 321,716,595

6. 874,263,815

7. 734,216,300

8. 426,385,196

9. 582,306,039

10. 750,000,465

11. 853,071,000

12. 639,211,007

13. 206,500,317

14. 500,023,700

15. 375,005,041

16. 458,072,005

17. 404,400,040

18. 440,004,400

19. 400,044,040

20. 400,404,004

The population of the United States has grown rapidly since 1790. The table at the right gives the population of the United States at different times.

21. When was the population the least?

22. When was the population the greatest?

23. What was the population in 1910?

24. What is the last year on the table when the population was less than 200 million?

25. What is the first year on the table when the population was more than 100 million?

26. In what year was the population just over 150 million?

U.S. Population

Year	Population
1790	3,929,214
1810	7,239,881
1830	12,638,453
1850	23,191,876
1870	39,818,449
1890	62,947,714
1910	91,972,266
1930	122,775,046
1950	151,325,798
1970	203,211,926

CHAPTER CHECKUP

Round to the nearest ten. [pages 24–25]

1. 74   **2.** 55   **3.** 167   **4.** 203   **5.** 345

Round to the nearest hundred. [pages 24–25]

6. 75   **7.** 126   **8.** 348   **9.** 550   **10.** 619

What does the red digit stand for? [pages 26–27]
Give two answers.

11. 9682   **12.** 3574   **13.** 6172   **14.** 4839

[pages 28–29]
Which digit is in the

15. ten thousands place?

16. thousands place?

17. hundred thousands place?

< or >? [pages 32–33]

18. 838 ● 829   **19.** 2385 ● 2386   **20.** 9748 ● 9874

21. 35,261 ● 35,172   **22.** 24,078 ● 24,178   **23.** 369,152 ● 369,143

Round to the nearest thousand. [pages 34–35]

24. 7953   **25.** 128,581   **26.** 396,483

Project

Secret messages are often sent in code. If only the sender and receiver know the code, the message will stay secret. One way to make a code is to assign a number pattern to the alphabet.

1. Copy and complete the code for all letters of the alphabet.

A	B	C	D	E	F	G	H
2	4	6	8	10	12	14	16

2. Using the code above, decode this message.

SECRET MESSAGE

50|30|42☆28|30|46☆22|28|30|46☆

16|30|46☆40|30☆8|10|6|30|8|10☆

2☆26|10|38|38|2|14|10

3. **a.** Here is a more difficult code. Complete the code. *Hint:* Add 1, add 2, add 1, add 2, etc.

A	B	C	D	E	F	G	H	I	J	K
1	2	4	5	7	8	10	11	13	14	16

   b. Write the message with this code.

4. **a.** With a classmate, use a number pattern and invent your own code.
   b. Each of you send a message in code to the other.
   c. Decode one word of each message. See if other classmates can decode the message.

1. There are ? hundreds.

2. The 6 stands for 6 tens, or ? .

3. 368 rounded to the nearest ten is ? .

4. 368 rounded to the nearest hundred is ? .

5. The 1 stands for ? .

6. The 8 stands for ? .

7. Pictured above are two thousand one hundred ? blocks.

8. 8146 rounded to the nearest thousand is ? .

Which digit is in the

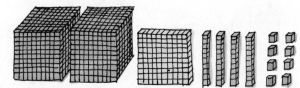

9. ten thousands place?

10. hundred thousands place?

Less than (<) or greater than (>)?

11. **5267** ⬤ **5248**
    ↑ GREATER   ↑

12. 537 ⬤ 548

13. 906 ⬤ 839

14. 2178 ⬤ 2164

15. 3752 ⬤ 3706

16. 29,135 ⬤ 29,456

17. 674,291 ⬤ 674,189

CHAPTER CHALLENGE

Roman numerals were used for hundreds of years.
Roman numerals are written with letters.

I	II	III	IV	V	VI	VII	VIII	IX	X
1	2	3	4	5	6	7	8	9	10

Look at the Roman numerals for 4 and 9.

Since the I is before the V, subtract 1 from 5.

Since the I is before the X, subtract 1 from 10.

Study these Roman numerals.

XI 10+1
11

XIX 10+9
19

XX 10+10
20

XXIV 20+4
24

XXXIX 30+9
39

Write Roman numerals.

1. 4   2. 5   3. 10   4. 9   5. 8   6. 13

7. 14   8. 17   9. 25   10. 32   11. 36   12. 29

Write standard numerals.

13. XII   14. XIV   15. XVIII   16. XXI   17. XXIV   18. XXIX

19. XXX   20. XXXII   21. XXXV   22. XXXVI   23. XXXIV   24. XXXIX

Answer with Roman numerals.

25. How old are you?

26. How many boys in your class?

27. How many girls in your class?

28. How many desks in your class?

41

	a	b	c	d		a	b	c	d			a	b	c	d		a	b	c	d		a	b	c	d
14					34						14					4					30				
15	a	b	c	d										c	d				b	c	31	a	b	c	d
							a	b	c																

MAJOR CHECKUP
Standardized Format

Choose the correct letter.

1. Add.

　　6
　　+9

    a. 14
    b. 16
    c. 15
    d. none of these

2. In $3 + 5 = 8$, the addends are

    a. 3 and 5
    b. 3 and 8
    c. 5 and 8
    d. none of these

3. Add.

　　6
　　3
　　4
　　7
　　+2

    a. 24
    b. 23
    c. 21
    d. 22

4. $\underline{?} + 3 = 8$
The missing number is

    a. 11
    b. 3
    c. 5
    d. none of these

5. Subtract.

　　16
　　− 9

    a. 7
    b. 6
    c. 8
    d. 9

6. $13 - (6 - 2) = \underline{?}$
The missing number is

    a. 5
    b. 9
    c. 4
    d. none of these

7. The standard numeral for four hundred six is

    a. 460
    b. 466
    c. 406
    d. none of these

8. 234 rounded to the nearest ten is

    a. 230
    b. 240
    c. 200
    d. none of these

9. 750 rounded to the nearest hundred is

    a. 760
    b. 700
    c. 800
    d. none of these

10. The standard numeral for four thousand two hundred two is

    a. 4202
    b. 4022
    c. 4220
    d. none of these

11. In 328,174 the 2 stands for

    a. 20
    b. 2000
    c. 200
    d. none of these

12. Which number is the greatest?

    a. 536,784
    b. 497,983
    c. 536,872
    d. 540,000

3
Addition
and
Subtraction

READY OR NOT !

Add.

1. 6
  +6

2. 9
  +7

3. 2
  +9

4. 3
  +7

5. 9
  +6

6. 8
  +8

7. 7
  +7

8. 3
  +8

9. 7
  +8

10. 8
   +9

11. 9
   +3

12. 5
   +8

Subtract.

13. 15
   − 8

14. 11
   − 5

15. 18
   − 9

16. 12
   − 4

17. 15
   − 6

18. 14
   − 5

19. 13
   − 4

20. 16
   − 7

21. 10
   − 4

22. 14
   − 6

23. 13
   − 9

24. 17
   − 9

Adding without regrouping

You can find the total number of blocks by adding in columns.

EXAMPLE 1.   63
              + 24

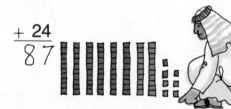

Step 1. Add in ones column.

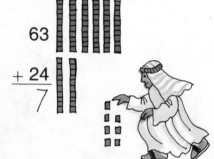

63
+ 24
  7

Step 2. Add in tens column.

63
+ 24
 87

EXAMPLE 2.   213
              +145
              ─────
               358

EXAMPLE 3.   38291
              + 10304
              ───────
               48,595

44

EXERCISES

Add.

1. 42
    +21

2. 38
    +30

3. 56
    +41

4. 65
    +24

5. 76
    +13

6. 356
    +221

7. 403
    +174

8. 206
    + 21

9. 405
    +390

10. 226
    +430

11. 205
    +483

12. 274
    +425

13. 674
    +215

14. 511
    + 46

15. 46
    +511

16. 5214
    + 653

17. 3608
    +2101

18. 1284
    +8510

19. 7653
    + 304

20. 5326
    +2401

21. 32864
    + 5031

22. 87400
    + 2405

23. 43215
    + 453

24. 64102
    +23243

25. 54103
    +10782

26. 583243
    +415214

27. 402032
    +453647

28. 727134
    + 52601

29. 43856
    +914022

30. 642354
    +150410

```
3469+230=

3469
 230
3699
```

Give each sum.

31. 54 + 21
32. 36 + 42
33. 251 + 306
34. 740 + 38
35. 3912 + 5003
36. 4235 + 421
37. 53614 + 21052
38. 376042 + 11823

45

Adding with regrouping

In this example, 10 ones are regrouped for 1 ten.

Step 1. Add ones. **Step 2.** Regroup. **Step 3.** Add tens.

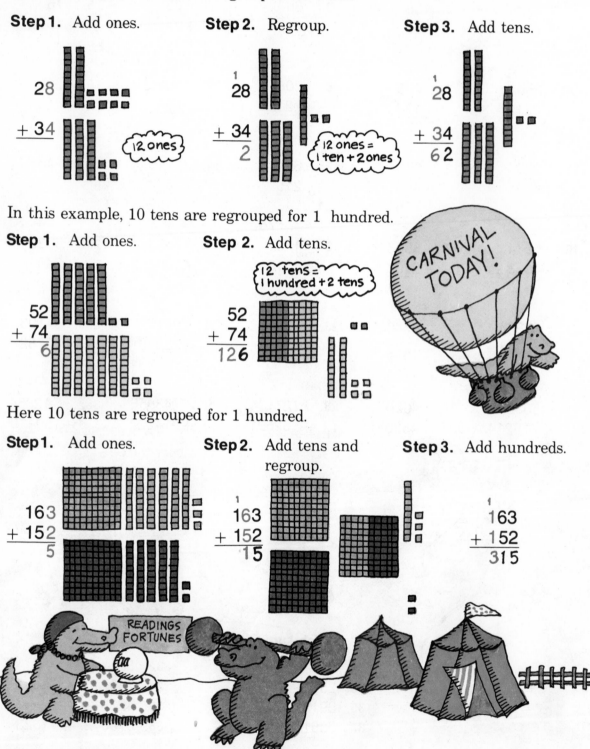

$$\begin{array}{r} 28 \\ + 34 \\ \hline \end{array}$$
12 ones

$$\begin{array}{r} 28 \\ + 34 \\ \hline 2 \end{array}$$
12 ones = 1 ten + 2 ones

$$\begin{array}{r} 28 \\ + 34 \\ \hline 62 \end{array}$$

In this example, 10 tens are regrouped for 1 hundred.

Step 1. Add ones. **Step 2.** Add tens.

$$\begin{array}{r} 52 \\ + 74 \\ \hline 6 \end{array}$$

12 tens = 1 hundred + 2 tens

$$\begin{array}{r} 52 \\ + 74 \\ \hline 126 \end{array}$$

CARNIVAL TODAY!

Here 10 tens are regrouped for 1 hundred.

Step 1. Add ones. **Step 2.** Add tens and regroup. **Step 3.** Add hundreds.

$$\begin{array}{r} 163 \\ + 152 \\ \hline 5 \end{array}$$

$$\begin{array}{r} 163 \\ + 152 \\ \hline 15 \end{array}$$

$$\begin{array}{r} 163 \\ + 152 \\ \hline 315 \end{array}$$

READINGS FORTUNES

EXERCISES

Add.

1. 38
   +25

2. 56
   +39

3. 21
   +49

4. 28
   +69

5. 55
   + 7

6. 48
   +21

7. 56
   +29

8. 56
   +39

9. 37
   +45

10. 45
    +37

11. 68
    +91

12. 53
    +72

13. 52
    +80

14. 75
    +43

15. 86
    +72

16. 253
    +481

17. 162
    +284

18. 363
    +576

19. 492
    +184

20. 273
    +581

21. 329
    +408

22. 133
    +557

23. 205
    +366

24. 429
    +534

25. 437
    +419

26. 842
    + 93

27. 68
    +51

28. 74
    +18

29. 39
    +448

30. 536
    +147

31.

COLA 25¢   55¢
How much for both?

32. The fourth-grade class sold 128 tickets for the school carnival. The fifth-grade class sold 119. How many tickets did they sell in all?

33. Three hundred fifty-two people came to the carnival the first night. Two hundred ninety-one came the second night. How many people came the first two nights?

Regrouping more than once

Sometimes you have to regroup more than once when adding. Study these examples.

EXAMPLE 1.

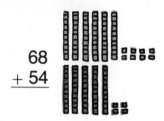

$$\begin{array}{r} 68 \\ + 54 \\ \hline \end{array}$$

Step 1. Add ones and regroup.

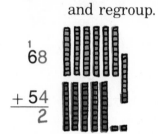

$$\begin{array}{r} \overset{1}{6}8 \\ + 54 \\ \hline 2 \end{array}$$

Step 2. Add tens and regroup.

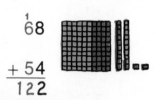

$$\begin{array}{r} \overset{1}{6}8 \\ + 54 \\ \hline 1\,2\,2 \end{array}$$

EXAMPLE 2.

$$\begin{array}{r} 258 \\ + 175 \\ \hline \end{array}$$

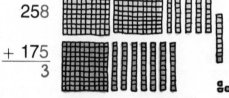

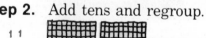

Step 1. Add ones and regroup.

$$\begin{array}{r} \overset{1}{2}58 \\ + 175 \\ \hline 3 \end{array}$$

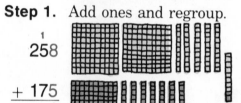

Step 2. Add tens and regroup.

$$\begin{array}{r} \overset{1\ 1}{2}58 \\ + 175 \\ \hline 3\,3 \end{array}$$

Step 3. Add hundreds.

$$\begin{array}{r} \overset{1}{2}58 \\ + 175 \\ \hline 4\,3\,3 \end{array}$$

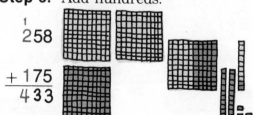

48

EXERCISES

Add.

1. 75
    +68

2. 39
    +83

3. 76
    +79

4. 97
    +44

5. 69
    +58

6. 486
    + 95

7. 567
    + 93

8. 48
    +387

9. 59
    +469

10. 258
    + 68

11. 275
    +438

12. 579
    +285

13. 368
    +245

14. 693
    +208

15. 572
    +198

Remember that money is added in the same way.

16. $3.75
    +1.21

17. $5.98
    +2.62

18. $5.37
    +1.95

19. $2.99
    +4.08

20. $4.29
    +1.82

21. $6.20
    +2.95

22. $4.08
    +3.69

23. $7.49
    +1.87

Solve.

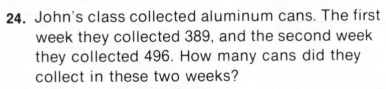

24. John's class collected aluminum cans. The first week they collected 389, and the second week they collected 496. How many cans did they collect in these two weeks?

25. The class set a goal of 950 cans during the third and fourth weeks. They collected 419 cans the third week and 537 the fourth week. Did they reach their goal?

Find the missing digits.

★26. 3⬛6
     +249
     605

★27. 486
     +17⬛
     6⬛5

★28. 37⬛
     +5⬛4
     902

49

Estimating sums

When you estimate an answer, you think about what number the answer is near. Sometimes an estimate is called an "educated guess." An estimate can help you decide whether or not you have made a mistake.

To estimate
this sum:

58	Round to nearest 10	60
+ 29	Round to nearest 10	+ 30
		90

The sum is about 90.

To estimate
this sum:

526	Round to nearest 100	500
+ 385	Round to nearest 100	+ 400
		900

Problem		Estimate
62	Round to	60
+ 39	Round to	+ 40
		100

The sum is near 100. Do you think the sum is less than 100 or greater than 100?

Problem		Estimate
493	Round to	500
+ 178	Round to	+ 200
		700

Is the sum less than or greater than 700?

Problem		Estimate
74	Round to	70
+ 85	Round to	+ 90
		160

The sum is near 160. Do you think the sum is less than 160 or greater than 160?

Problem		Estimate
621	Round to	600
+ 295	Round to	+ 300
		900

Is the sum less than or greater than 900?

EXERCISES

Round each addend to the nearest ten.
Estimate the sum.

1. 38 +53	2. 47 +19	3. 56 +20	4. 25 +54
5. 62 +19	6. 63 +81	7. 65 +53	8. 31 +83
9. 76 +64	10. 54 +83	11. 62 +78	12. 93 +89

Round each addend to the nearest hundred.
Estimate the sum.

13. 574 +238	14. 621 +308	15. 482 +278	16. 609 + 82
17. 59 +342	18. 259 +340	19. 150 +438	20. 346 +590
21. 438 +549	22. 623 +106	23. 387 +605	24. 817 +481

First estimate the final sum.
Add across. Add down.

25.

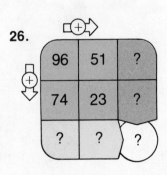

26.

1. 14 − 8	2. 11 − 7
3. 15 − 8	4. 13 − 6
5. 12 − 7	6. 16 − 7
7. 16 − 8	8. 10 − 6
9. 14 − 7	10. 17 − 9
11. 13 − 5	12. 12 − 6
13. 15 − 9	14. 11 − 3
15. 12 − 8	16. 11 − 5
17. 14 − 9	18. 18 − 9

51

Adding larger numbers

Remember to regroup when a sum is 10 or greater.

Step 1. Add ones.

```
  573
+ 785
    8
```

Step 2. Add tens and regroup.

```
   ¹
  573
+ 785
   58
```

Step 3. Add hundreds and regroup.

```
   ¹
  573
+ 785
 1358
```

In this problem we have to regroup in each step.

Step 1. Add and regroup.

```
   ¹
 5287
+ 4963
    0
```

Step 2. Add and regroup.

```
  ¹ ¹
 5287
+ 4963
   50
```

Step 3. Add and regroup.

```
  ¹ ¹ ¹
 5287
+ 4963
  250
```

Step 4. Add and regroup.

```
  ¹ ¹ ¹
 5287
+ 4963
 10,250
```

You add larger numbers the same way.

```
  ¹ ¹ ¹ ¹
 734 695
 194 385
 929,080
```

EXERCISES
Add.

1. 638
   +257

2. 519
   +324

3. 743
   +896

4. 547
   +968

5. 658
   +729

6. 472
   +298

7. 799
   +948

8. 973
   +918

9. 4618
   +3812

10. 3957
   + 384

11. 3219
   +2537

12. 6765
   +1805

13. 5674
   +6384

14. 7038
   +8299

15. 8078
   +9951

16. 346
   +6528

17. $63.52
   +74.98

18. $78.56
   +59.74

19. $95.26
   + 6.97

20. $83.77
   +41.69

21. 32781
   +14625

22. 83175
   + 9654

23. 75263
   + 7491

24. 63826
   +17941

25. 381724
   + 97382

26. 658725
   +234983

27. 493785
   +176594

28. 759638
   +472359

Find the missing digits.

★29.   7▮382
    +29 5▮3
    103,92▮

★30. 481▮9▮
    +24▮357
    7▮0,653

Adding three or more numbers

Before adding three or more numbers, practice the following addition shortcut.

```
  38
+  9
  47
```

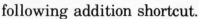

I know the ones digit is 7. When I regroup, the tens digit will be 1 greater.

```
  27        39        43
+  8       + 6       + 8
```

```
  52     36     58     64     45     28     37     49
+  9    + 5    + 7    + 8    + 9    + 8    + 9    + 5
```

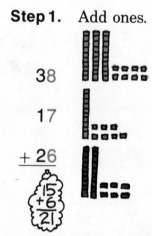

Step 1. Add ones.

```
  38
  17
+ 26
```
5
+6
21

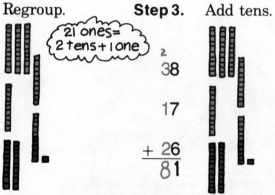

Step 2. Regroup.

```
   2
  38
  17
+ 26
   1
```

21 ones = 2 tens + 1 one

Step 3. Add tens.

```
   2
  38
  17
+ 26
  81
```

Other examples.

```
   2
  43          21          31
  59         352         291
  28         167         783
+ 65        + 894        462
 195        1413        + 597
                        2133
```

54

Add.

1. 43 56 +19	2. 43 78 +62	3. 53 79 +18	4. 59 48 + 7	5. 38 74 +16

6. 62 35 +17	7. 85 74 +91	8. 46 27 +58	9. 38 19 + 8	10. 49 35 +27

11. 13 38 44 +22	12. 85 6 71 +53	13. 97 34 48 +71	14. 19 22 55 +63	15. 46 36 84 + 8

16. 128 426 +234	17. 373 519 +267	18. 286 452 +635	19. 578 341 +824	20. 769 33 +247

21. 231 742 591 +280	22. 162 303 244 + 15	23. 425 103 241 +153	24. $2.43 2.56 1.45 +1.58	25. $3.59 2.16 3.05 + .56

26.

How much for both?

27. Maria had 478 stamps. She bought 36 stamps, and a friend gave her 19. How many stamps did she have then?

28. Alex had 279 stamps. His father gave him 24 stamps each week for 3 weeks. How many stamps did he have then?

Problem solving

Many people work for airlines. Some fly the planes. Others work directly with passengers. Still others service the planes to keep them in top condition.

Modern jets can fly long distances, making several stops, in only a few hours. The chart on page 57 shows the air distance in kilometers between certain cities of the world.

Air Distance in Kilometers Between Cities

City	Bangkok	Cairo	Chicago	Hong Kong	London	Montreal	Moscow	New York	Paris	Peking	San Francisco	Stockholm	Washington, D.C.
Bangkok		7237	13,712	1723	9510	13,341	7022	13,870	9403	3274	12,690	8142	14,091
Cairo	7237		9826	8106	3496	8683	2885	8990	3197	7517	11,946	3354	9315
Chicago	13,712	9826		12,475	6333	1192	7979	1142	6629	10,566	2974	6930	954
Hong Kong	1723	8106	12,475		9584	12,378	7099	12,896	9584	1947	11,048	8101	13,048
London	9510	3496	6333	9584		5206	2502	5550	342	8118	8587	1507	5878
Montreal	13,341	8683	1192	12,378	5206		7042	530	5941	10,422	4069	5942	782
Moscow	7022	2885	7979	7099	2502	7042		7493	2486	5771	9416	1146	7802
New York	13,870	8990	1142	12,896	5550	530	7493		5818	10,950	4115	6378	328
Paris	9403	3197	6629	9584	342	5491	2486	5818		8192	8923	1605	6144
Peking	3274	7517	10,566	1947	8118	10,422	5771	10,950	8192		9469	6613	11,107
San Francisco	12,690	11,946	2974	11,048	8587	4069	9416	4115	8923	9469		8638	3906
Stockholm	8142	3354	6930	8101	1507	5942	1146	6378	1605	6613	8638		6693
Washington, D.C.	14,091	9315	954	13,048	5878	782	7802	328	6144	11,107	3906	6693	

How far is it from

1. Bangkok to Cairo?

2. Peking to Moscow?

3. London to Montreal?

4. San Francisco to Washington, D.C.?

Give the total kilometers for the following flights.

5. New York–London–Paris

6. San Francisco–Chicago–New York

7. Stockholm–London–New York

8. Moscow–Washington, D.C.–San Francisco

9. Paris–Moscow–Peking

10. New York–Chicago–San Francisco–Hong Kong

11. London–Montreal–Chicago–San Francisco

12. Hong Kong–Moscow–Paris–Stockholm

Subtracting without regrouping

You can find differences by subtracting in columns.

EXAMPLE 1.

$$\begin{array}{r} 68 \\ -\ 23 \\ \hline \end{array}$$

Step 1. Subtract in ones column.

$$\begin{array}{r} 68 \\ -\ 23 \\ \hline 5 \end{array}$$

Step 2. Subtract in tens column.

$$\begin{array}{r} 68 \\ -\ 23 \\ \hline 45 \end{array}$$

EXAMPLE 2.

$$\begin{array}{r} 457 \\ -\ 243 \\ \hline \end{array}$$

Step 1. Subtract ones.

$$\begin{array}{r} 457 \\ -\ 243 \\ \hline 4 \end{array}$$

Step 2. Subtract tens.

$$\begin{array}{r} 457 \\ -\ 243 \\ \hline 14 \end{array}$$

Step 3. Subtract hundreds.

$$\begin{array}{r} 457 \\ -\ 243 \\ \hline 214 \end{array}$$

EXAMPLE 3.

$$\begin{array}{r} 5896 \\ -\ 2140 \\ \hline 3756 \end{array}$$

EXAMPLE 4.

$$\begin{array}{r} 73529 \\ -\ 51203 \\ \hline 22{,}326 \end{array}$$

EXAMPLE 5.

$$\begin{array}{r} 679381 \\ -\ 152041 \\ \hline 527{,}340 \end{array}$$

EXERCISES
Subtract.

1. 85
   − 32

2. 81
   − 41

3. 69
   − 33

4. 77
   − 12

5. 98
   − 56

6. 359
   − 246

7. 478
   − 123

8. 527
   − 205

9. 694
   − 423

10. 975
   − 125

11. 753
   − 42

12. 826
   − 301

13. 588
   − 26

14. 590
   − 150

15. 967
   − 245

16. 5634
   − 3500

17. 7827
   − 4305

18. 9740
   − 6240

19. 6558
   − 2123

20. 4369
   − 1023

21. 78293
   − 2030

22. 57608
   − 3604

23. 92735
   − 30402

24. 46918
   − 12604

25. 37925
   − 12404

26. 382195
   − 120084

27. 946361
   − 311240

28. 295348
   − 102113

29. 886307
   − 351204

30. 568974
   − 213421

Give each difference.

SECRETARY'S NOTES
5978 − 316

```
  5978
 − 316
  5662
```

31. 78 − 23

32. 59 − 14

33. 594 − 211

34. 465 − 15

35. 3842 − 1510

36. 5864 − 324

37. 74381 − 22130

38. 894637 − 162514

Subtracting with regrouping

In this example, 1 ten is regrouped for 10 ones.

Step 1. Not enough ones.

$$\begin{array}{r} 5\,4 \\ -\,2\,9 \\ \hline \end{array}$$

Step 2. Regroup 1 ten for 10 ones.

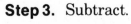

$$\begin{array}{r} {}^{4}\,{}^{14} \\ \cancel{5}\,\cancel{4} \\ -\,2\,9 \\ \hline \end{array}$$

Step 3. Subtract.

$$\begin{array}{r} {}^{4}\,{}^{14} \\ \cancel{5}\,\cancel{4} \\ -\,2\,9 \\ \hline 2\,5 \end{array}$$

Here 1 hundred is regrouped for 10 tens.

Step 1. Subtract ones.

$$\begin{array}{r} 4\,2\,6 \\ -\,1\,5\,2 \\ \hline 4 \end{array}$$

Step 2. Not enough tens. Regroup 1 hundred for 10 tens.

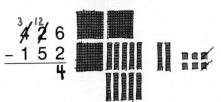

$$\begin{array}{r} {}^{3}\,{}^{12} \\ \cancel{4}\,\cancel{2}\,6 \\ -\,1\,5\,2 \\ \hline 4 \end{array}$$

Step 3. Subtract tens.

$$\begin{array}{r} {}^{3}\,{}^{12} \\ \cancel{4}\,\cancel{2}\,6 \\ -\,1\,5\,2 \\ \hline 7\,4 \end{array}$$

Step 4. Subtract hundreds.

$$\begin{array}{r} {}^{3}\,{}^{12} \\ \cancel{4}\,\cancel{2}\,6 \\ -\,1\,5\,2 \\ \hline 2\,7\,4 \end{array}$$

EXERCISES

Subtract.

1.   24
   − 18
	2. 73
	   − 44
		3. 92
		   − 46
			4. 70
			   − 25
				5. 84
				   − 39

6.   78
   − 29
	7. 87
	   − 26
		8. 65
		   − 19
			9. 93
			   − 58
				10. 81
				   − 74

11.   742
   − 216
	12. 586
	   − 48
		13. 753
		   − 628
			14. 978
			   − 49
				15. 684
				   − 212

16.   528
   − 152
	17. 406
	   − 231
		18. 753
		   − 61
			19. 517
			   − 303
				20. 856
				   − 574

21.   753
   − 219
	22. 647
	   − 481
		23. 958
		   − 223
			24. 526
			   − 373
				25. 838
				   − 529

26.   678
   − 595
	27. 895
	   − 462
		28. 463
		   − 229
			29. 742
			   − 715
				30. 527
				   − 275

31. How much change?

$1.29

32. 24 chocolate cookies
36 peanut butter cookies
How many in all?

33. 56 oatmeal cookies
128 sugar cookies
Sold 39. How many left?

Regrouping more than once

Sometimes you have to regroup more than once
when subtracting. Study these examples.

Step 1. Regroup one ten for
10 ones.

Step 1. There are no tens. So
regroup 1 hundred for
10 tens.

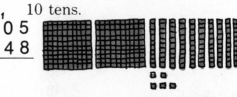

Step 2. Subtract ones.

$$\begin{array}{r} 5\,2\,4 \\ -2\,5\,8 \\ \hline 6 \end{array}$$

Step 2. Regroup 1 ten for 10 ones.

Step 3. Regroup one hundred for
10 tens.

$$\begin{array}{r} 5\,2\,4 \\ -2\,5\,8 \\ \hline 6 \end{array}$$

Step 3. Subtract ones.

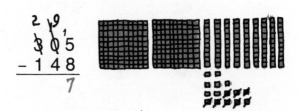

Step 4. Subtract tens.

$$\begin{array}{r} 5\,2\,4 \\ -2\,5\,8 \\ \hline 6\,6 \end{array}$$

Step 4. Subtract tens.

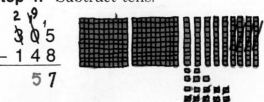

Step 5. Subtract hundreds.

$$\begin{array}{r} 5\,2\,4 \\ -2\,5\,8 \\ \hline 2\,6\,6 \end{array}$$

Step 5. Subtract hundreds.

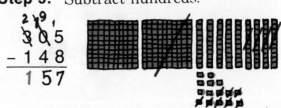

62

EXERCISES
Subtract.

1. 641
    − 259

2. 381
    − 193

3. 823
    − 485

4. 426
    − 358

5. 750
    − 467

6. 712
    − 359

7. 512
    − 458

8. 633
    − 275

9. 510
    − 394

10. 746
    − 268

11. 635
    − 367

12. 816
    − 608

13. 930
    − 718

14. 924
    − 501

15. 842
    − 375

16. $8.03
    − 4.58

17. $7.04
    − 3.69

18. $6.01
    − 1.74

19. $9.05
    − 6.29

You subtract money in the same way that you subtract whole numbers.

20. $7.01
    − 4.26

21. $5.02
    − 2.75

22. $9.00
    − 3.58

23. $8.00
    − 6.29

Solve.

24. The Allens drove 452 kilometers the first day and 379 kilometers the second day. How much farther did they drive the first day?

25. On their trip Nancy saw this road sign:

OAKVILLE 74 km   ANDERSON 102 km

How far apart are the two cities?

Give the missing digits.

26. 521
    − 37▢
    ▢ 47

27. 6▢1
    − ▢58
    163

28. ▢02
    − 4▢9
    24▢

Estimating differences

You learned to round to estimate sums. Rounding can help you estimate differences, too. An estimate can help you decide whether you made a mistake subtracting.

Each number was rounded to the nearest ten. Then the difference was estimated.

The difference is about 60.

This difference is about 30.

83	Round to	80
− 47	Round to	− 50
		30

This difference is about 50.

92	Round to	90
− 35	Round to	− 40
		50

Each of these numbers was rounded to the nearest hundred.

This difference is about 300.

742	Round to	700
− 388	Round to	− 400
		300

Is the difference less than or greater than 300?

This difference is about 300.

803	Round to	800
− 475	Round to	− 500
		300

Is the difference less than or greater than 300?

EXERCISES

Round each number to the nearest ten. Then estimate the difference.

1. 58 − 17	2. 64 − 39	3. 53 − 21	4. 82 − 47	5. 75 − 57
6. 65 − 18	7. 75 − 47	8. 80 − 53	9. 78 − 32	10. 64 − 25

Round each number to the nearest hundred. Then estimate the difference.

11. 529 − 242	12. 782 − 365	13. 604 − 427	14. 813 − 385	15. 922 − 409
16. 743 − 575	17. 682 − 429	18. 900 − 675	19. 529 − 372	20. 857 − 689
21. 538 − 169	22. 817 − 683	23. 891 − 497	24. 965 − 327	25. 983 − 714

Keeping Skills Sharp

Less than (<) or greater than (>)?

1. 456 ● 465

2. 312 ● 409

3. 856 ● 850

4. 3617 ● 3528

5. 5263 ● 5438

6. 2674 ● 3200

7. 26,174 ● 26,274

8. 38,061 ● 38,056

9. 59,274 ● 58,374

10. 618,321 ● 617,493

11. 583,274 ● 590,003

12. 99,999 ● 100,000

Subtracting larger numbers

Larger numbers are subtracted in the same way as smaller numbers. Study these examples.

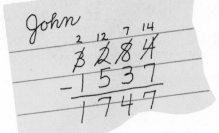

Patsy remembered that subtraction is finding a missing addend. So, to check her subtraction, she did this addition:

What numbers would you add to check John's subtraction? To check Sarah's?

EXERCISES
Subtract.

1. 5735	2. 3529	3. 8375	4. 9782
− 2168	− 1674	− 2694	− 3597

5. 6581	6. 5029	7. 3406	8. 5003
− 4259	− 1382	− 1658	− 4475

First subtract.

Then check your work by addition.

9. 86215
   − 34802

10. 73052
   − 58629

11. 94160
   − 41387

12. 75384
   − 38965

13. 62415
   − 5658

14. 90346
   − 2918

15. 78002
   − 35146

16. 50000
   − 16742

Subtract.

17. 378219
   −   3948

18. 564381
   − 64592

19. 901276
   − 340561

20. 828391
   − 352675

21. 756550
   − 437891

22. 544602
   − 257284

23. 637082
   − 305674

24. 710028
   − 529674

25. 999999
   − 538215

★26. 1000000
   − 538216

Who am I?

27. If you add me to 3872, you get 8526.

28. If you subtract 14,974 from me, you get 3865.

67

Problem solving

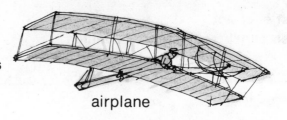

airplane

Inventors: Orville
and Wilbur Wright
Year: 1903

How many years ago were these things invented?

1. adding machine

2. pendulum clock

3. steam piston engine

4. radar

5. slide rule

6. steam car

7. How many years after the steam car was invented was the gasoline car invented?

8. How many years before the airplane was invented was the gasoline-powered car invented?

9. How many years before radar was invented was the thermometer invented?

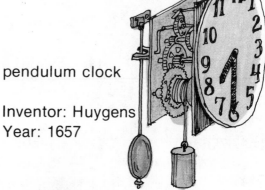

pendulum clock

Inventor: Huygens
Year: 1657

automobile
(gasoline-powered)

Inventor: Daimler
Year: 1887

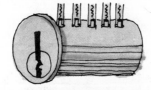

cylinder lock

Inventor: Yale
Year: 1865

bicycle

Inventor: Starley
Year: 1871

thermometer

Inventor: Galileo
Year: 1593

steam piston engine

Inventor: Newcomen
Year: 1705

10. Which was invented first, the Starley bicycle or the cylinder lock? How many years were there between these two inventions?

11. The gasoline engine was invented one hundred sixty-seven years after the steam piston engine. In what year was the gasoline engine invented?

12. The long-playing record was invented sixty-one years after the cylinder record. In what year was the long-playing record invented?

adding machine

Inventor: Pascal
Year: 1642

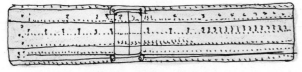

slide rule

Inventor: Oughtred
Year: 1620

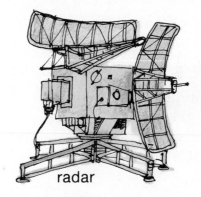

radar

Inventors: Taylor and Young
Year: 1922

cylinder record

Inventors: Bell and Tainter
Year: 1887

steam car

Inventor: Cugnot
Year: 1770

Addition and subtraction

Remember: Do the work inside the grouping symbols first.

EXAMPLE. $(278 + 456) - 532 = 202$

$$\begin{array}{r} \overset{1}{2}78 \\ +456 \\ \hline 734 \\ -532 \\ \hline 202 \end{array}$$

EXERCISES
Compute.

1. $(375 + 296) + 492$ 2. $375 + (296 + 492)$

3. $(693 - 281) - 105$ 4. $693 - (281 - 105)$

5. $(856 + 395) - 399$ 6. $(408 - 275) + 856$

7. $(927 + 384) - 384$ 8. $(759 - 257) + 578$

9. $867 + (795 - 426)$ 10. $876 - (253 + 125)$

Make up a story.   PROBLEM SOLVING

NUMBER NEWS $563 - 285 = \boxed{}$

NAILS

Skill Game

Build the greatest difference.

$$\begin{array}{r} \overset{9}{5}\,\overset{2}{\cancel{3}}\,\overset{\cancel{10}}{\cancel{0}}\,\overset{\cancel{13}}{\cancel{3}} \\ -4\ 1\ 9\ 8 \\ \hline 1\ 1\ 0\ 5 \end{array}$$

$$\begin{array}{r} \overset{7}{\cancel{8}}\,\overset{11}{\cancel{1}}\,5\,4 \\ -3\ 9\ 0\ 3 \\ \hline 4\ 2\ 5\ 1 \end{array}$$
greater difference

Tell which difference is greater.

1.
$$\begin{array}{r} 8\ 0\ 7\ 5 \\ -3\ 9\ 2\ 1 \\ \hline \end{array}\qquad \begin{array}{r} 9\ 7\ 8\ 1 \\ -2\ 3\ 0\ 5 \\ \hline \end{array}$$

2.
$$\begin{array}{r} 6\ 3\ 8\ 5 \\ -1\ 2\ 9\ 4 \\ \hline \end{array}\qquad \begin{array}{r} 9\ 8\ 3\ 1 \\ -5\ 2\ 4\ 6 \\ \hline \end{array}$$

3.
$$\begin{array}{r} 6\ 4\ 0\ 7 \\ -3\ 1\ 2\ 4 \\ \hline \end{array}\qquad \begin{array}{r} 7\ 0\ 4\ 4 \\ -2\ 6\ 1\ 3 \\ \hline \end{array}$$

4.
$$\begin{array}{r} 4\ 6\ 8\ 5 \\ -1\ 5\ 6\ 3 \\ \hline \end{array}\qquad \begin{array}{r} 8\ 3\ 1\ 6 \\ -5\ 4\ 5\ 6 \\ \hline \end{array}$$

Play the game.

1. Make two cards for each of the digits.

2. Choose a leader.

3. Draw a table like this:

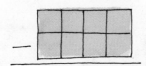

4. As the leader picks the digits, fill in your table.
   Caution: Try to have a greater number on top.

5. Repeat step 4 until your table is filled in.

6. The player who has the greatest difference wins the game.

71

Problem solving

Your body gets energy from the food you eat. A dietitian can tell you which foods are good for you and how much of each you should eat. The amount of energy in food is measured in calories. Study this chart.

food	calories
apple, 1 medium	100
beans, green, 1 cup	30
blueberry muffin, 1	150
bun, hamburger	100
butter pat	50
cole slaw, 1 cup	110
corn flakes, 1 cup	50
egg, boiled	100
hamburger patty	200
ice cream	150
lettuce	15
milk, 1 cup	150
noodle soup, 1 cup	50
oatmeal	100
orange juice, 1 cup	100
peas	75
potato, baked	90
strawberry shortcake	300
sirloin steak, 3 oz.	225
toast, 1 slice	75
tomato, 1 medium	40

Use the chart to find the total number of calories in each of these meals.

1.

2.

3.

4. Do these three meals total more or less than 2000 calories? How many calories more or less than 2000?

5. From the list, "order" a breakfast, a lunch, and a dinner. Find the total calories of your order.

CHAPTER CHECKUP

Add. [pages 44–54]

1. 58 +21	**2.** 65 +29	**3.** 58 +96	**4.** 243 +164
5. 593 +369	**6.** 758 +695	**7.** 3921 +7865	**8.** 5934 +8476
9. 35891 +26748	**10.** 532168 +293857	**11.** 694 359 +786	**12.** 428 139 357 +275

Subtract. [pages 58–67]

13. 95 −42	**14.** 73 −45	**15.** 456 −283	**16.** 572 −156
17. 603 −429	**18.** 800 −614	**19.** 5916 −2358	**20.** 7146 −3958
21. 63941 −28056	**22.** 90131 −28464	**23.** 529108 −256795	**24.** 650081 −281374

Solve. [pages 56–57, 68–69, 72–73]

25.

$7.95

$4.79

What is the total price?

26. Mary had $7.40. She bought a jersey for $3.98 and some socks for $1.75. How much money did she have left?

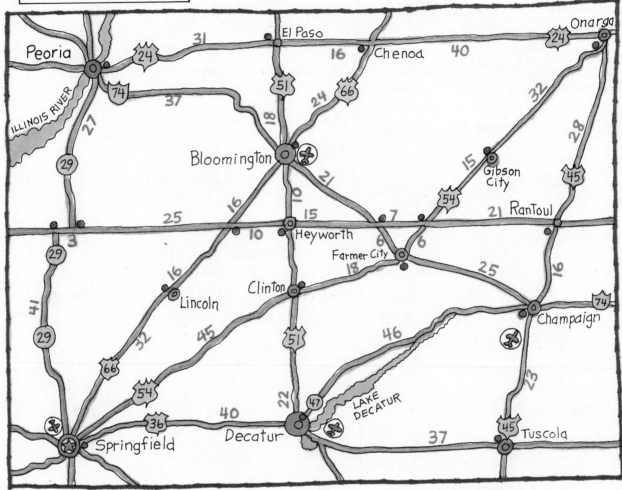

Project

Study this map to see how to find the distance between two cities.

1. How far is it from Bloomington to Peoria?
2. What is the distance from Champaign to Bloomington?
3. **a.** Get a map of your state.
   b. List four cities in your state that you would like to visit.
   c. Use your map to see how far you would have to travel to visit all four cities and return home. Did you plan the shortest trip?
4. Plan some other trips. See how far you would travel on each trip.

HIGHWAY MAP

HIGHWAY MARKERS
UNITED STATES 50 INTER-STATE 70 STATE 98

⊛ STATE CAPITAL

✈ SCHEDULED AIRLINE STOPS

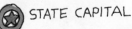 TOTAL MILEAGE BETWEEN DOTS

CHAPTER REVIEW

Add.

Regroup 10 ones for 1 ten.

$$\begin{array}{r} \overset{1}{6}8 \\ +25 \\ \hline 93 \end{array}$$

1. 56
   +19

2. 48
   +48

3. 259
   +128

Regroup 10 tens for 1 hundred.

$$\begin{array}{r} \overset{1}{3}82 \\ +153 \\ \hline 535 \end{array}$$

4. 572
   +253

5. 621
   +195

6. 463
   +384

Regroup more than once.

$$\begin{array}{r} \overset{1}{3}\overset{1}{5}96 \\ +2458 \\ \hline 6054 \end{array}$$

7. 4678
   +3917

8. 35925
   +65426

9. 389275
   +654897

Subtract.

Regroup 1 ten for 10 ones.

$$\begin{array}{r} \overset{6}{7}\overset{12}{2} \\ -38 \\ \hline 34 \end{array}$$

10. 92
    −56

11. 80
    −36

12. 262
    −129

Regroup more than once.

$$\begin{array}{r} \overset{7}{8}\overset{11}{2}\overset{13}{3} \\ -259 \\ \hline 564 \end{array}$$

13. 752
    −386

14. 2914
    −1859

15. 6243
    −4858

$$\begin{array}{r} \overset{4}{5}\overset{11}{2}\overset{9}{0}\overset{16}{6} \\ -1429 \\ \hline 3777 \end{array}$$

16. 56234
    −38175

17. 76048
    −41293

18. 320413
    −154289

CHAPTER CHALLENGE

1. **a.** Add the numbers in each row.
   b. Add the numbers in each column.
   c. Add the numbers along each diagonal.

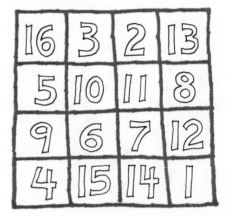

16	3	2	13
5	10	11	8
9	6	7	12
4	15	14	1

Since all the sums are the same, it is a magic square.

2. Copy and complete this magic square.
   Hint: First find the magic sum.

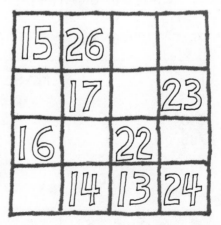

15	26		
	17		23
16		22	
	14	13	24

MAJOR CHECKUP
Standardized Format

Choose the correct letter.

1. In $7 + 2 = 9$,
   which number is
   the sum?

   a. 7
   b. 2
   c. 9
   d. none of these

2. $4 + \underline{?} = 9$
   The missing
   number is

   a. 13
   b. 5
   c. 14
   d. none of these

3. $12 - (8 - 4) = \underline{?}$
   The missing
   number is

   a. 0
   b. 4
   c. 6
   d. none of these

4. 426 rounded to the
   nearest ten is

   a. 420
   b. 430
   c. 400
   d. none of these

5. 559 rounded to the
   nearest hundred is

   a. 500
   b. 550
   c. 560
   d. 600

6. The standard
   numeral for three
   thousand
   thirty-three is

   a. 3033
   b. 3330
   c. 3303
   d. none of these

7. Which digit in
   265,340 is in the
   ten thousands
   place?

   a. 2
   b. 6
   c. 5
   d. 3

8. Which number is
   greatest?

   a. 537,824
   b. 521,979
   c. 540,793
   d. 541,988

9. Add.
   5962
   +3879

   a. 9841
   b. 9831
   c. 8731
   d. 9731

10. Add.
    526
    348
    +789

    a. 1643
    b. 1663
    c. 1543
    d. none of these

11. Subtract.
    8216
    − 2549

    a. 5667
    b. 6333
    c. 5777
    d. none of these

12. Subtract.
    4028
    − 1694

    a. 2434
    b. 3434
    c. 3334
    d. none of these

4
Time
and
Money

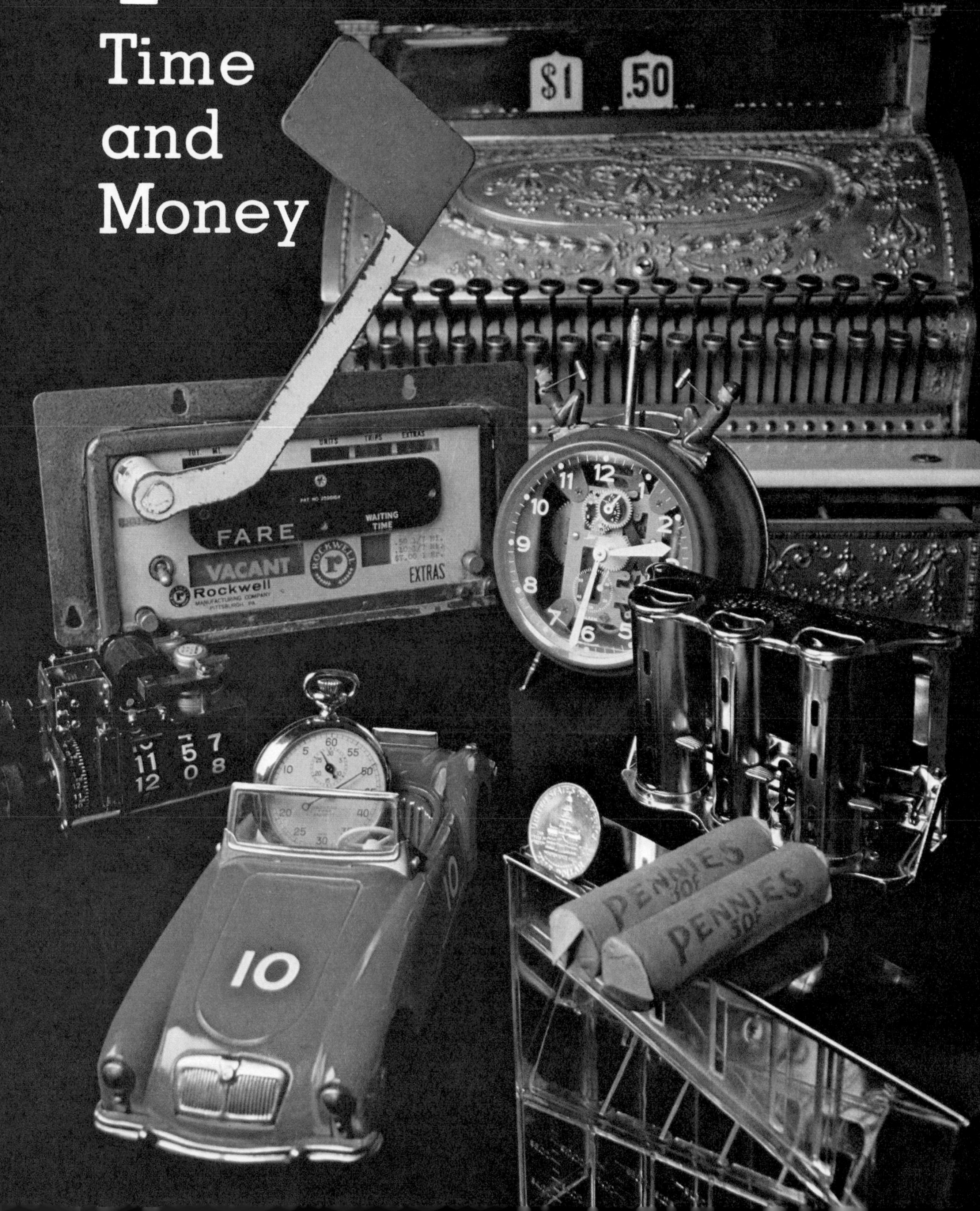

Hours and minutes

There are 60 minutes in 1 hour. The examples
show different ways to tell time.

We can say two thirty
or thirty minutes after two
or half past two.

We write 2:30.

We can say four forty-two
or eighteen minutes to five.

We write 4:42.

We can say ten fifteen
or fifteen minutes after ten
or quarter past ten.

We write 10:15.

We can say eleven forty-five
or fifteen minutes to twelve
or quarter to twelve.

We write 11:45.

EXERCISES
Write each time.

1.

2.
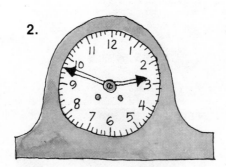

3.

Copy and complete.

4.

a. nine _?_
b. twenty-six minutes _?_ _?_

5.

a. four _?_
b. thirty minutes _?_ _?_
c. half _?_ _?_

6.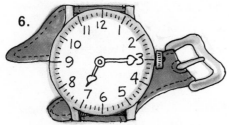

a. seven _?_
b. fifteen minutes _?_ _?_
c. quarter _?_ _?_

7.

a. twelve _?_
b. fifteen minutes _?_ _?_
c. quarter _?_ _?_

8.

a. eleven _?_
b. _?_ minutes to twelve

9.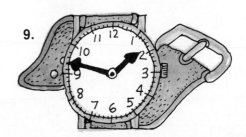

a. one _?_
b. _?_ minutes to two

Match.

10. 4:12   a. ten minutes to five

11. 4:50   b. quarter to three

12. 2:45   c. eight minutes after four

13. 3:48   d. twelve minutes to four

14. 3:15   e. quarter past three

15. 4:08   f. twelve minutes after four

A.M. and P.M.

There are 60 seconds in one minute.

The **second hand** goes around once in one minute.

There are 60 minutes in one hour.

The **minute hand** goes around once in one hour.

There are 24 hours in 1 day.

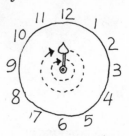

The **hour hand** goes around twice in one day.

A.M. is used for times after 12:00 midnight and before 12:00 noon.

P.M. is used for times after 12:00 noon and before 12:00 midnight.

12:00 MIDNIGHT · A.M. · 12:00 NOON · P.M. · 12:00 MIDNIGHT

EXERCISES
Daylight or dark?

1. 12:00 midnight
2. 12:00 noon
3. 3:00 A.M.
4. 3:00 P.M.
5. 11:45 A.M.
6. 11:45 P.M.
7. 2:36 A.M.
8. 2:36 P.M.
9. 10:30 A.M.
10. 10:30 P.M.

How many

11. hours in a day?

12. minutes in an hour?

13. seconds in a minute?

14. seconds in two minutes?

15. minutes in a quarter hour?

16. minutes in a half hour?

Use A.M. or P.M. in your answers. What time did you (or will you)

17. get up today?

18. eat breakfast?

19. leave for school?

20. arrive at school?

21. have morning recess?

22. eat lunch?

23. have afternoon recess?

24. get out of school?

25. get home?

26. eat dinner?

27. go to bed?

1. $\begin{array}{r} 26 \\ +13 \\ \hline \end{array}$

2. $\begin{array}{r} 37 \\ +58 \\ \hline \end{array}$

3. $\begin{array}{r} 96 \\ +57 \\ \hline \end{array}$

4. $\begin{array}{r} 243 \\ +159 \\ \hline \end{array}$

5. $\begin{array}{r} 575 \\ +868 \\ \hline \end{array}$

6. $\begin{array}{r} 351 \\ +999 \\ \hline \end{array}$

7. $\begin{array}{r} 786 \\ +954 \\ \hline \end{array}$

8. $\begin{array}{r} 3821 \\ +4675 \\ \hline \end{array}$

9. $\begin{array}{r} 3982 \\ +7465 \\ \hline \end{array}$

10. $\begin{array}{r} 8974 \\ +5628 \\ \hline \end{array}$

More about time

Maria woke up at:

She had to be in school at:

How much time did she have?
Here are two ways to get the answer.

Wake-up time   School time

7:15 →[15 minutes]→ 7:30 →[1 hour]→ 8:30

1 hour and 15 minutes

Wake-up time   School time

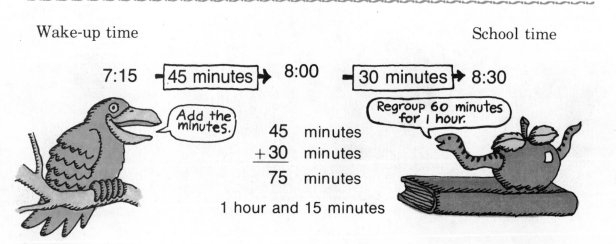

7:15 →[45 minutes]→ 8:00 →[30 minutes]→ 8:30

Add the minutes.

```
 45  minutes
+30  minutes
 75  minutes
```

1 hour and 15 minutes

Regroup 60 minutes for 1 hour.

EXERCISES

Give the time that is

1. 20 minutes later than 3:10.

2. 15 minutes later than 2:50.

3. 23 minutes later than 11:45.

4. 10 minutes earlier than 8:25.

5. 15 minutes earlier than 6:47.

6. 20 minutes earlier than 11:12.

How many minutes from

7. 2:15 to 3:00?   8. 7:45 to 8:30?

9. 11:15 to 12:15?   10. 4:25 to 5:00?

11. 6:03 to 7:00?   12. 1:05 to 1:57?

Solve.

13. School begins at 8:20. Susan got to school at 8:05. How many minutes early was she?

14. The television show started at 7:30. Mark turned it on at 7:45. How many minutes did he miss?

15. Jon left for the ball game at 7:45. He arrived at 8:10. How long did it take him to get there?

16. Julie started raking leaves at 4:15. She finished at 5:35. How long did she work?

How much sleep?

17. Bedtime   Wake-up time

18. Bedtime   Wake-up time

Money

twenty-dollar bill

$20 or $20.00

ten-dollar bill

$10 or $10.00

half-dollar

50¢ or $.50

quarter

25¢ or $.25

five-dollar bill

$5 or $5.00

one-dollar bill

$1 or $1.00

dime   nickel

10¢ or $.10   5¢ or $.05

penny

1¢ or $.01

EXERCISES
How much money?

1.

2.

86

3.

4.

5.

6.

Give each total.

									TOTAL
7.			1	1	1		1		3	?
8.		1		3		2		1		?
9.	1		1		1		2		4	?
10.	1	1				1	3	2	3	?
11.	1		1	2		2	4	1	1	?
12.	1	1	2	3	1		2	3	5	?

Study the clues. Then tell what is in each bank.

13.

35¢
3 coins

★**14.**

$1.54
1 bill
6 coins

★**15.**

$2.45
1 bill
6 coins

Making change

Sales clerks must know how to operate a cash register. They must also be able to give customers the correct change. The example shows the method that most clerks use to count change.

Terry bought this shirt for $3.79. She gave the clerk a five-dollar bill.

Here is how the clerk "counted out" Terry's change.

$3.79 $3.80 $3.90 $4.00 $5.00

Terry's change was $1.21.

ORAL EXERCISES

Touch the money needed as you "count out" the change.

1. You have   You spend

2. You have   You spend

3. You have   You spend

4. You have   You spend

5. You have   You spend
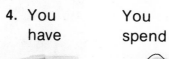

6. You have   You spend
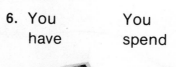

7. You have   You spend

8. You have   You spend

89

Earning money

1. Alan delivers 126 papers each morning and 87 papers each evening. How many papers does he deliver each day?

2. How many more papers does he deliver in the morning?

3. One afternoon Alan started his delivery at 3:45 and finished at 4:50. How long did it take him to deliver his papers?

4. He collects $.85 from Ted Lewis each week for the morning paper. How much should he collect for two weeks?

5. The morning and evening papers cost $1.25 each week. How much should he collect for three weeks?

6. Ms. Thomas takes both the morning and evening papers. She paid for two weeks and gave Alan a 25¢ tip. What was the total?

7. Mr. Franklin owed $4.25. He gave Alan a five-dollar bill. How much change did Alan owe Mr. Franklin?

8. One week Alan collected $86.35. The bill for his papers was $67.80. How much money did he have left?

9. Another week Alan collected $92.00. His bill was $66.45. He gave his friend $8.00 for helping. How much did he have left?

★10. Mrs. Jacobson owed $2.55. She gave Alan a five-dollar bill. He gave her three coins and two bills. What were they?

CHAPTER CHECKUP

What time is shown? [pages 80–83]

1.

2.

3.

Match. [pages 80–83]

4. fifteen minutes after six

5. thirty minutes after six

6. fifteen minutes to six

a. quarter to six

b. half past six

c. quarter past six

Answer the questions. [pages 82–83]

7. How many seconds are in 1 minute?

8. How many minutes are in 1 hour?

9. How many hours are in 1 day?

10. Is 8:30 in the morning 8:30 A.M. or 8:30 P.M.?

How many minutes from [pages 84–85]

11. 3:45 to 4:30?

12. 7:08 to 8:00?

13. 2:06 to 2:43?

How much money? [pages 86–89]

14.

15.

16.

Project

Have you ever seen a grandfather clock? Did you see the part that swings back and forth? It is called a **pendulum.** A pendulum can be used to measure time.

1. Work with a classmate and make a pendulum as shown above. You will need a book, a thumbtack, a piece of string, a paper clip, and an eraser.

2. Adjust the string so that the eraser is 20 centimeters from the thumbtack. Start the eraser swinging and count the number of "back and forth" swings in a minute.

3. Repeat step 2 using other pendulum lengths. Keep a record of the pendulum lengths and the number of swings.

4. Make a graph of your findings.

5. List some things shown by your graph.

6. About how long should the pendulum be to swing back and forth once every second?

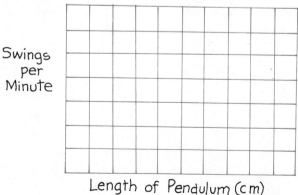

Swings per Minute

Length of Pendulum (cm)

CHAPTER REVIEW

Match.

1. quarter past one

2. half past one

3. quarter to one

a.

b.

c.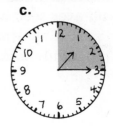

True or false?

4. There are 60 seconds in 1 minute.

5. There are 60 minutes in 1 hour.

6. There are 12 hours in 1 day.

7. 4:45 P.M. is in the afternoon.

How many minutes?

8. from   to

9. from   to

How much money?

10.

11.

12.

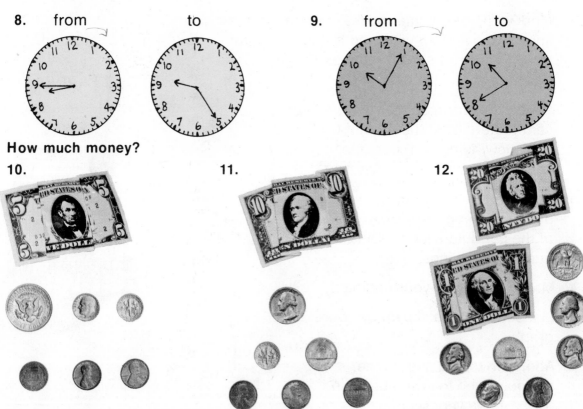

CHAPTER CHALLENGE

Our armed forces and some European countries use a different method of telling time. They use a "24-hour" clock, or 24-hour time. A.M. and P.M. are not used. Study these examples.

8:30 A.M.

12:00 noon

4:15 P.M.

24-hour time:

0830

This is generally read as "oh-eight-thirty."

1200

"twelve hundred"

1615

"sixteen fifteen"

Give the 24-hour time.

1. 5:20 A.M.   2. 6:00 A.M.   3. 9:57 A.M.

4. 10:30 A.M.   5. 11:45 A.M.   6. 12:00 noon

7. 1:00 P.M.   8. 2:00 P.M.   9. 4:00 P.M.

10. 6:25 P.M.   11. 8:45 P.M.   12. 10:40 P.M.

Write each time using A.M. or P.M.

13. 0100   14. 0430   15. 0950

16. 1140   17. 1245   18. 1330

19. 1545   20. 1605   21. 1900

22. 2130   23. 2245   24. 2315

Form W

	a	b	c	d		a	b	c	d		a	b	c	d		a	b	c	d		a	b	c	d
14					34					14					4					30				
15	a	b	c	d												c	d			31	a	b	c	d

MAJOR CHECKUP
Standardized Format

Choose the correct letter.

1. In $17 - 9 = 8$, which number is the difference?

    a. 17
    b. 9
    c. 8
    d. none of these

2. Complete.
$9 - (6 + 2) = \underline{?}$

    a. 6
    b. 1
    c. 5
    d. none of these

3. The standard numeral for twenty-nine thousand five hundred fifty is:
    a. 29,550
    b. 29,055
    c. 29,505
    d. none of these

4. 38,656 rounded to the nearest ten is

    a. 38,700
    b. 38,650
    c. 38,660
    d. 38,600

5. Which number is the smallest?

    a. 58,984
    b. 65,894
    c. 68,435
    d. 58,899

6. Add.
789
+256

    a. 935
    b. 1045
    c. 945
    d. none of these

7. Add.
76
93
45
+28

    a. 242
    b. 222
    c. 243
    d. 241

8. Subtract.
521
− 386

    a. 145
    b. 135
    c. 265
    d. 235

9. Subtract.
6204
− 3587

    a. 2627
    b. 2717
    c. 3627
    d. 2617

10. What time is shown?

    a. quarter to five
    b. quarter after five
    c. quarter to six
    d. quarter after six

11. How much time from 7:30 to 8:45?

    a. 15 minutes
    b. 45 minutes
    c. 1 hour 15 minutes
    d. none of these

12. How much money in all?

1 five-dollar bill
2 one-dollar bills
2 quarters
3 dimes

    a. $6.80
    b. $7.55
    c. $7.70
    d. none of these

5
Multiplication and Division Facts

Multiplying 0, 1, and 2

The numbers you multiply are called **factors**. The answer is called the **product**.

$$3 \times 2 = 6$$

Read as "Three times two equals six."

$$4 \times 1 = 4 \qquad\qquad 2 \times 0 = 0$$

EXERCISES
Multiply.

1. 4×2

2. 3×0

3. 5×1

4. 3×1

5. 5×2

6. 1×0

7. 6×1

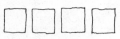

8. 4×0

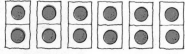

9. 6×2

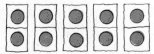

98

Give each product.

10. 5×1 11. 1×1 12. 7×0 13. 9×0

14. 4×0 15. 8×1 16. 2×2 17. 1×2

18. 3×1 19. 6×1 20. 8×0 21. 2×0

22. 3×2 23. 4×2 24. 7×2 25. 1×0

26. 7×1 27. 6×0 28. 8×2 29. 5×2

30. 2×1 31. 9×2 32. 5×0 33. 3×0

34. 4×1 35. 6×2 36. 9×1 37. 9×2

Solve.

38. 2 cupcakes in a package
    6 packages
    How many cupcakes?

39. 2 cupcakes in one package
    6 cupcakes in another
    How many cupcakes?

40. 8 packages of erasers
    2 erasers in each package
    How many erasers?

41. 8 red erasers
    2 green erasers
    How many more red erasers?

Follow the path.
Find the end number.

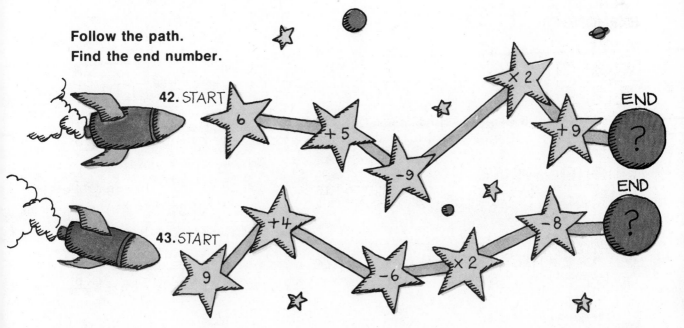

42. START   6   + 5   − 9   × 2   + 9   END ?

43. START   9   + 4   − 6   × 2   − 8   END ?

99

Multiplying 3, 4, and 5

$$\begin{array}{r} 3 \\ \times 4 \\ \hline 12 \end{array}$$

$$\begin{array}{r} 5 \\ \times 3 \\ \hline 15 \end{array}$$

$$\begin{array}{r} 4 \\ \times 5 \\ \hline 20 \end{array}$$

EXERCISES
Multiply.

1. $\begin{array}{r}3\\ \times 3\\ \hline\end{array}$	2. $\begin{array}{r}4\\ \times 6\\ \hline\end{array}$	3. $\begin{array}{r}3\\ \times 9\\ \hline\end{array}$	4. $\begin{array}{r}3\\ \times 1\\ \hline\end{array}$	5. $\begin{array}{r}4\\ \times 7\\ \hline\end{array}$	6. $\begin{array}{r}3\\ \times 6\\ \hline\end{array}$
7. $\begin{array}{r}4\\ \times 5\\ \hline\end{array}$	8. $\begin{array}{r}5\\ \times 6\\ \hline\end{array}$	9. $\begin{array}{r}4\\ \times 1\\ \hline\end{array}$	10. $\begin{array}{r}5\\ \times 4\\ \hline\end{array}$	11. $\begin{array}{r}3\\ \times 5\\ \hline\end{array}$	12. $\begin{array}{r}4\\ \times 3\\ \hline\end{array}$
13. $\begin{array}{r}3\\ \times 2\\ \hline\end{array}$	14. $\begin{array}{r}4\\ \times 2\\ \hline\end{array}$	15. $\begin{array}{r}3\\ \times 7\\ \hline\end{array}$	16. $\begin{array}{r}3\\ \times 4\\ \hline\end{array}$	17. $\begin{array}{r}3\\ \times 8\\ \hline\end{array}$	18. $\begin{array}{r}4\\ \times 8\\ \hline\end{array}$
19. $\begin{array}{r}5\\ \times 7\\ \hline\end{array}$	20. $\begin{array}{r}5\\ \times 5\\ \hline\end{array}$	21. $\begin{array}{r}4\\ \times 9\\ \hline\end{array}$	22. $\begin{array}{r}5\\ \times 9\\ \hline\end{array}$	23. $\begin{array}{r}4\\ \times 4\\ \hline\end{array}$	24. $\begin{array}{r}5\\ \times 8\\ \hline\end{array}$

Give each product.

25. $\begin{array}{r}1\\ \times 7\\\hline\end{array}$	26. $\begin{array}{r}3\\ \times 6\\\hline\end{array}$	27. $\begin{array}{r}5\\ \times 3\\\hline\end{array}$	28. $\begin{array}{r}3\\ \times 4\\\hline\end{array}$	29. $\begin{array}{r}2\\ \times 3\\\hline\end{array}$	30. $\begin{array}{r}4\\ \times 9\\\hline\end{array}$
31. $\begin{array}{r}3\\ \times 2\\\hline\end{array}$	32. $\begin{array}{r}5\\ \times 5\\\hline\end{array}$	33. $\begin{array}{r}4\\ \times 6\\\hline\end{array}$	34. $\begin{array}{r}1\\ \times 5\\\hline\end{array}$	35. $\begin{array}{r}2\\ \times 5\\\hline\end{array}$	36. $\begin{array}{r}5\\ \times 4\\\hline\end{array}$
37. $\begin{array}{r}5\\ \times 6\\\hline\end{array}$	38. $\begin{array}{r}4\\ \times 3\\\hline\end{array}$	39. $\begin{array}{r}1\\ \times 6\\\hline\end{array}$	40. $\begin{array}{r}2\\ \times 6\\\hline\end{array}$	41. $\begin{array}{r}4\\ \times 2\\\hline\end{array}$	42. $\begin{array}{r}2\\ \times 4\\\hline\end{array}$
43. $\begin{array}{r}3\\ \times 7\\\hline\end{array}$	44. $\begin{array}{r}5\\ \times 7\\\hline\end{array}$	45. $\begin{array}{r}2\\ \times 7\\\hline\end{array}$	46. $\begin{array}{r}3\\ \times 5\\\hline\end{array}$	47. $\begin{array}{r}5\\ \times 8\\\hline\end{array}$	48. $\begin{array}{r}4\\ \times 8\\\hline\end{array}$
49. $\begin{array}{r}0\\ \times 8\\\hline\end{array}$	50. $\begin{array}{r}3\\ \times 3\\\hline\end{array}$	51. $\begin{array}{r}1\\ \times 8\\\hline\end{array}$	52. $\begin{array}{r}4\\ \times 1\\\hline\end{array}$	53. $\begin{array}{r}2\\ \times 9\\\hline\end{array}$	54. $\begin{array}{r}5\\ \times 1\\\hline\end{array}$
55. $\begin{array}{r}4\\ \times 4\\\hline\end{array}$	56. $\begin{array}{r}5\\ \times 9\\\hline\end{array}$	57. $\begin{array}{r}4\\ \times 7\\\hline\end{array}$	58. $\begin{array}{r}1\\ \times 1\\\hline\end{array}$	59. $\begin{array}{r}1\\ \times 4\\\hline\end{array}$	60. $\begin{array}{r}3\\ \times 1\\\hline\end{array}$
61. $\begin{array}{r}1\\ \times 9\\\hline\end{array}$	62. $\begin{array}{r}3\\ \times 8\\\hline\end{array}$	63. $\begin{array}{r}2\\ \times 8\\\hline\end{array}$	64. $\begin{array}{r}3\\ \times 9\\\hline\end{array}$	65. $\begin{array}{r}5\\ \times 2\\\hline\end{array}$	66. $\begin{array}{r}4\\ \times 5\\\hline\end{array}$

Solve.

67.

How much will 8 cost?

68.

How much will 6 cost?

69.

How much will 5 cost?

70.

How much will 9 cost?

Multiplying 6 and 7

If you know some facts, you can use this shortcut
to find other facts.

6
×2
——
12

6
×3

This must be 6 more.
So, this product is 18.

7
×5
——
35

7
×6

7 times 5 is 35, and
7 times 6 is 7 more.
So, 7 times 6 is 42.

EXERCISES
Use the first fact to find the other product.

1.
6	6
×5	×6
30	

2.
7	7
×2	×3
14	

3.
7	7
×4	×5
28	

4.
6	6
×8	×7
48	

5.
7	7
×6	×7
42	

6.
5	5
×6	×7
30	

7.
5	5
×9	×8
45	

8.
6	6
×3	×4
18	

9.
7	7
×8	×9
56	

Multiply.

10.   4
   ×5
	11. 5
	   ×5
		12. 7
		   ×5
			13. 4
			   ×4
				14. 6
				   ×1
					15. 6
					   ×7

16.   3
   ×6
	17. 6
	   ×6
		18. 3
		   ×7
			19. 7
			   ×3
				20. 5
				   ×6
					21. 3
					   ×9

22.   7
   ×6
	23. 4
	   ×6
		24. 6
		   ×2
			25. 4
			   ×7
				26. 3
				   ×8
					27. 7
					   ×2

28.   5
   ×4
	29. 6
	   ×3
		30. 5
		   ×7
			31. 7
			   ×8
				32. 4
				   ×9
					33. 6
					   ×5

34.   6
   ×8
	35. 7
	   ×4
		36. 5
		   ×2
			37. 5
			   ×9
				38. 7
				   ×1
					39. 5
					   ×3

40.   6
   ×9
	41. 4
	   ×8
		42. 6
		   ×4
			43. 7
			   ×7
				44. 5
				   ×8
					45. 7
					   ×9

Copy and complete.

46.

weeks	1	2	3	4	5	6	7	8	9
days	7								

47.

nickels	1	2	3	4	5	6	7	8	9
cents	5								

Who am I?

48. If you add us, you get 11. If you multiply us, you get 28.

49. If you subtract us, you get 0. If you multiply us, you get 36.

103

Multiplying 8 and 9

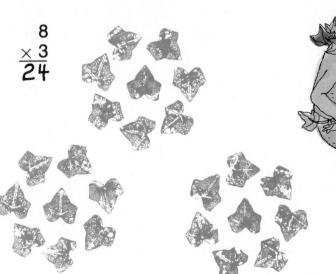

$$\begin{array}{r} 8 \\ \times 3 \\ \hline 24 \end{array}$$

5 times 9 would be 9 more, or 45.

SHORTCUT

$$\begin{array}{r} 9 \\ \times 4 \\ \hline 36 \end{array}$$

EXERCISES
Multiply.

1. $\begin{array}{r} 8 \\ \times 2 \\ \hline \end{array}$	2. $\begin{array}{r} 9 \\ \times 1 \\ \hline \end{array}$	3. $\begin{array}{r} 8 \\ \times 9 \\ \hline \end{array}$	4. $\begin{array}{r} 8 \\ \times 1 \\ \hline \end{array}$	5. $\begin{array}{r} 7 \\ \times 9 \\ \hline \end{array}$	6. $\begin{array}{r} 9 \\ \times 4 \\ \hline \end{array}$
7. $\begin{array}{r} 9 \\ \times 6 \\ \hline \end{array}$	8. $\begin{array}{r} 7 \\ \times 5 \\ \hline \end{array}$	9. $\begin{array}{r} 8 \\ \times 3 \\ \hline \end{array}$	10. $\begin{array}{r} 6 \\ \times 7 \\ \hline \end{array}$	11. $\begin{array}{r} 9 \\ \times 8 \\ \hline \end{array}$	12. $\begin{array}{r} 6 \\ \times 6 \\ \hline \end{array}$
13. $\begin{array}{r} 8 \\ \times 8 \\ \hline \end{array}$	14. $\begin{array}{r} 8 \\ \times 4 \\ \hline \end{array}$	15. $\begin{array}{r} 7 \\ \times 4 \\ \hline \end{array}$	16. $\begin{array}{r} 9 \\ \times 2 \\ \hline \end{array}$	17. $\begin{array}{r} 6 \\ \times 5 \\ \hline \end{array}$	18. $\begin{array}{r} 8 \\ \times 7 \\ \hline \end{array}$
19. $\begin{array}{r} 6 \\ \times 8 \\ \hline \end{array}$	20. $\begin{array}{r} 9 \\ \times 3 \\ \hline \end{array}$	21. $\begin{array}{r} 7 \\ \times 3 \\ \hline \end{array}$	22. $\begin{array}{r} 8 \\ \times 5 \\ \hline \end{array}$	23. $\begin{array}{r} 7 \\ \times 6 \\ \hline \end{array}$	24. $\begin{array}{r} 7 \\ \times 8 \\ \hline \end{array}$
25. $\begin{array}{r} 9 \\ \times 5 \\ \hline \end{array}$	26. $\begin{array}{r} 6 \\ \times 9 \\ \hline \end{array}$	27. $\begin{array}{r} 8 \\ \times 6 \\ \hline \end{array}$	28. $\begin{array}{r} 9 \\ \times 9 \\ \hline \end{array}$	29. $\begin{array}{r} 7 \\ \times 7 \\ \hline \end{array}$	30. $\begin{array}{r} 9 \\ \times 7 \\ \hline \end{array}$

31. Copy and complete this multiplication table.
(Multiply the "red numbers.")

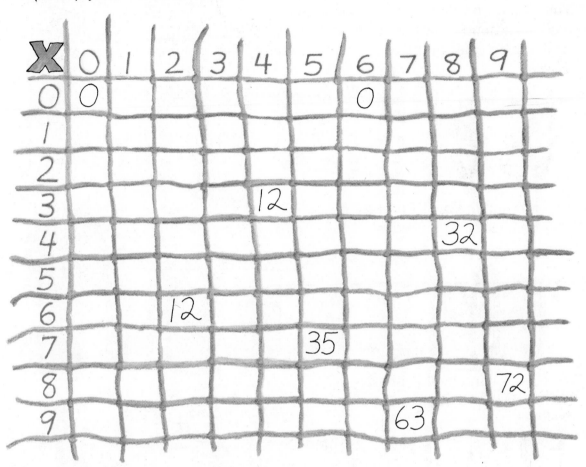

Keep your multiplication table to review the multiplication facts.

6¢ EACH

Solve.

32. How much for all the minnows?

33. 8 bottles in a carton
7 cartons
How many bottles?

34. 6 hooks per package
9 packages
How many hooks?

Multiplication Properties

You may think that there are too many multiplication facts to remember. There are some simple properties that make it easier to remember the facts.

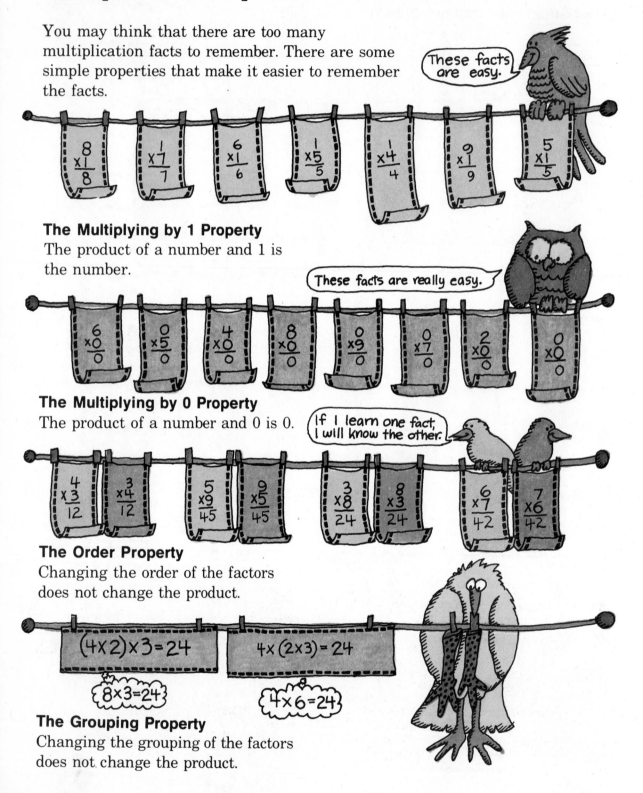

The Multiplying by 1 Property
The product of a number and 1 is the number.

The Multiplying by 0 Property
The product of a number and 0 is 0.

The Order Property
Changing the order of the factors does not change the product.

The Grouping Property
Changing the grouping of the factors does not change the product.

Complete.

1. If
$$\begin{array}{r} 6 \\ \times 8 \\ \hline 48 \end{array}$$
then
$$\begin{array}{r} 8 \\ \times 6 \\ \hline ? \end{array}$$

2. If
$$\begin{array}{r} 9 \\ \times 7 \\ \hline 63 \end{array}$$
then
$$\begin{array}{r} 7 \\ \times 9 \\ \hline ? \end{array}$$

3. If
$$\begin{array}{r} 9 \\ \times 8 \\ \hline 72 \end{array}$$
then
$$\begin{array}{r} 8 \\ \times 9 \\ \hline ? \end{array}$$

4. If
$$\begin{array}{r} 7 \\ \times 8 \\ \hline 56 \end{array}$$
then
$$\begin{array}{r} 8 \\ \times 7 \\ \hline ? \end{array}$$

5. If
$$\begin{array}{r} 7 \\ \times 6 \\ \hline 42 \end{array}$$
then
$$\begin{array}{r} 6 \\ \times 7 \\ \hline ? \end{array}$$

6. If
$$\begin{array}{r} 9 \\ \times 6 \\ \hline 54 \end{array}$$
then
$$\begin{array}{r} 6 \\ \times 9 \\ \hline ? \end{array}$$

Compute.

7. 3×9
8. 7×8
9. 5×6

10. 9×7
11. 8×8
12. 9×5

13. 4×6
14. 5×9
15. 6×9

16. $(4 \times 2) \times 3$
17. $(3 \times 3) \times 7$
18. $(2 \times 4) \times 9$

19. $3 \times (2 \times 2)$
20. $7 \times (3 \times 2)$
21. $6 \times (4 \times 2)$

22. $8 \times (9 - 2)$
23. $7 \times (8 - 2)$
24. $(9 \times 6) - 1$

25. $9 \times (3 + 4)$
26. $(8 \times 6) + 2$
27. $(10 - 6) - 2$

28. $10 - (6 - 2)$
29. $(8 - 4) \times 5$
30. $(3 \times 5) - 6$

$6 \times 8 = \triangle$

NUMBER NEWS

Make up a story.

Problem solving

These steps will help you to solve problems.

1. Read the problem carefully.

2. Picture in your mind what is happening.

3. What is the question?

4. What information is given?

5. Do you add, subtract, or multiply?

EXERCISES
Use the steps to solve these problems.

1. 8 baskets
   6 eggs in each basket
   How many eggs?

2. 8 eggs in one basket
   6 eggs in another basket
   How many eggs?

3. 8 eggs in one basket
   6 eggs in another basket
   How many more eggs in
   the first basket?

4. 8 eggs in a basket
   6 eggs are broken
   How many eggs left?

5. 7 apples
   6¢ for each apple
   How much for the apples?

6. 9 pears
   8¢ apiece
   How much for the pears?

Make up a story to fit the headline.

NUMBER NEWS

$8 \times 7 = \boxed{}$

Have someone time you. How fast can you do each
set? Can you do each set in less than a minute?  SPEED DRILL

A.

1. 3 ×2	2. 5 ×1	3. 4 ×4	4. 3 ×3	5. 4 ×1	6. 2 ×3
7. 1 ×2	8. 1 ×1	9. 5 ×2	10. 8 ×2	11. 4 ×2	12. 3 ×4
13. 0 ×0	14. 3 ×0	15. 4 ×3	16. 1 ×3	17. 2 ×4	18. 0 ×5
19. 5 ×3	20. 2 ×2	21. 4 ×5	22. 2 ×5	23. 0 ×3	24. 7 ×2

B.

1. 6 ×4	2. 9 ×7	3. 8 ×5	4. 5 ×6	5. 7 ×5	6. 6 ×3
7. 9 ×6	8. 6 ×8	9. 7 ×3	10. 7 ×4	11. 8 ×7	12. 8 ×3
13. 9 ×4	14. 8 ×6	15. 9 ×5	16. 7 ×7	17. 8 ×4	18. 5 ×7
19. 5 ×5	20. 4 ×9	21. 7 ×6	22. 6 ×5	23. 6 ×7	24. 9 ×3

C.

1. 4 ×5	2. 7 ×8	3. 9 ×9	4. 8 ×4	5. 6 ×3	6. 8 ×9
7. 3 ×2	8. 4 ×3	9. 8 ×2	10. 8 ×8	11. 2 ×4	12. 7 ×6
13. 6 ×4	14. 5 ×5	15. 6 ×5	16. 8 ×7	17. 7 ×7	18. 4 ×4
19. 9 ×4	20. 0 ×3	21. 6 ×6	22. 1 ×6	23. 5 ×9	24. 3 ×8

Multiples

3	3	3	3	3
× 0	× 1	× 2	× 3	× 4
0	3	6	9	12

0, 3, 6, 9, and 12 are **multiples of 3.**

What is the next multiple of 3?

19 is not a multiple of 3, because there is no whole number that you can multiply 3 by to get 19.

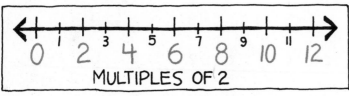

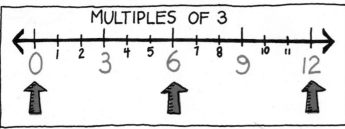

0, 6, and 12 are multiples of *both* 2 and 3. They are called **common multiples**. What is the next common multiple of 2 and 3?

EXERCISES

1. 0, 2, 4, 6, 8, 10, 12, and 14 are multiples of what number?

2. 0, 5, 10, 15, 20, 25, and 30 are multiples of what number?

3. Give the first ten multiples of 3.

4. Give the first ten multiples of 4.

5. Look at your answers to exercises 3 and 4. Give the first three *common multiples* of 3 and 4.

6. Give the first two *common multiples* of 2 and 4.

True or false?

7. 25 is a multiple of 5.

8. 30 is a multiple of 4.

9. 54 is a multiple of 9.

10. 45 is a multiple of 7.

11. 24 is a common multiple of 4 and 6.

12. 36 is a common multiple of 4 and 6.

Multiples of 2 are called **even numbers**. Whole numbers that are not multiples of 2 are called **odd numbers**.

Even or odd?

13. 6	**14.** 7	**15.** 9	**16.** 12	**17.** 18
18. 13	**19.** 16	**20.** 19	**21.** 23	**22.** 26
23. 51	**24.** 66	**25.** 67	**26.** 68	**27.** 69
28. 135	**29.** 168	**30.** 241	**31.** 257	**32.** 904

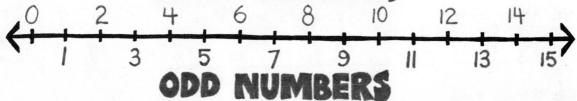

Keeping Skills Sharp

1. 23 52 +18	**2.** 29 35 +46	**3.** 72 58 +94	**4.** 82 37 +10	**5.** 75 75 +75
6. 213 478 +369	**7.** 526 237 +158	**8.** 356 147 +628	**9.** 503 742 +390	**10.** 628 956 +749

Missing factors

EXERCISES

Give each missing factor.

1. $8 \times \underline{?} = 16$
2. $9 \times \underline{?} = 27$
3. $6 \times \underline{?} = 0$

4. $7 \times \underline{?} = 21$
5. $5 \times \underline{?} = 30$
6. $5 \times \underline{?} = 25$

7. $5 \times \underline{?} = 45$
8. $6 \times \underline{?} = 18$
9. $8 \times \underline{?} = 32$

10. $8 \times \underline{?} = 56$
11. $4 \times \underline{?} = 36$
12. $6 \times \underline{?} = 36$

13. $9 \times \underline{?} = 72$
14. $8 \times \underline{?} = 40$
15. $8 \times \underline{?} = 64$

16. $8 \times \underline{?} = 48$
17. $9 \times \underline{?} = 81$
18. $7 \times \underline{?} = 49$

19. $7 \times \underline{?} = 63$
20. $6 \times \underline{?} = 42$
21. $6 \times \underline{?} = 54$

22. $5 \times \underline{?} = 35$
23. $7 \times \underline{?} = 28$
24. $3 \times \underline{?} = 24$

Give each missing factor.

25. $4 \times \underline{?} = 12$

26. $6 \times \underline{?} = 48$

27. $9 \times \underline{?} = 63$

28. $\underline{?} \times 5 = 20$

29. $\underline{?} \times 9 = 18$

30. $\underline{?} \times 5 = 15$

31. $7 \times \underline{?} = 56$

32. $5 \times \underline{?} = 40$

33. $9 \times \underline{?} = 54$

34. $\underline{?} \times 2 = 14$

35. $\underline{?} \times 7 = 35$

36. $\underline{?} \times 4 = 24$

37. $9 \times \underline{?} = 45$

38. $7 \times \underline{?} = 42$

39. $4 \times \underline{?} = 32$

40. $\underline{?} \times 2 = 12$

41. $\underline{?} \times 4 = 0$

42. $\underline{?} \times 4 = 16$

43. $3 \times \underline{?} = 27$

44. $4 \times \underline{?} = 28$

45. $8 \times \underline{?} = 72$

Solve.

46. A baseball card costs 4¢. How many cards can be bought for 32¢?

47. Three tennis balls fill a can. How many cans can be filled with 25 balls? How many balls will be left over?

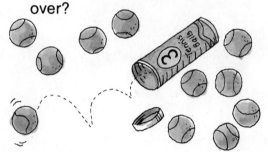

Copy and complete.

48.
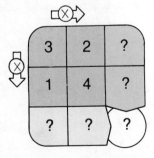

49.
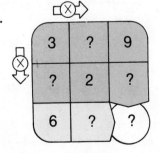

50.
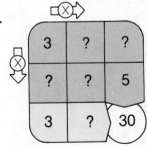

113

Problem solving

A fourth-grade class decided to raise money by collecting aluminum cans for two weeks. They used a picture graph to show the number of cans that they collected each day.

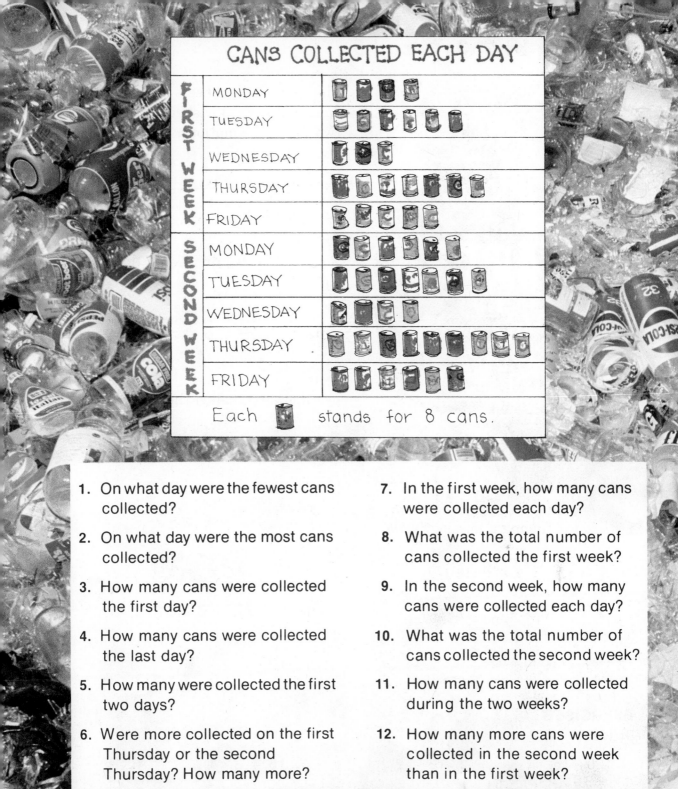

CANS COLLECTED EACH DAY

FIRST WEEK	MONDAY	
	TUESDAY	
	WEDNESDAY	
	THURSDAY	
	FRIDAY	
SECOND WEEK	MONDAY	
	TUESDAY	
	WEDNESDAY	
	THURSDAY	
	FRIDAY	

Each ☐ stands for 8 cans.

1. On what day were the fewest cans collected?

2. On what day were the most cans collected?

3. How many cans were collected the first day?

4. How many cans were collected the last day?

5. How many were collected the first two days?

6. Were more collected on the first Thursday or the second Thursday? How many more?

7. In the first week, how many cans were collected each day?

8. What was the total number of cans collected the first week?

9. In the second week, how many cans were collected each day?

10. What was the total number of cans collected the second week?

11. How many cans were collected during the two weeks?

12. How many more cans were collected in the second week than in the first week?

Dividing by 2, 3, 4, and 5

The candies have been divided equally among 3 baskets. Study the two division equations.

candies		baskets		candies in each basket
12	÷	3	=	4

Read as "twelve divided by three equals four."

candies		candies in each basket		baskets
12	÷	4	=	3

The answer is called the **quotient**.

Division is finding a missing factor.

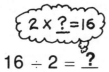

$$16 \div 2 = \underline{?}$$

The quotient is 8.

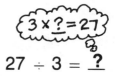

$$27 \div 3 = \underline{?}$$

The quotient is 9.

EXERCISES
Divide.

1. $20 \div 5$ 2. $12 \div 2$ 3. $15 \div 3$ 4. $16 \div 2$

5. $24 \div 3$ 6. $28 \div 4$ 7. $21 \div 3$ 8. $35 \div 5$

9. $14 \div 2$ 10. $30 \div 5$ 11. $18 \div 3$ 12. $32 \div 4$

116

Give each quotient.

13. $25 \div 5$ **14.** $10 \div 5$ **15.** $6 \div 3$

16. $12 \div 4$ **17.** $12 \div 3$ **18.** $18 \div 2$

19. $8 \div 4$ **20.** $5 \div 5$ **21.** $36 \div 4$

22. $27 \div 3$ **23.** $24 \div 4$ **24.** $9 \div 3$

25. $4 \div 2$ **26.** $40 \div 5$ **27.** $45 \div 5$

28. $4 \div 4$ **29.** $20 \div 4$ **30.** $16 \div 4$

31. $6 \div 2$ **32.** $8 \div 2$ **33.** $3 \div 3$

34. $10 \div 2$ **35.** $15 \div 5$ **36.** $2 \div 2$

Solve.

37. 15 golf balls
3 in a package
How many packages?

38. 20 buttons
4 cards with same number of buttons
How many buttons on a card?

39. Jill collected 18 soda bottles, which filled 3 cartons.
How many bottles were in a carton?

40. Jeff bought 24 stamps. He pasted the same number of stamps on 4 pages of his stamp book. How many stamps did he paste on each page?

Find the missing numbers.

41.

42.

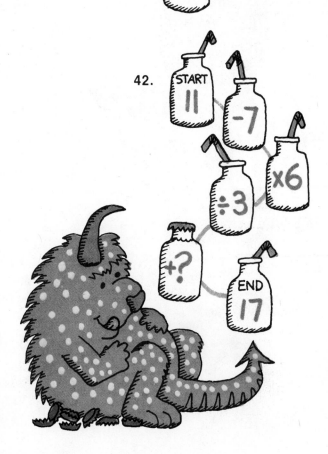

117

More about division

Here is another way to write division.

$$\overset{5}{4\overline{)20}}\ \text{trays}$$ ice cream scoops
↑
ice cream
scoops in
each tray

$$\overset{4}{5\overline{)20}}\ \text{ice cream scoops in each tray}$$ ice cream scoops
↑
Trays

 $$\overset{0}{3\overline{)0}}$$

 $$0\overline{)6}$$ 0 times any number is 0, not 6. So, we don't divide by 0.

   $$\overset{7}{1\overline{)7}}$$ 1 times any number is the number.

EXERCISES
Divide.

1. $3\overline{)18}$ 2. $3\overline{)21}$ 3. $1\overline{)6}$ 4. $3\overline{)24}$ 5. $5\overline{)25}$

6. $3\overline{)15}$ 7. $4\overline{)24}$ 8. $5\overline{)30}$ 9. $3\overline{)27}$ 10. $3\overline{)12}$

11. $4\overline{)28}$ 12. $1\overline{)7}$ 13. $3\overline{)0}$ 14. $1\overline{)4}$ 15. $4\overline{)12}$

16. $5\overline{)35}$ 17. $4\overline{)0}$ 18. $5\overline{)40}$ 19. $4\overline{)16}$ 20. $4\overline{)36}$

21. $1\overline{)5}$ 22. $4\overline{)20}$ 23. $4\overline{)32}$ 24. $1\overline{)9}$ 25. $5\overline{)45}$

Give each quotient.

26. $2\overline{)0}$ 27. $4\overline{)8}$ 28. $3\overline{)6}$ 29. $5\overline{)5}$ 30. $3\overline{)21}$

31. $3\overline{)18}$ 32. $2\overline{)14}$ 33. $5\overline{)10}$ 34. $2\overline{)4}$ 35. $5\overline{)15}$

36. $3\overline{)24}$ 37. $1\overline{)3}$ 38. $4\overline{)24}$ 39. $5\overline{)30}$ 40. $5\overline{)0}$

41. $2\overline{)12}$ 42. $4\overline{)28}$ 43. $3\overline{)3}$ 44. $5\overline{)25}$ 45. $1\overline{)6}$

46. $5\overline{)20}$ 47. $2\overline{)16}$ 48. $3\overline{)12}$ 49. $4\overline{)36}$ 50. $2\overline{)6}$

51. $4\overline{)12}$ 52. $5\overline{)35}$ 53. $2\overline{)8}$ 54. $3\overline{)21}$ 55. $5\overline{)40}$

56. $4\overline{)16}$ 57. $2\overline{)10}$ 58. $4\overline{)0}$ 59. $3\overline{)9}$ 60. $4\overline{)20}$

61. $4\overline{)32}$ 62. $3\overline{)0}$ 63. $2\overline{)18}$ 64. $5\overline{)45}$ 65. $1\overline{)9}$

Add, subtract, multiply, or divide?

66. Ann picked ■ tulips. She gave her mother ■ tulips. How many tulips did she have left?

67. Jerry baked ■ cookies one day and ■ cookies the next day. How many cookies did he bake?

68. Mark earned $■ a day. He worked ■ Saturdays. How much did he earn?

69. Felicia bought ■ tomato plants. She put ■ plants in each row. How many rows did she plant?

Copy and complete so that each "middle" number is the product of the "corner" numbers.

70. ★71. ★72.

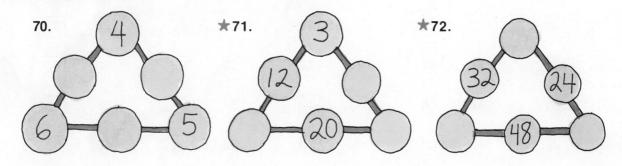

Dividing by 6 and 7

Plants in each row

$$6 \overline{\smash{)}24}\ \ \begin{array}{c}4\end{array}$$ plants

↑ rows

$$4 \overline{\smash{)}24}\ \ \begin{array}{c}6\end{array}$$ rows plants

↑ Plants in each row

EXERCISES
Divide.

1. $3\overline{\smash{)}21}$ 2. $7\overline{\smash{)}14}$ 3. $3\overline{\smash{)}24}$ 4. $7\overline{\smash{)}21}$ 5. $4\overline{\smash{)}16}$

6. $5\overline{\smash{)}25}$ 7. $7\overline{\smash{)}28}$ 8. $2\overline{\smash{)}18}$ 9. $5\overline{\smash{)}20}$ 10. $6\overline{\smash{)}18}$

11. $4\overline{\smash{)}20}$ 12. $4\overline{\smash{)}8}$ 13. $6\overline{\smash{)}24}$ 14. $4\overline{\smash{)}24}$ 15. $7\overline{\smash{)}35}$

16. $3\overline{\smash{)}15}$ 17. $3\overline{\smash{)}18}$ 18. $5\overline{\smash{)}15}$ 19. $5\overline{\smash{)}30}$ 20. $4\overline{\smash{)}36}$

21. $6\overline{\smash{)}36}$ 22. $4\overline{\smash{)}28}$ 23. $5\overline{\smash{)}10}$ 24. $3\overline{\smash{)}27}$ 25. $6\overline{\smash{)}42}$

26. $4\overline{\smash{)}32}$ 27. $7\overline{\smash{)}42}$ 28. $6\overline{\smash{)}12}$ 29. $7\overline{\smash{)}49}$ 30. $5\overline{\smash{)}45}$

31. $5\overline{\smash{)}35}$ 32. $6\overline{\smash{)}48}$ 33. $3\overline{\smash{)}12}$ 34. $6\overline{\smash{)}6}$ 35. $2\overline{\smash{)}16}$

36. $6\overline{\smash{)}30}$ 37. $5\overline{\smash{)}40}$ 38. $7\overline{\smash{)}63}$ 39. $6\overline{\smash{)}54}$ 40. $7\overline{\smash{)}56}$

Solve.

41.

How many stamps can you buy?

42.

How many stamps can you buy?

43.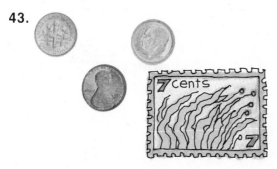

How many stamps can you buy?

44.

How many stamps can you buy?

Solve.

45. How many 6¢ stamps can you buy with 24¢?

46. You have a quarter and a dime. How many 7¢ stamps can you buy?

47. Which costs more, nine 3¢ stamps or six 4¢ stamps?

48. You have a half-dollar. You buy four 7¢ stamps. How much money will you have left?

Who am I?

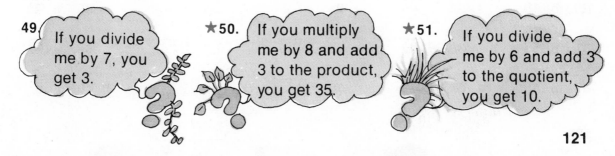

49. If you divide me by 7, you get 3.

★50. If you multiply me by 8 and add 3 to the product, you get 35.

★51. If you divide me by 6 and add 3 to the quotient, you get 10.

121

Dividing by 8 and 9

$$6 \overset{\text{feathers on}}{\underset{\text{each wing}}{}}$$

wings $9\overline{)54}$ feathers

feathers on each wing $6\overline{)54}$ $\overset{9 \text{ wings}}{}$ feathers

EXERCISES
Divide.

1. $3\overline{)27}$　　2. $6\overline{)24}$　　3. $3\overline{)24}$　　4. $8\overline{)8}$　　5. $7\overline{)21}$

6. $9\overline{)18}$　　7. $8\overline{)24}$　　8. $7\overline{)42}$　　9. $6\overline{)30}$　　10. $8\overline{)32}$

11. $7\overline{)14}$　　12. $7\overline{)28}$　　13. $5\overline{)35}$　　14. $9\overline{)27}$　　15. $7\overline{)35}$

16. $8\overline{)16}$　　17. $9\overline{)36}$　　18. $6\overline{)36}$　　19. $4\overline{)36}$　　20. $8\overline{)48}$

21. $4\overline{)32}$　　22. $8\overline{)40}$　　23. $7\overline{)56}$　　24. $9\overline{)0}$　　25. $5\overline{)40}$

26. $6\overline{)18}$　　27. $7\overline{)49}$　　28. $9\overline{)54}$　　29. $8\overline{)64}$　　30. $6\overline{)42}$

31. $8\overline{)56}$　　32. $9\overline{)63}$　　33. $6\overline{)54}$　　34. $5\overline{)45}$　　35. $9\overline{)81}$

36. $9\overline{)45}$　　37. $6\overline{)48}$　　38. $8\overline{)72}$　　39. $9\overline{)72}$　　40. $7\overline{)63}$

Give each quotient.

41. $4\overline{)32}$ 42. $3\overline{)21}$ 43. $4\overline{)16}$ 44. $8\overline{)8}$ 45. $9\overline{)81}$

46. $5\overline{)30}$ 47. $4\overline{)20}$ 48. $2\overline{)16}$ 49. $9\overline{)9}$ 50. $9\overline{)72}$

51. $4\overline{)28}$ 52. $5\overline{)20}$ 53. $3\overline{)15}$ 54. $8\overline{)64}$ 55. $7\overline{)56}$

56. $5\overline{)25}$ 57. $3\overline{)18}$ 58. $5\overline{)15}$ 59. $9\overline{)63}$ 60. $6\overline{)36}$

61. $4\overline{)24}$ 62. $2\overline{)18}$ 63. $2\overline{)14}$ 64. $7\overline{)49}$ 65. $6\overline{)42}$

Solve.

66. 8 candles in a package
    9 packages
    How many candles?

67. 54 cookies
    9 cookies in a package
    How many packages?

68. Earned $2.25
    Spent $1.69
    How much left?

69. Had $4.56
    Earned $1.75 more
    How much in all?

Keeping Skills Sharp

1. $\begin{array}{r} 58 \\ -\ 24 \\ \hline \end{array}$
2. $\begin{array}{r} 60 \\ -\ 37 \\ \hline \end{array}$
3. $\begin{array}{r} 379 \\ -\ 146 \\ \hline \end{array}$
4. $\begin{array}{r} 572 \\ -\ 249 \\ \hline \end{array}$
5. $\begin{array}{r} 625 \\ -\ 467 \\ \hline \end{array}$

6. $\begin{array}{r} 302 \\ -\ 186 \\ \hline \end{array}$
7. $\begin{array}{r} 500 \\ -\ 374 \\ \hline \end{array}$
8. $\begin{array}{r} 8371 \\ -\ 2593 \\ \hline \end{array}$
9. $\begin{array}{r} 6025 \\ -\ 3748 \\ \hline \end{array}$
10. $\begin{array}{r} 9211 \\ -\ 6987 \\ \hline \end{array}$

Addition, subtraction, multiplication, and division

Work inside the grouping symbols first.

$$(12 \div 4) + 2 = 5$$

$$12 \div (4 + 2) = 2$$

EXERCISES
Compute.

1. $(18 \div 6) + 3$
2. $18 \div (6 + 3)$
3. $(18 \div 6) \div 3$

4. $(16 \div 4) + 4$
5. $16 \div (4 + 4)$
6. $(24 \div 8) - 2$

7. $24 \div (8 - 2)$
8. $9 + (6 \div 3)$
9. $(9 + 6) \div 3$

10. $(15 - 6) \times 2$
11. $15 - (6 \times 2)$
12. $(36 \div 4) \times 8$

13. $(48 \div 8) + 7$
14. $(42 \div 6) \times 6$
15. $(9 + 8) - 8$

16. $(54 \div 9) \times 9$
17. $(8 + 7) - 7$
18. $(5 \times 9) \div 9$

Copy, and draw the path.

★19.

★20.

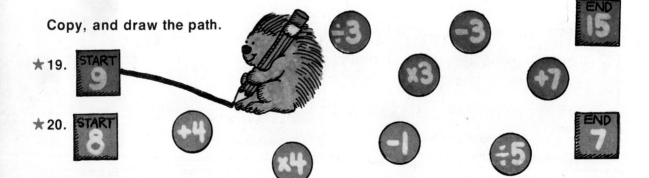

TARGET NUMBER

You can add, subtract, multiply, or divide. Can you use the three numbers to build the target number?

1. target number: **4**

 2 3 6

 {(2×6)÷3}

2. target number: **8**

9 6 7

3. target number: **3**

2 4 5

4. target number: **6**

 8 2 4

5. target number: **1**

 2 5 3

6. target number: **9**

 1 3 6

Play the game.

1. Prepare digit cards for 0 through 9.

2. Choose a leader.

3. Divide the class into two teams, team A and team B.

4. Without looking, the leader picks a target-number card and three other cards.

5. If team A can build the target number using the other three numbers, it scores 1 point.

6. The leader chooses new cards and the next team plays.

7. The first team to get 12 points wins the game.

125

Division with remainder

Some divisions do not come out evenly.

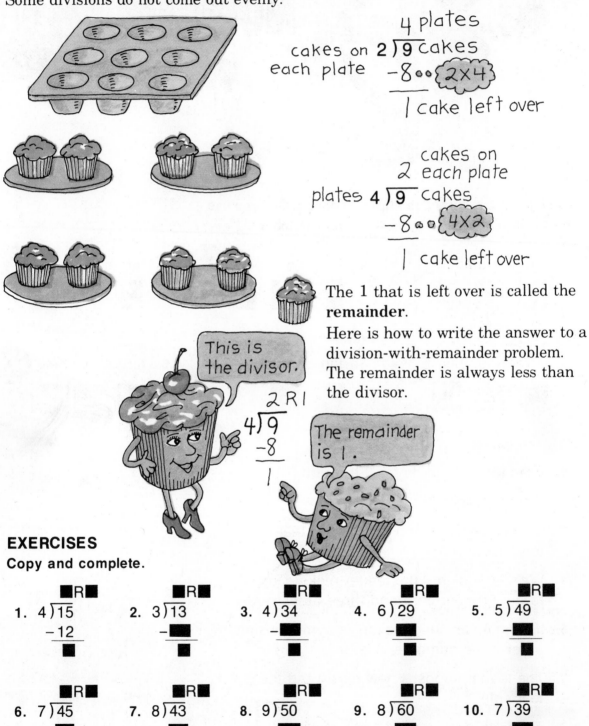

4 plates

cakes on 2)9 cakes
each plate   −8 ∘∘ {2×4}
             —————
             | cake left over

              cakes on
         2 each plate
plates 4)9 cakes
        −8 ∘∘ {4×2}
        —————
        | cake left over

The 1 that is left over is called the **remainder**.

Here is how to write the answer to a division-with-remainder problem. The remainder is always less than the divisor.

This is the divisor.

2 R 1
4)9
−8
——
1

The remainder is 1.

EXERCISES
Copy and complete.

1. ■R■
   4)15
   −12
   ——
   ■

2. ■R■
   3)13
   −■
   ——
   ■

3. ■R■
   4)34
   −■
   ——
   ■

4. ■R■
   6)29
   −■
   ——
   ■

5. ■R■
   5)49
   −■
   ——
   ■

6. ■R■
   7)45
   −■
   ——
   ■

7. ■R■
   8)43
   −■
   ——
   ■

8. ■R■
   9)50
   −■
   ——
   ■

9. ■R■
   8)60
   −■
   ——
   ■

10. ■R■
    7)39
    −■
    ——
    ■

126

Give each quotient and remainder.

Who am I?

11. 5)29   12. 9)20   13. 2)17

14. 5)27   15. 6)50   16. 9)50

17. 7)43   18. 4)37   19. 8)25

20. 7)30   21. 8)46   22. 9)35

23. 6)45   24. 4)30   25. 8)67

26. 7)15   27. 6)39   28. 9)25

29. 7)45   30. 5)49   31. 3)20

32. 7)54   33. 8)35   34. 9)80

39. If you divide me by 6, you get a quotient of 5 and a remainder of 4.

40. If you divide my by 9, you get a quotient of 3 and a remainder of 7.

★41. I am less than 20. If you divide me by 5, you get a remainder of 2. If you divide me by 6, you get a remainder of 5.

Solve.

35. 26 players
    4 on a team
    How many teams?
    How many left over?

36. 47 eggs
    6 in a carton
    How many cartons?
    How many left over?

37. 50 tires
    6 for each truck
    How many trucks?
    How many left over?

38. 43 desks
    8 in each row
    How many rows?
    How many left over?

Problem solving

These steps can help you solve problems.

Step 1. Read the problem.

Step 2. What facts are given?

Step 3. What is the question?

Step 4. Add, subtract, multiply, or divide?

1. Mr. Johnson bought a shovel for $6.75 and a rake for $5.29. What was the total cost?

2. Mrs. Johnson bought a hose for $3.45. She gave the clerk $10. How much change did she get?

3. Julie spent $.65 for carrot seeds, $.48 for radish seeds, and $1.85 for tomato plants. How much did she spend?

4. Matt had $4.60. He bought some pepper plants for $1.29 and some tomato plants for $1.85. How much money did he have left?

5. Mr. Johnson had 42 tulip bulbs. He ordered two bags of tulip bulbs. There are 30 bulbs in a bag. How many tulip bulbs did he have then?

6. The store had 6 cabbage plants in each tray. The Johnsons decided to buy 24 plants. How many trays did they buy?

7. Julie and Matt planted 3 rows of tomato plants with 9 plants in each row. How many tomato plants did they plant?

8. Julie planted 7 watermelon seeds in each of 8 hills. How many watermelon seeds did she plant?

9. Matt planted 72 onion sets. He planted the same number in each of 9 rows. How many did he plant in each row?

10. Julie has 20 pepper plants. She wants to plant them in rows of 6. How many rows will she have? How many plants will she have left over?

CHAPTER CHECKUP

Multiply. [pages 98–107, 109]

1. 8 $\times 6$	2. 5 $\times 0$	3. 9 $\times 6$	4. 7 $\times 8$	5. 8 $\times 8$	6. 6 $\times 8$
7. 6 $\times 6$	8. 7 $\times 6$	9. 8 $\times 7$	10. 6 $\times 9$	11. 9 $\times 9$	12. 8 $\times 9$
13. 5 $\times 9$	14. 8 $\times 5$	15. 9 $\times 7$	16. 7 $\times 7$	17. 5 $\times 7$	18. 5 $\times 5$

Divide. [pages 116–120, 122–123]

19. $6\overline{)36}$	20. $3\overline{)27}$	21. $6\overline{)30}$	22. $8\overline{)72}$	23. $7\overline{)49}$
24. $8\overline{)24}$	25. $6\overline{)54}$	26. $5\overline{)35}$	27. $8\overline{)56}$	28. $9\overline{)81}$
29. $9\overline{)63}$	30. $9\overline{)45}$	31. $6\overline{)48}$	32. $5\overline{)40}$	33. $6\overline{)42}$

Give each quotient and remainder. [pages 126–127]

34. $5\overline{)34}$	35. $9\overline{)60}$	36. $6\overline{)33}$	37. $8\overline{)29}$	38. $6\overline{)45}$
39. $4\overline{)23}$	40. $6\overline{)40}$	41. $5\overline{)19}$	42. $7\overline{)65}$	43. $4\overline{)35}$
44. $7\overline{)52}$	45. $9\overline{)75}$	46. $6\overline{)17}$	47. $8\overline{)70}$	48. $5\overline{)43}$

Solve. [pages 108, 114–115, 121, 128–129]

49. 6 puppies in a cage
    4 cages
    How many puppies?

50. 9 pencils in a package
    7 packages
    How many pencils?

51. 42 people
    6 people in each car
    How many cars?

52. 52 bottles
    8 bottles fill a carton
    How many cartons?
    How many bottles left over?

1

2

3

4

Project

Jane

number	number of rectangles
1	1
2	1
3	1
4	2
5	
6	

1. Get a piece of graph paper.

2. Stay on the grid lines and draw as many different rectangles as you can for each of the numbers. Each rectangle you draw should have a *different shape*.

3. Keep a record of what you found.

4. The numbers greater than one that have only one rectangle are called **prime numbers**. What prime numbers did you find?

CHAPTER REVIEW

Multiply.

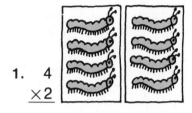 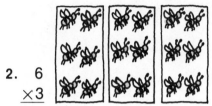 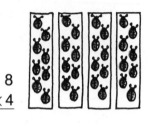

1. 4
   ×2

2. 6
   ×3

3. 8
   ×4

4. 7
   ×3

5. 6
   ×5

6. 4
   ×9

7. 5
   ×8

8. 7
   ×7

9. 7
   ×8

10. 5
    ×7

11. 8
    ×8

12. 7
    ×9

13. 8
    ×9

14. 6
    ×9

15. 7
    ×6

Divide.

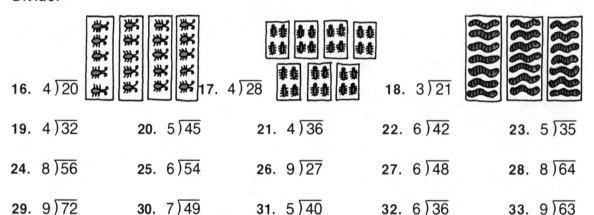

16. 4)20

17. 4)28

18. 3)21

19. 4)32

20. 5)45

21. 4)36

22. 6)42

23. 5)35

24. 8)56

25. 6)54

26. 9)27

27. 6)48

28. 8)64

29. 9)72

30. 7)49

31. 5)40

32. 6)36

33. 9)63

Give each quotient and remainder.

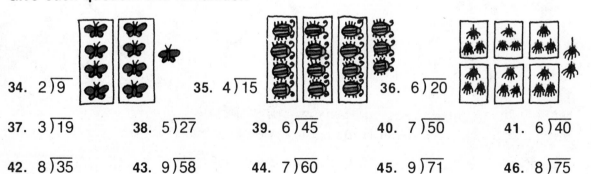

34. 2)9

35. 4)15

36. 6)20

37. 3)19

38. 5)27

39. 6)45

40. 7)50

41. 6)40

42. 8)35

43. 9)58

44. 7)60

45. 9)71

46. 8)75

CHAPTER CHALLENGE

Here is a factor tree.

First, 30 was written as 5 × 6. Then, 6 was written as 3 × 2.

Copy and complete each factor tree.
Do not use 1 as a factor.

1.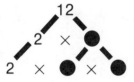

2.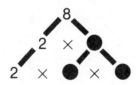

3.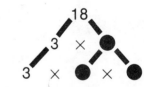

4.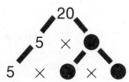

5.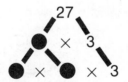

6.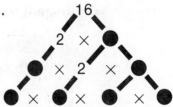

Make a factor tree for each of these numbers. Make each tree as large as possible. Do not use 1 as a factor.

7. 14   8. 30   9. 54   10. 32   11. 48   12. 64

MAJOR CHECKUP
Standardized Format

Choose the correct letter.

1. 708 rounded to the nearest ten is

    a. 700
    b. 710
    c. 800
    d. none of these

2. 448 rounded to the nearest hundred is

    a. 450
    b. 400
    c. 500
    d. none of these

3. Which digit in 793,465 is in the hundred thousands place?

    a. 7
    b. 3
    c. 9
    d. 4

4. The standard numeral for five hundred five thousand seventy-seven is

    a. 55,077
    b. 550,077
    c. 505,707
    d. none of these

5. Which number is the greatest?

    a. 78,397
    b. 654,261
    c. 645,368
    d. 656,207

6. Add.
$$\begin{array}{r} \$9.63 \\ +2.57 \\ \hline \end{array}$$

    a. $12.20
    b. $11.10
    c. $11.20
    d. none of these

7. Add.
$$\begin{array}{r} 593 \\ 269 \\ +742 \\ \hline \end{array}$$

    a. 1494
    b. 1604
    c. 1504
    d. none of these

8. Subtract.
$$\begin{array}{r} 5362 \\ -1785 \\ \hline \end{array}$$

    a. 3577
    b. 4423
    c. 4687
    d. none of these

9. To check this subtraction, you can add
$$\begin{array}{r} 603 \\ -259 \\ \hline 344 \end{array}$$

    a. 344 and 603
    b. 259 and 603
    c. 344 and 259
    d. none of these

10. What time is it?

    a. quarter to three
    b. quarter past three
    c. quarter to ten
    d. quarter past ten

11. How many minutes from 11:45 A.M. to 12:25 P.M.?

    a. 40
    b. 30
    c. 50
    d. 20

12. Which is the greatest amount of money?

    a. 3 quarters
    b. 1 half-dollar, 4 dimes
    c. 3 quarters, 3 dimes
    d. 1 dollar bill

6
Fractions

Fractions and regions

3 parts are blue
4 equal parts

numerator ⟶ $\dfrac{3}{4}$ is blue
denominator ⟶

Read as "three fourths."

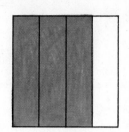

The same amount is shaded in both squares. So the fractions are **equivalent**.

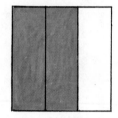 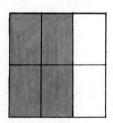

$$\frac{2}{3} \quad = \quad \frac{4}{6}$$

EXERCISES

What fraction is colored?

1.

2.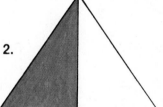

3.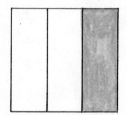

4.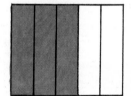

5.

6.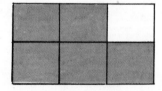

7.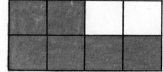

8.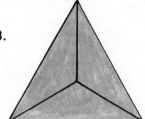

9.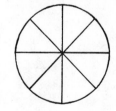

Give the equivalent fractions that are pictured.

10.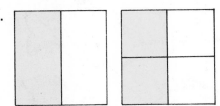

11.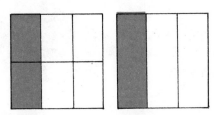

12.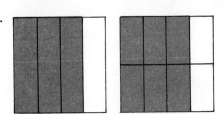

13.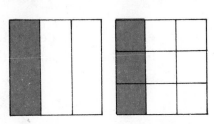

14.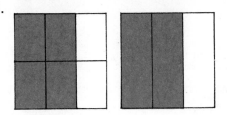

15.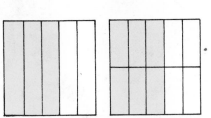

Who am I?

16. My numerator is 3 and my denominator is 4.

17. My denominator is 5 and my numerator is 2.

Complete. If you need to, draw pictures.

18. $\frac{1}{2} = \frac{?}{4}$ 19. $\frac{1}{2} = \frac{?}{6}$ 20. $\frac{1}{2} = \frac{?}{8}$ 21. $\frac{1}{2} = \frac{?}{10}$

22. $\frac{1}{3} = \frac{?}{6}$ 23. $\frac{1}{3} = \frac{?}{9}$ 24. $\frac{1}{4} = \frac{?}{8}$ 25. $\frac{1}{4} = \frac{?}{12}$

Fractions and sets

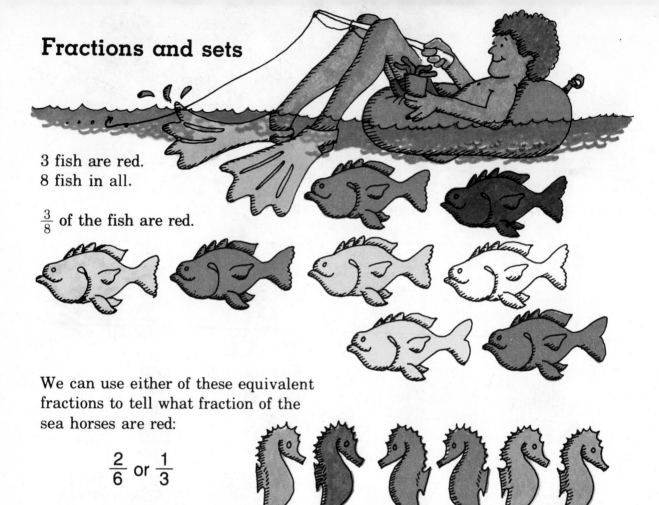

3 fish are red.
8 fish in all.

$\frac{3}{8}$ of the fish are red.

We can use either of these equivalent
fractions to tell what fraction of the
sea horses are red:

$$\frac{2}{6} \text{ or } \frac{1}{3}$$

Give two fractions that tell what fraction of the
sea horses are green.

EXERCISES

1.

a. What fraction of the shells
are red?

b. What fraction of the shells
are blue?

2.

a. What fraction of the star-
fish are green?

b. What fraction of the star-
fish are yellow?

3.

What fraction are

- **a.** red?
- **b.** yellow?
- **c.** blue?
- **d.** not blue?
- **e.** not yellow?

4.

What fraction are

- **a.** green?
- **b.** red?
- **c.** blue?
- **d.** not blue?
- **e.** not red?

Give *two* fractions that tell what fraction of the toys are red.

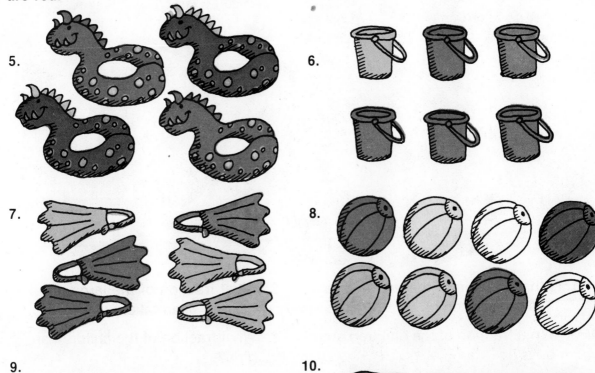

5.

6.

7.

8.

9.

10.

Problem solving

1. What fraction of the large pizza has been taken?

2. What fraction of the large pizza has not been taken?

3. What fraction of the children are boys?

4. What fraction of the children are girls?

5. What fraction of the small pizza has not been taken?

6. What fraction of the small pizza has been taken?

7. What fraction of the children are drinking root beer?

8. What fraction of the children are drinking milk?

1. 5
   ×4

2. 8
   ×3

3. 5
   ×6

4. 4
   ×5

5. 6
   ×4

6. 4
   ×8

7. 3
   ×7

8. 7
   ×4

9. 5
   ×5

10. 6
    ×6

11. 3
    ×9

12. 4
    ×9

13. 7
    ×5

14. 7
    ×9

15. 6
    ×7

16. 7
    ×8

17. 6
    ×8

18. 9
    ×8

9. What fraction of the boys are drinking milk?

10. What fraction of the girls are not drinking milk?

11. When two more pieces of the small pizza are taken, what fraction of the pizza will be left? Give two answers.

12. When three more pieces of the large pizza are taken, what fraction of the pizza will be left? Give two answers.

Fraction of a number

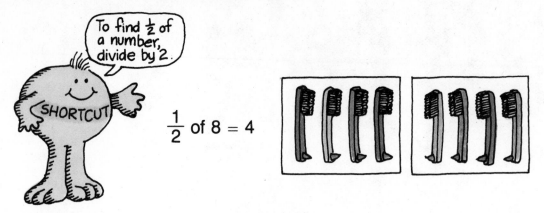

To find $\frac{1}{2}$ of a number, divide by 2.

$\frac{1}{2}$ of 8 = 4

To find $\frac{1}{3}$ of a number, divide by 3.

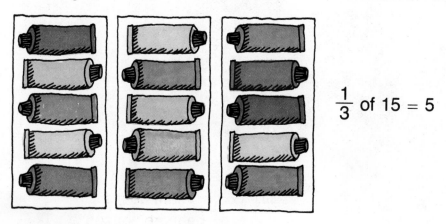

$\frac{1}{3}$ of 15 = 5

EXERCISES
Complete.

1. $\frac{1}{2}$ of 12 = _?_

2. $\frac{1}{2}$ of 10 = _?_

3. $\frac{1}{3}$ of 9 = _?_

4. $\frac{1}{3}$ of 12 = _?_

5. $\frac{1}{4}$ of 12 = _?_

6. $\frac{1}{4}$ of 20 = _?_

Compute.

7. $\frac{1}{2}$ of 4

8. $\frac{1}{3}$ of 6

9. $\frac{1}{5}$ of 25

10. $\frac{1}{6}$ of 18

11. $\frac{1}{4}$ of 8

12. $\frac{1}{2}$ of 8

13. $\frac{1}{4}$ of 28

14. $\frac{1}{5}$ of 30

15. $\frac{1}{3}$ of 21

16. $\frac{1}{6}$ of 24

17. $\frac{1}{2}$ of 6

18. $\frac{1}{8}$ of 24

19. $\frac{1}{5}$ of 40

20. $\frac{1}{4}$ of 36

21. $\frac{1}{3}$ of 24

22. $\frac{1}{3}$ of 18

23. $\frac{1}{8}$ of 48

24. $\frac{1}{4}$ of 32

1 dozen = 12

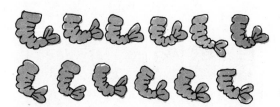

25. $\frac{1}{2}$ of a dozen = $\underline{\ ?\ }$

26. $\frac{1}{3}$ of a dozen = $\underline{\ ?\ }$

27. $\frac{1}{4}$ of a dozen = $\underline{\ ?\ }$

28. $\frac{1}{6}$ of a dozen = $\underline{\ ?\ }$

Solve.

29. 12 bicycles
$\frac{1}{3}$ of them are red
How many are red?

30. 12 ice cream cones
$\frac{1}{2}$ of them are chocolate
How many are chocolate?

31. Susan baked a dozen cupcakes.
She gave $\frac{1}{3}$ of them to a friend.
How many did she give away?
How many did she have left?

32. David baked 3 dozen cookies.
He burned $\frac{1}{4}$ of them.
How many were not burned?

PROBLEM SOLVING

Make up a story.

143

Fraction of a number

To find a fraction of a number: divide the number
by the denominator; then multiply by the
numerator.

EXAMPLE. $\frac{2}{3}$ of $12 = 8$

Step 1. Divide by 3 to find $\frac{1}{3}$.

$12 \div 3 = 4$

Step 2. Multiply the quotient by 2
to find $\frac{2}{3}$.

$4 \times 2 = 8$

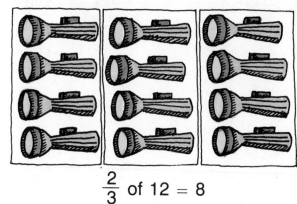

$\frac{2}{3}$ of $12 = 8$

$\frac{3}{4}$ of $12 = 9$

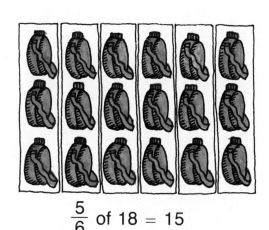

$\frac{5}{6}$ of $18 = 15$

EXERCISES

Complete.

1. $\frac{2}{3}$ of $9 = \underline{\ ?\ }$

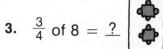

2. $\frac{2}{3}$ of $15 = \underline{\ ?\ }$

3. $\frac{3}{4}$ of $8 = \underline{\ ?\ }$

4. $\frac{3}{4}$ of $16 = \underline{\ ?\ }$

144

Compute.

5. $\frac{1}{3}$ of 18

6. $\frac{2}{3}$ of 18

7. $\frac{3}{3}$ of 18

8. $\frac{1}{4}$ of 20

9. $\frac{2}{4}$ of 20

10. $\frac{3}{4}$ of 20

11. $\frac{1}{5}$ of 30

12. $\frac{2}{5}$ of 30

13. $\frac{3}{5}$ of 30

14. $\frac{1}{6}$ of 42

15. $\frac{1}{8}$ of 40

16. $\frac{3}{8}$ of 24

17. $\frac{3}{8}$ of 8

18. $\frac{5}{6}$ of 36

19. $\frac{5}{8}$ of 32

20. $\frac{5}{6}$ of 30

21. $\frac{7}{8}$ of 16

22. $\frac{5}{9}$ of 18

Find the sale price.

23. $\frac{2}{3}$ of marked price

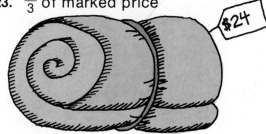

$24

24. $\frac{3}{4}$ of marked price

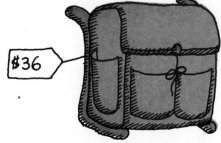

$36

25. $\frac{3}{4}$ of marked price

$32

26. $\frac{2}{3}$ of marked price

$27

Solve.

27. Sally went on a 15-kilometer hike. At the end of 3 hours, she had hiked $\frac{2}{3}$ of the way. How many kilometers had she hiked?

28. John had $12. He spent $\frac{2}{3}$ of it for a camping knife. Later, he bought a canteen for $2.79. How much money did he have left?

Problem solving

Price tags shown on the items:
- Lock: $5, $\frac{1}{5}$ OFF
- Brake lever: $\frac{1}{3}$ OFF, $3
- Reflector: $\frac{1}{5}$ OFF, $.45
- Rack: $\frac{1}{3}$ OFF, $12
- Handle grips: $12, $\frac{1}{4}$ OFF
- Bicycle: $92.50

1. Sarah wanted to buy the bicycle. She had $62.75. How much more money did she need?

2. The store owner offered Juan $37.50 for his old bicycle. How much more money would Juan need to buy the new bicycle?

3. Before the sale, what was the total price of a bell and a reflector?

4. Before the sale, how much more did the bell cost than the handle grips?

5. a. What is the regular price of the lock?
   b. How many dollars off on sale?
   c. What is the sale price?

6. a. What is the regular price of the pump?
   b. How many dollars off on sale?
   c. What is the sale price?

7. What is the sale price of the basket?

8. What is the sale price of the fender?

9. Eric bought a kickstand and a rack. What was the total price?

10. Dave bought a chain and a light. What was the total price?

11. Paul had $5. He bought a horn. How much money did he have left?

✻12. Mary had $9.40. She bought a lock and a kickstand. How much money did she have left?

Equivalent fractions

If you multiply the numerator and denominator of a fraction by the same number (not 0), you get an equivalent fraction.

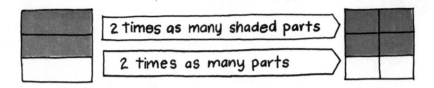

$$\frac{2}{3} = \frac{4}{6}$$

EXERCISES
Complete.

1.

$$\frac{1}{2} \xrightarrow{\times 2} \frac{?}{?} \xleftarrow{\times 2}$$

2.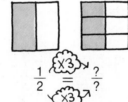

$$\frac{1}{2} \xrightarrow{\times 3} \frac{?}{?} \xleftarrow{\times 3}$$

3.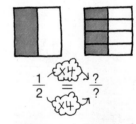

$$\frac{1}{2} \xrightarrow{\times 4} \frac{?}{?} \xleftarrow{\times 4}$$

4.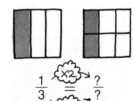

$$\frac{1}{3} \xrightarrow{\times 2} \frac{?}{?} \xleftarrow{\times 2}$$

5.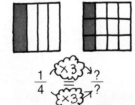

$$\frac{1}{4} \xrightarrow{\times 3} \frac{?}{?} \xleftarrow{\times 3}$$

6.

$$\frac{2}{3} \xrightarrow{\times 3} \frac{?}{?} \xleftarrow{\times 3}$$

7.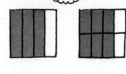

$$\frac{3}{4} \xrightarrow{\times 2} \frac{?}{?} \xleftarrow{\times 2}$$

8.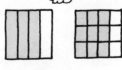

$$\frac{3}{4} \xrightarrow{\times 3} \frac{?}{?} \xleftarrow{\times 3}$$

9.

$$\frac{5}{5} \xrightarrow{\times 2} \frac{?}{?} \xleftarrow{\times 2}$$

148

Complete.

10. $\frac{1}{4}$  ×2 = ×2 → $\frac{?}{?}$

11. $\frac{1}{3}$ ×3 = ×3 → $\frac{?}{?}$

12. $\frac{1}{2}$ ×5 = ×5 → $\frac{?}{?}$

13. $\frac{2}{3}$ ×4 = ×4 → $\frac{?}{?}$

14. $\frac{2}{2}$ ×2 = ×2 → $\frac{?}{?}$

15. $\frac{2}{5}$ ×3 = ×3 → $\frac{?}{?}$

16. $\frac{1}{6}$ ×3 = think! → $\frac{?}{?}$

17. $\frac{1}{8}$ ×2 = think! → $\frac{?}{?}$

18. $\frac{3}{8}$ think! = ×2 → $\frac{?}{?}$

19. **Copy and complete this equivalent fractions table.**

	×2	×3	×4	×5
$\frac{1}{2}$	$\frac{2}{4}$	$\frac{3}{6}$		
$\frac{1}{3}$				
$\frac{2}{3}$				
$\frac{1}{4}$				
$\frac{3}{4}$				

BUBBLE GUM

Copy and complete.

20. $\frac{1}{2} = \frac{?}{10}$

21. $\frac{1}{3} = \frac{?}{12}$

22. $\frac{3}{5} = \frac{?}{10}$

23. $\frac{2}{3} = \frac{?}{6}$

24. $\frac{2}{3} = \frac{?}{9}$

25. $\frac{3}{4} = \frac{?}{8}$

26. $\frac{3}{8} = \frac{?}{16}$

27. $\frac{5}{8} = \frac{?}{24}$

149

Reducing fractions to lower terms

If you divide the numerator and denominator of a fraction by the same number, you get an equivalent fraction.

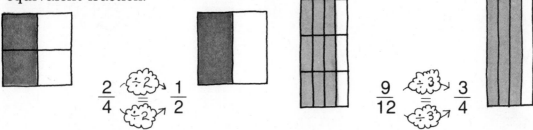

$$\frac{2}{4} \underset{\div 2}{\overset{\div 2}{=}} \frac{1}{2} \qquad \frac{9}{12} \underset{\div 3}{\overset{\div 3}{=}} \frac{3}{4}$$

Notice that we got a fraction with a smaller numerator and denominator. We call this **reducing a fraction to lower terms**. A fraction that cannot be reduced to lower terms is in **lowest terms**.

EXERCISES
Complete.

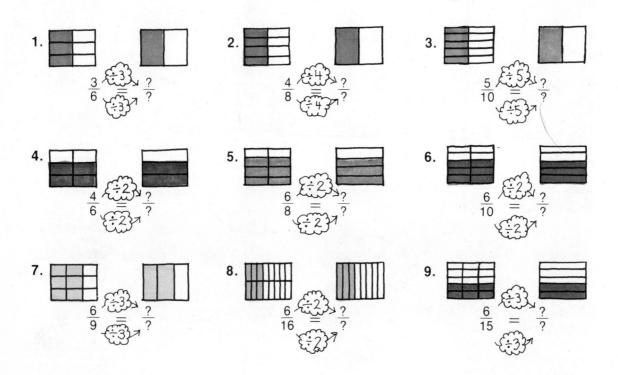

1. $\dfrac{3}{6} \underset{\div 3}{\overset{\div 3}{=}} \dfrac{?}{?}$

2. $\dfrac{4}{8} \underset{\div 4}{\overset{\div 4}{=}} \dfrac{?}{?}$

3. $\dfrac{5}{10} \underset{\div 5}{\overset{\div 5}{=}} \dfrac{?}{?}$

4. $\dfrac{4}{6} \underset{\div 2}{\overset{\div 2}{=}} \dfrac{?}{?}$

5. $\dfrac{6}{8} \underset{\div 2}{\overset{\div 2}{=}} \dfrac{?}{?}$

6. $\dfrac{6}{10} \underset{\div 2}{\overset{\div 2}{=}} \dfrac{?}{?}$

7. $\dfrac{6}{9} \underset{\div 3}{\overset{\div 3}{=}} \dfrac{?}{?}$

8. $\dfrac{6}{16} \underset{\div 2}{\overset{\div 2}{=}} \dfrac{?}{?}$

9. $\dfrac{6}{15} \underset{\div 3}{\overset{\div 3}{=}} \dfrac{?}{?}$

Complete.

10. $\dfrac{5}{10}$ 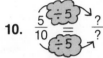 $\begin{array}{c}\div 5 \to \dfrac{?}{?} \\ \div 5 \to \end{array}$

11. $\dfrac{3}{9}$ $\begin{array}{c}\div 3 \to \dfrac{?}{?} \\ \div 3 \to \end{array}$

12. $\dfrac{6}{12}$ $\begin{array}{c}\div 6 \to \dfrac{?}{?} \\ \div 6 \to \end{array}$

13. $\dfrac{3}{12}$ $\begin{array}{c}\div 3 \to \dfrac{?}{?} \\ \div 3 \to \end{array}$

14. $\dfrac{6}{10}$ $\begin{array}{c}\div 2 \to \dfrac{?}{?} \\ \div 2 \to \end{array}$

15. $\dfrac{4}{12}$ $\begin{array}{c}\div 4 \to \dfrac{?}{?} \\ \div 4 \to \end{array}$

16. $\dfrac{10}{16}$ $\begin{array}{c}\div 2 \to \dfrac{?}{?} \\ \text{think} \to \end{array}$

17. $\dfrac{12}{16}$ $\begin{array}{c}\text{think} \to \dfrac{?}{?} \\ \div 4 \to \end{array}$

18. $\dfrac{8}{8}$ $\begin{array}{c}\div 8 \to \dfrac{?}{?} \\ \text{think} \to \end{array}$

Reduce to lowest terms.

19. $\dfrac{2}{4}$

20. $\dfrac{2}{10}$

21. $\dfrac{3}{9}$

22. $\dfrac{4}{6}$

23. $\dfrac{5}{10}$

24. $\dfrac{2}{12}$

25. $\dfrac{2}{6}$

26. $\dfrac{6}{8}$

27. $\dfrac{3}{6}$

28. $\dfrac{9}{12}$

29. $\dfrac{2}{16}$

30. $\dfrac{10}{15}$

31. $\dfrac{8}{12}$

32. $\dfrac{6}{6}$

33. $\dfrac{4}{12}$

34. $\dfrac{6}{9}$

35. $\dfrac{4}{8}$

36. $\dfrac{15}{20}$

Who am I?

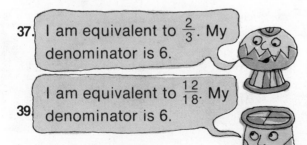

37. I am equivalent to $\dfrac{2}{3}$. My denominator is 6.

38. I am equivalent to $\dfrac{3}{4}$. My numerator is 12.

39. I am equivalent to $\dfrac{12}{18}$. My denominator is 6.

40. I am equivalent to $\dfrac{16}{24}$. I am in lowest terms.

151

Reducing fractions to lowest terms

You can reduce a fraction to lowest terms by dividing both numerator and denominator by the greatest possible number,

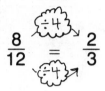

$$\frac{8}{12} = \frac{2}{3}$$

or

by dividing by a smaller number, then another smaller number, and so on, until the fraction is in lowest terms.

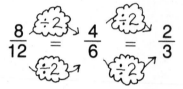

$$\frac{8}{12} = \frac{4}{6} = \frac{2}{3}$$

EXERCISES
Reduce to lowest terms.

1. $\frac{5}{10}$ 2. $\frac{9}{12}$ 3. $\frac{15}{20}$ 4. $\frac{24}{36}$ 5. $\frac{15}{25}$ 6. $\frac{15}{30}$

7. $\frac{16}{24}$ 8. $\frac{16}{18}$ 9. $\frac{12}{18}$ 10. $\frac{12}{16}$ 11. $\frac{9}{24}$ 12. $\frac{6}{24}$

13. $\frac{9}{36}$ 14. $\frac{8}{24}$ 15. $\frac{18}{27}$ 16. $\frac{18}{24}$ 17. $\frac{42}{56}$ 18. $\frac{35}{40}$

19. $\frac{27}{36}$ 20. $\frac{24}{48}$ 21. $\frac{72}{81}$ 22. $\frac{56}{72}$ 23. $\frac{48}{56}$ 24. $\frac{40}{56}$

$\frac{6}{9}$ $\frac{6}{24}$ $\frac{5}{15}$ $\frac{6}{8}$ $\frac{1}{4}$ $\frac{8}{12}$ $\frac{1}{3}$

$\frac{2}{3}$ $\frac{10}{15}$ $\frac{2}{4}$ $\frac{3}{6}$ $\frac{12}{16}$ $\frac{2}{6}$ $\frac{16}{24}$

$\frac{3}{9}$ $\frac{2}{8}$ $\frac{9}{12}$ $\frac{4}{16}$ $\frac{18}{24}$ $\frac{5}{20}$ $\frac{5}{10}$

$\frac{3}{12}$ $\frac{15}{20}$ $\frac{4}{12}$ $\frac{4}{6}$ $\frac{12}{18}$ $\frac{3}{4}$ $\frac{6}{18}$

Are the two fractions equivalent?

1. $\frac{1}{2}$ $\frac{3}{6}$ 2. $\frac{4}{6}$ $\frac{2}{3}$ 3. $\frac{3}{9}$ $\frac{1}{2}$ 4. $\frac{4}{16}$ $\frac{1}{4}$

PLAY THE GAME

1. Divide the class into two teams, team A and team B.

2. A player from team A picks two cards. If the fractions are equivalent, team A gets one point. If the fractions are not equivalent, team A loses a point.

3. A player from team B picks two of the cards that are left.

4. The teams take turns until only two cards are left. Then the game ends.

5. The team with more points wins.

More about equivalent fractions

Some of the points on the number lines below have been labeled with fractions. The fractions that "line up" are equivalent fractions. They all name the same number.

Here we go!

EXERCISES

Copy and complete. Check your work by using the number lines above.

1. $\frac{1}{2} = \frac{?}{8}$

2. $\frac{6}{6} = \frac{?}{3}$

3. $\frac{1}{2} = \frac{?}{6}$

4. $\frac{1}{2} = \frac{?}{4}$

5. $\frac{1}{3} = \frac{?}{6}$

6. $\frac{4}{8} = \frac{?}{4}$

7. $\frac{2}{8} = \frac{?}{4}$

8. $\frac{1}{4} = \frac{?}{8}$

9. $\frac{0}{8} = \frac{?}{2}$

10. $\frac{6}{8} = \frac{?}{4}$

11. $\frac{5}{4} = \frac{?}{8}$

12. $\frac{4}{3} = \frac{?}{6}$

13. $\frac{6}{6} = \frac{?}{2}$

14. $\frac{3}{4} = \frac{?}{8}$

15. $\frac{4}{8} = \frac{?}{2}$

16. $\frac{12}{8} = \frac{?}{4}$

154

17. **a.** Write five fractions equivalent to $\frac{1}{2}$.

b. Write five fractions equivalent to $\frac{1}{3}$.

c. Pick a fraction from the first list and a fraction from the second list that have the same denominator.

18. **a.** Write five fractions equivalent to $\frac{2}{3}$.

b. Write five fractions equivalent to $\frac{1}{4}$.

c. Pick a fraction from the first list and a fraction from the second list that have the same denominator.

19. **a.** Write five fractions equivalent to $\frac{3}{4}$.

b. Write five fractions equivalent to $\frac{1}{5}$.

c. Pick a fraction from the first list and a fraction from the second list that have the same denominator.

PROBLEM SOLVING

Number News
$$\frac{1}{2} = \frac{3}{6}$$

Keeping Skills Sharp

Find each product.

1. 5×7	2. 3×8	3. 9×4	4. 5×6
5. 8×4	6. 9×5	7. 5×8	8. 6×7
9. 9×3	10. 5×5	11. 4×7	12. 3×7
13. 7×8	14. 8×8	15. 9×9	16. 7×7
17. 6×9	18. 4×4	19. 9×8	20. 7×8

Make up a story.

Comparing fractions

Pictures can help you to compare fractions.

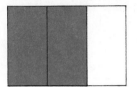 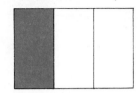 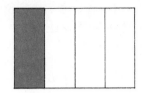 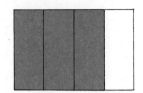

$$\frac{2}{3} > \frac{1}{3}$$

(is greater than)

$$\frac{1}{4} < \frac{3}{4}$$

(is less than)

Numbers get greater.

$$\frac{0}{4} \quad \frac{1}{4} \quad \frac{2}{4} \quad \frac{3}{4} \quad \frac{4}{4} \quad \frac{5}{4} \quad \frac{6}{4} \quad \frac{7}{4} \quad \frac{8}{4}$$

$$\frac{0}{2} \quad \frac{1}{2} \quad \frac{2}{2} \quad \frac{3}{2} \quad \frac{4}{2}$$

Numbers get less.

$$\frac{1}{4} < \frac{1}{2} \qquad\qquad \frac{3}{4} > \frac{1}{2}$$

EXERCISES

< or >?

1.

$$\frac{1}{2} \bigcirc \frac{1}{3}$$

2.

$$\frac{1}{2} \bigcirc \frac{1}{4}$$

3.

$$\frac{1}{5} \bigcirc \frac{1}{3}$$

4.

$$\frac{1}{6} \bigcirc \frac{1}{3}$$

5.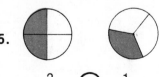

$$\frac{2}{4} \bigcirc \frac{1}{3}$$

6.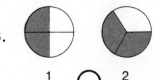

$$\frac{1}{2} \bigcirc \frac{2}{3}$$

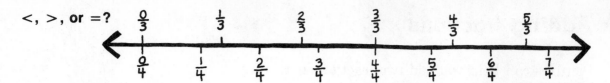

<, >, or =?

7. $\frac{1}{3}$ ◯ $\frac{2}{3}$ **8.** $\frac{4}{3}$ ◯ $\frac{3}{3}$ **9.** $\frac{5}{3}$ ◯ $\frac{1}{3}$ **10.** $\frac{2}{4}$ ◯ $\frac{0}{4}$

11. $\frac{1}{4}$ ◯ $\frac{3}{4}$ **12.** $\frac{0}{3}$ ◯ $\frac{0}{4}$ **13.** $\frac{5}{4}$ ◯ $\frac{1}{4}$ **14.** $\frac{6}{4}$ ◯ $\frac{4}{4}$

15. $\frac{1}{3}$ ◯ $\frac{1}{4}$ **16.** $\frac{3}{4}$ ◯ $\frac{2}{3}$ **17.** $\frac{5}{4}$ ◯ $\frac{4}{3}$ **18.** $\frac{3}{3}$ ◯ $\frac{4}{4}$

<, >, or =?

19. $\frac{1}{2}$ ◯ $\frac{3}{2}$ **20.** $\frac{5}{4}$ ◯ $\frac{3}{4}$ **21.** $\frac{3}{8}$ ◯ $\frac{5}{8}$ **22.** $\frac{2}{3}$ ◯ $\frac{3}{3}$

23. $\frac{1}{2}$ ◯ $\frac{1}{4}$ **24.** $\frac{1}{6}$ ◯ $\frac{1}{3}$ **25.** $\frac{5}{6}$ ◯ $\frac{1}{2}$ **26.** $\frac{1}{4}$ ◯ $\frac{3}{8}$

Which would you rather have

27. $\frac{1}{3}$ of a dozen cookies or $\frac{2}{3}$ of a dozen cookies?

28. $\frac{1}{2}$ of a dollar or $\frac{1}{4}$ of a dollar?

Which is shorter

29. $\frac{1}{2}$ of an hour or $\frac{3}{4}$ of an hour?

30. $\frac{2}{3}$ of a day or $\frac{3}{4}$ of a day?

Which is more

31. $\frac{1}{3}$ of a dozen or $\frac{1}{4}$ of a dozen?

32. $\frac{2}{3}$ of 24 children or $\frac{3}{4}$ of 24 children?

157

Adding fractions

Pictures can help you add two fractions with the same denominator.

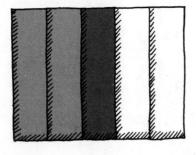 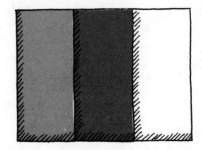

$$\frac{2}{5} + \frac{1}{5} = \frac{3}{5} \qquad \frac{1}{3} + \frac{1}{3} = \frac{2}{3}$$

When adding two fractions that have the same denominator:

Step 1. Add the numerators to get the numerator of the sum.

Step 2. Use the same denominator for the denominator of the sum.

EXERCISES
Give each sum.

1.

$$\frac{1}{4} + \frac{1}{4}$$

2.

$$\frac{2}{5} + \frac{2}{5}$$

3.

$$\frac{3}{5} + \frac{1}{5}$$

4.

$$\frac{1}{6} + \frac{1}{6}$$

5.

$$\frac{2}{6} + \frac{3}{6}$$

6.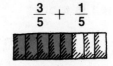

$$\frac{3}{8} + \frac{2}{8}$$

7.

$$\frac{2}{4} + \frac{1}{4}$$

8.

$$\frac{3}{7} + \frac{2}{7}$$

9.

$$\frac{2}{5} + \frac{3}{5}$$

Give each sum.

10. $\dfrac{4}{3} + \dfrac{1}{3}$

11. $\dfrac{2}{5} + \dfrac{2}{5}$

12. $\dfrac{0}{2} + \dfrac{3}{2}$

13. $\dfrac{3}{9} + \dfrac{2}{9}$

14. $\dfrac{1}{8} + \dfrac{4}{8}$

15. $\dfrac{3}{8} + \dfrac{2}{8}$

16. $\dfrac{1}{10} + \dfrac{6}{10}$

17. $\dfrac{2}{5} + \dfrac{1}{5}$

Add.

18. $\dfrac{0}{4}$
$+\dfrac{3}{4}$

19. $\dfrac{4}{6}$
$+\dfrac{1}{6}$

20. $\dfrac{4}{7}$
$+\dfrac{2}{7}$

21. $\dfrac{2}{5}$
$+\dfrac{4}{5}$

22. $\dfrac{1}{3}$
$+\dfrac{1}{3}$

23. $\dfrac{2}{9}$
$+\dfrac{5}{9}$

24. $\dfrac{1}{6}$
$+\dfrac{5}{6}$

25. $\dfrac{0}{12}$
$+\dfrac{5}{12}$

26. $\dfrac{4}{12}$
$+\dfrac{3}{12}$

27. $\dfrac{2}{8}$
$+\dfrac{3}{8}$

28. $\dfrac{3}{9}$
$+\dfrac{5}{9}$

29. $\dfrac{1}{6}$
$+\dfrac{4}{6}$

Add. Then reduce the answer to lowest terms.

30. $\dfrac{1}{4}$
$+\dfrac{1}{4}$

31. $\dfrac{1}{8}$
$+\dfrac{1}{8}$

32. $\dfrac{1}{6}$
$+\dfrac{1}{6}$

33. $\dfrac{1}{10}$
$+\dfrac{1}{10}$

34. $\dfrac{5}{8}$
$+\dfrac{1}{8}$

35. $\dfrac{2}{9}$
$+\dfrac{4}{9}$

Keeping Skills Sharp

1. $3\overline{)18}$

2. $5\overline{)20}$

3. $4\overline{)24}$

4. $7\overline{)21}$

5. $3\overline{)24}$

6. $3\overline{)27}$

7. $5\overline{)25}$

8. $7\overline{)28}$

9. $6\overline{)48}$

10. $6\overline{)54}$

11. $4\overline{)32}$

12. $8\overline{)40}$

13. $5\overline{)35}$

14. $8\overline{)72}$

15. $6\overline{)36}$

16. $7\overline{)49}$

17. $4\overline{)36}$

18. $7\overline{)56}$

19. $9\overline{)45}$

20. $9\overline{)81}$

21. $9\overline{)63}$

22. $6\overline{)42}$

23. $8\overline{)64}$

24. $8\overline{)48}$

25. $6\overline{)42}$

More about adding

The fractions on each strip are equivalent.

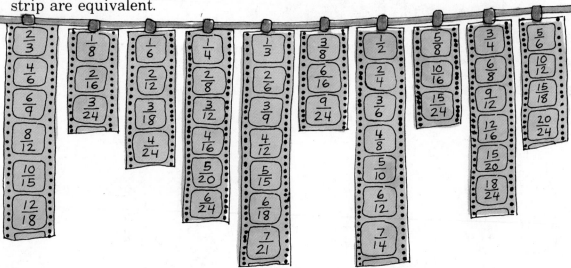

EXAMPLE 1. The steps show how to add fractions that have different denominators.

$$\frac{1}{8} + \frac{1}{4}$$

Step 1. Find equivalent fractions so that both denominators are the same.

$$\frac{1}{8} + \frac{1}{4}$$

Step 2. Think about the fractions that have the same denominator. Add.

$$\frac{1}{8} + \frac{1}{4} = \frac{3}{8}$$

$$\frac{1}{8} + \frac{2}{8}$$

EXAMPLE 2.

Step 1. $\frac{1}{2} + \frac{3}{8}$

Step 2. $\frac{1}{2} + \frac{3}{8} = \frac{7}{8}$

$$\frac{4}{8} + \frac{3}{8}$$

EXERCISES
Give each sum.

1. $\frac{1}{3} + \frac{1}{6}$

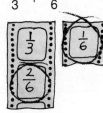

2. $\frac{3}{8} + \frac{1}{4}$

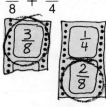

3. $\frac{1}{6} + \frac{2}{3}$

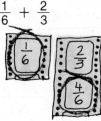

4. $\frac{1}{4} + \frac{1}{6}$

5. $\frac{3}{8} + \frac{1}{2}$

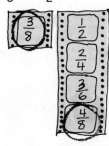

6. $\frac{3}{4} + \frac{1}{8}$

Give each sum. If you need to, use the fraction strips.

7. $\frac{1}{2} + \frac{1}{4}$

8. $\frac{1}{4} + \frac{1}{2}$

9. $\frac{1}{2} + \frac{1}{6}$

10. $\frac{5}{8} + \frac{1}{4}$

11. $\frac{1}{4} + \frac{3}{8}$

12. $\frac{1}{8} + \frac{3}{4}$

13. $\frac{1}{6} + \frac{1}{3}$

14. $\frac{1}{6} + \frac{2}{3}$

15. $\frac{1}{4} + \frac{1}{8}$

Solve.

16. Robert mowed $\frac{1}{2}$ of his lawn before dinner and $\frac{1}{4}$ of it after dinner. What fraction of the lawn did he mow?

17. Jan bought $\frac{1}{4}$ pound of Swiss cheese and $\frac{5}{8}$ pound of American cheese. How many pounds of cheese did she buy?

Give each sum in lowest terms.

18. $\frac{1}{3}$
$+\frac{1}{2}$

19. $\frac{1}{4}$
$+\frac{1}{3}$

20. $\frac{2}{3}$
$+\frac{1}{4}$

21. $\frac{3}{4}$
$+\frac{1}{6}$

22. $\frac{3}{8}$
$+\frac{1}{6}$

23. $\frac{1}{6}$
$+\frac{5}{8}$

Subtracting fractions

You can draw pictures to help you subtract fractions.

$\dfrac{2}{3}$

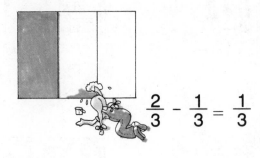

$\dfrac{2}{3} - \dfrac{1}{3} = \dfrac{1}{3}$

$\dfrac{4}{5}$

$\dfrac{4}{5} - \dfrac{1}{5} = \dfrac{3}{5}$

When subtracting two fractions that have the same denominator:

Step 1. Subtract the numerators to get the numerator of the difference.

Step 2. Use the same denominator for the denominator of the difference.

EXERCISES
Give each difference.

1. $\dfrac{3}{4} - \dfrac{2}{4}$

2. 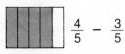 $\dfrac{4}{5} - \dfrac{3}{5}$

3. $\dfrac{4}{5} - \dfrac{2}{5}$

4. $\dfrac{5}{7} - \dfrac{2}{7}$

5. 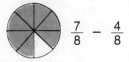 $\dfrac{7}{8} - \dfrac{4}{8}$

6. $\dfrac{4}{6} - \dfrac{3}{6}$

7. $\frac{7}{5} - \frac{2}{5}$ 8. $\frac{5}{5} - \frac{1}{5}$ 9. $\frac{7}{6} - \frac{2}{6}$ 10. $\frac{2}{3} - \frac{1}{3}$

11. $\frac{7}{4} - \frac{6}{4}$ 12. $\frac{9}{3} - \frac{2}{3}$ 13. $\frac{5}{8} - \frac{2}{8}$ 14. $\frac{3}{5} - \frac{3}{5}$

Subtract.

15. $\frac{4}{9}$ 16. $\frac{9}{8}$ 17. $\frac{2}{10}$ 18. $\frac{4}{5}$ 19. $\frac{5}{8}$ 20. $\frac{3}{6}$
$-\frac{1}{9}$ $-\frac{4}{8}$ $-\frac{1}{10}$ $-\frac{3}{5}$ $-\frac{0}{8}$ $-\frac{2}{6}$

21. $\frac{8}{9}$ 22. $\frac{5}{6}$ 23. $\frac{9}{12}$ 24. $\frac{7}{12}$ 25. $\frac{8}{10}$ 26. $\frac{7}{8}$
$-\frac{3}{9}$ $-\frac{4}{6}$ $-\frac{2}{12}$ $-\frac{2}{12}$ $-\frac{5}{10}$ $-\frac{7}{8}$

Copy and complete.

27.

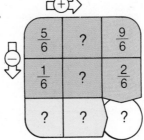

28.

29.

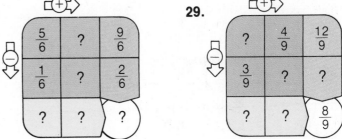

Subtract. Then reduce the answer to lowest terms.

30. $\frac{5}{8}$ 31. $\frac{7}{4}$ 32. $\frac{5}{6}$ 33. $\frac{7}{8}$ 34. $\frac{8}{9}$ 35. $\frac{10}{12}$
$-\frac{1}{8}$ $-\frac{5}{4}$ $-\frac{3}{6}$ $-\frac{1}{8}$ $-\frac{2}{9}$ $-\frac{2}{12}$
$\frac{4}{8} = \frac{1}{2}$

More about subtracting

You can use these equivalent-fraction strips to subtract fractions with different denominators.

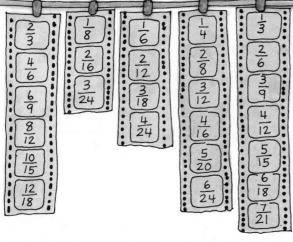

Step 1. Find equivalent fractions so that both denominators are the same.

$$\frac{5}{8} - \frac{1}{4}$$

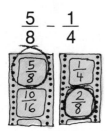

Step 2. Think about the fractions that have the same denominator. Subtract.

$$\frac{5}{8} - \frac{1}{4} = \frac{3}{8}$$

$$\frac{5}{8} - \frac{2}{8}$$

EXERCISES
Give each difference.

1. $\frac{1}{2} - \frac{3}{8}$

2. $\frac{5}{8} - \frac{1}{2}$

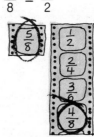

3. $\frac{5}{6} - \frac{1}{3}$

164

Give each difference. If you need to, use the fraction strips.

4. $\frac{1}{2} - \frac{1}{4}$ 5. $\frac{5}{8} - \frac{1}{4}$ 6. $\frac{2}{3} - \frac{1}{6}$ 7. $\frac{5}{6} - \frac{1}{2}$

8. $\frac{1}{2} - \frac{1}{8}$ 9. $\frac{5}{8} - \frac{1}{2}$ 10. $\frac{3}{4} - \frac{5}{8}$ 11. $\frac{3}{4} - \frac{1}{2}$

Add or subtract. Give your answers in lowest terms.

12. $\frac{3}{4}$ $+ \frac{3}{8}$ 13. $\frac{1}{4}$ $+ \frac{1}{8}$ 14. $\frac{5}{6}$ $- \frac{1}{3}$ 15. $\frac{3}{4}$ $- \frac{3}{8}$ 16. $\frac{5}{6}$ $- \frac{1}{2}$ 17. $\frac{5}{8}$ $+ \frac{1}{4}$

18. $\frac{5}{8}$ $+ \frac{3}{4}$ 19. $\frac{1}{2}$ $- \frac{1}{8}$ 20. $\frac{5}{8}$ $- \frac{1}{2}$ 21. $\frac{3}{8}$ $+ \frac{1}{4}$ 22. $\frac{5}{6}$ $- \frac{2}{3}$ 23. $\frac{3}{4}$ $- \frac{5}{8}$

Use the fraction strips to find these differences.

24. $\frac{1}{2}$ $- \frac{1}{3}$ 25. $\frac{2}{3}$ $- \frac{1}{2}$ 26. $\frac{3}{4}$ $- \frac{2}{3}$ 27. $\frac{5}{6}$ $- \frac{1}{4}$ 28. $\frac{5}{6}$ $- \frac{3}{4}$ 29. $\frac{5}{8}$ $- \frac{1}{6}$

Solve.

30. Alice bought $\frac{3}{8}$ yard of blue ribbon and $\frac{1}{2}$ yard of red ribbon. How many yards of ribbon did she buy?

31. Andrew had $\frac{2}{3}$ dozen eggs. He used $\frac{1}{6}$ dozen in a cake. What fraction of a dozen did he have left?

165

Adding and subtracting fractions

To add and subtract fractions with different denominators, you can make your own lists of equivalent fractions.

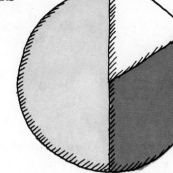

EXAMPLE 1. $\dfrac{1}{2} + \dfrac{1}{3}$

Step 1. Think about equivalent fractions.

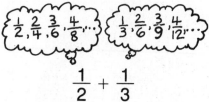

$$\dfrac{1}{2} + \dfrac{1}{3}$$

Step 2. Find fractions with the same denominator and add.

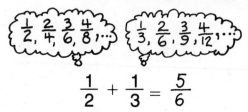

$$\dfrac{1}{2} + \dfrac{1}{3} = \dfrac{5}{6}$$

EXAMPLE 2. $\dfrac{1}{2} - \dfrac{1}{4}$

Step 1.

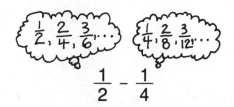

$$\dfrac{1}{2} - \dfrac{1}{4}$$

Step 2.

$$\dfrac{1}{2} - \dfrac{1}{4} = \dfrac{1}{4}$$

EXERCISES
Add or subtract. Watch the signs. Think about equivalent fractions.

1. $\dfrac{1}{3} + \dfrac{1}{6}$

2. $\dfrac{1}{3} - \dfrac{1}{6}$

3. $\dfrac{1}{2} + \dfrac{1}{4}$

4. $\dfrac{1}{2} - \dfrac{1}{4}$

5. $\dfrac{3}{4} - \dfrac{1}{2}$

6. $\dfrac{2}{3} - \dfrac{1}{2}$

7. $\dfrac{1}{3} + \dfrac{1}{4}$

8. $\dfrac{1}{3} - \dfrac{1}{4}$

9. $\dfrac{2}{3} + \dfrac{1}{4}$

10. $\dfrac{2}{3} - \dfrac{1}{4}$

11. $\dfrac{1}{2} + \dfrac{1}{5}$

12. $\dfrac{1}{2} - \dfrac{1}{5}$

13. $\frac{1}{2} + \frac{2}{5}$ **14.** $\frac{1}{2} - \frac{2}{5}$ **15.** $\frac{3}{5} - \frac{1}{2}$ **16.** $\frac{1}{3} - \frac{1}{5}$

17. $\frac{1}{3} + \frac{1}{5}$ **18.** $\frac{2}{3} + \frac{1}{5}$ **19.** $\frac{1}{3} + \frac{2}{5}$ **20.** $\frac{2}{3} - \frac{1}{5}$

Solve.

21. Bill ate $\frac{1}{2}$ of a candy bar. Jill ate $\frac{1}{4}$ of the candy bar. Together how much did they eat?

22. Karen ate $\frac{1}{2}$ of a pie. Larry ate $\frac{1}{4}$ of the pie. How much more did Karen eat?

23. Jody paid for $\frac{1}{2}$ of a pizza. Jenny paid for $\frac{1}{3}$ of the pizza. Judy paid for the rest of the pizza. What fraction of the pizza did Judy pay for?

24. Mary and Jack found a dozen eggs. Mary broke $\frac{1}{3}$ of the eggs. Jack broke $\frac{1}{4}$ of the eggs. What fraction of the eggs were left?

Make up a story.

NUMBER NEWS

$\frac{1}{4} + \frac{1}{3} = \boxed{}$

Mixed numbers

You have often used mixed numbers.

$2\frac{1}{4}$ glasses of milk

$1\frac{1}{2}$ sandwiches

You can use both mixed numbers and fractions.

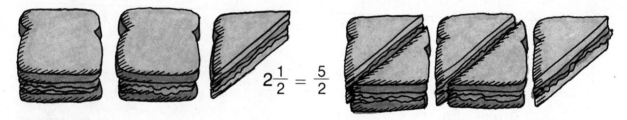

$2\frac{1}{2} = \frac{5}{2}$

EXERCISES

Write a mixed number and a fraction.

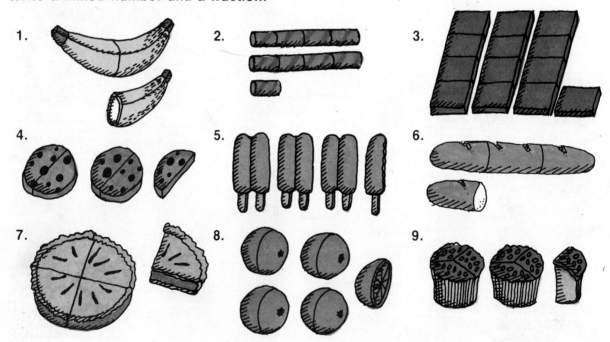

1.

2.

3.

4.

5.

6.

7.

8.

9.

10. Draw a picture to show that $1\frac{3}{4} = \frac{7}{4}$.

11. Draw a picture to show that $2\frac{1}{3} = \frac{7}{3}$.

Draw a picture. Then complete with a fraction.

12. $1\frac{1}{4} = \underline{?}$ **13.** $3\frac{1}{2} = \underline{?}$ **14.** $1\frac{2}{3} = \underline{?}$ **15.** $3\frac{1}{4} = \underline{?}$

I use this shortcut to change mixed numbers to fractions.

SHORTCUT

$2 \times 1 + 1$

$1\frac{1}{2} = \frac{3}{2}$

$4 \times 2 + 3$

$2\frac{3}{4} = \frac{11}{4}$

Change to fractions.

16. $1\frac{1}{3}$ **17.** $1\frac{1}{4}$ **18.** $1\frac{2}{3}$ **19.** $2\frac{1}{2}$ **20.** $2\frac{1}{3}$

21. $2\frac{1}{4}$ **22.** $2\frac{2}{3}$ **23.** $2\frac{3}{4}$ **24.** $3\frac{1}{2}$ **25.** $3\frac{1}{3}$

26. $3\frac{2}{3}$ **27.** $3\frac{1}{4}$ **28.** $3\frac{3}{4}$ **29.** $4\frac{1}{2}$ **30.** $5\frac{1}{2}$

Keeping Skills Sharp

Add or subtract. Watch the signs.

1. 526 $+238$	**2.** 431 -156	**3.** 827 -155	**4.** 363 $+151$	**5.** 462 $+155$
6. 503 -256	**7.** 783 $+159$	**8.** 864 $+118$	**9.** 286 $+99$	**10.** 566 -277
11. 421 $+288$	**12.** 277 $+193$	**13.** 468 $+232$	**14.** 674 -177	**15.** 300 -145

169

Changing fractions to mixed numbers

EXERCISES
Give the mixed number.

1. $\dfrac{3}{2}$ = ?

2. $\dfrac{5}{4}$ = ?

3. $\dfrac{5}{3}$ = ?

4. $\dfrac{9}{4}$ = ?

5. $\dfrac{4}{3}$ = ?

6. $\dfrac{5}{2}$ = ?

7. $\dfrac{6}{5}$ = ?

8. $\dfrac{7}{3}$ = ?

9. $\dfrac{5}{4}$ = ?

10. $\dfrac{6}{4}$ = ?

11. $\dfrac{7}{4}$ = ?

12. $\dfrac{8}{5}$ = ?

13. $\dfrac{9}{2}$ = ?

14. $\dfrac{11}{2}$ = ?

15. $\dfrac{13}{2}$ = ?

16. $\dfrac{15}{2}$ = ?

I use this shortcut to change a fraction to a mixed number.

Divide numerator by denominator.

NUMERATOR

DENOMINATOR

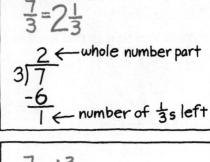

$$\frac{7}{3} = 2\frac{1}{3}$$

$$3\overline{)7}$$ ← whole number part
$$\underline{-6}$$
$$1$$ ← number of $\frac{1}{3}$s left

$$\frac{7}{4} = 1\frac{3}{4}$$

$$4\overline{)7}$$ ← whole number part
$$\underline{-4}$$
$$3$$ ← number of $\frac{1}{4}$s left

Change to mixed numbers.

17. $\frac{9}{4}$ **18.** $\frac{8}{5}$ **19.** $\frac{3}{2}$ **20.** $\frac{5}{4}$ **21.** $\frac{7}{5}$

22. $\frac{8}{3}$ **23.** $\frac{10}{3}$ **24.** $\frac{7}{3}$ **25.** $\frac{11}{5}$ **26.** $\frac{7}{2}$

27. $\frac{9}{5}$ **28.** $\frac{14}{3}$ **29.** $\frac{15}{4}$ **30.** $\frac{17}{5}$ **31.** $\frac{20}{3}$

Add. Give your answers as mixed numbers.

32. $\frac{5}{4}$ **33.** $\frac{2}{3}$ **34.** $\frac{3}{4}$ **35.** $\frac{5}{3}$ **36.** $\frac{3}{4}$ **37.** $\frac{3}{2}$
$+\frac{2}{4}$ $+\frac{2}{3}$ $+\frac{2}{4}$ $+\frac{2}{3}$ $+\frac{6}{4}$ $+\frac{4}{2}$

38. $\frac{5}{6}$ **39.** $\frac{3}{5}$ **40.** $\frac{4}{5}$ **41.** $\frac{4}{5}$ **42.** $\frac{7}{3}$ **43.** $\frac{2}{5}$
$+\frac{2}{6}$ $+\frac{3}{5}$ $+\frac{4}{5}$ $+\frac{3}{5}$ $+\frac{3}{3}$ $+\frac{7}{5}$

CHAPTER CHECKUP

What fraction is red? [pages 136–137]

1.

2.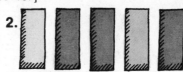

3.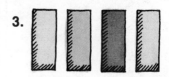

Complete. [pages 142–145]

4. $\frac{1}{2}$ of 8 = $\underline{\ ?\ }$

5. $\frac{1}{4}$ of 20 = $\underline{\ ?\ }$

6. $\frac{1}{3}$ of 18 = $\underline{\ ?\ }$

7. $\frac{2}{3}$ of 18 = $\underline{\ ?\ }$

8. $\frac{3}{4}$ of 12 = $\underline{\ ?\ }$

9. $\frac{5}{6}$ of 18 = $\underline{\ ?\ }$

Find the sale price. [pages 140–141, 146–147]

10. SALE: $\frac{2}{3}$ of marked price 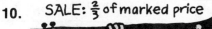 $24.00

11.  SALE: $\frac{1}{4}$ off marked price

Complete the equivalent fractions. [pages 148–155]

12. $\frac{1}{2} = \frac{?}{4}$

13. $\frac{1}{4} = \frac{?}{12}$

14. $\frac{2}{3} = \frac{?}{6}$

15. $\frac{6}{8} = \frac{?}{4}$

< or >? [pages 156–157]

16. $\frac{1}{2}$  $\frac{1}{3}$

17. $\frac{1}{8}$ ◯ $\frac{1}{4}$

18. $\frac{1}{2}$ ◯ $\frac{3}{4}$

19. $\frac{3}{8}$ ◯ $\frac{1}{4}$

Add. [pages 158–161]

20. $\frac{2}{5} + \frac{1}{5}$

21. $\frac{2}{8} + \frac{3}{8}$

22. $\frac{3}{8} + \frac{1}{2}$

23. $\frac{2}{3} + \frac{5}{6}$

Subtract. [pages 162–165]

24. $\frac{3}{8} - \frac{2}{8}$

25. $\frac{7}{4} - \frac{4}{4}$

26. $\frac{3}{4} - \frac{3}{8}$

27. $\frac{5}{6} - \frac{2}{3}$

Complete. [pages 168–171]

	28.	29.	30.	31.	32.	33.
Mixed number	$2\frac{1}{3}$	$3\frac{3}{4}$	?	?	$2\frac{1}{2}$	?
Fraction	?	?	$\frac{5}{3}$	$\frac{7}{2}$	?	$\frac{9}{4}$

Project

1. Get some graph paper.

2. Make and complete an equivalent-fractions table like the one shown.

3. Look for patterns in your table.

4. See if you can use your table to find these sums and differences.

   a. $\frac{1}{3} + \frac{1}{4}$

   b. $\frac{1}{2} + \frac{1}{5}$

   c. $\frac{1}{3} + \frac{1}{6}$

   d. $\frac{1}{2} - \frac{1}{8}$

   e. $\frac{1}{2} - \frac{1}{3}$

   f. $\frac{1}{3} - \frac{1}{4}$

MY EQUIVALENT FRACTION TABLE

FRACTION

	$\frac{1}{2}$	$\frac{1}{3}$	$\frac{1}{4}$	$\frac{1}{5}$	$\frac{1}{6}$	$\frac{1}{7}$	$\frac{1}{8}$	$\frac{1}{9}$	$\frac{1}{10}$	$\frac{1}{11}$	$\frac{1}{12}$
2	$\frac{1}{2}$										
3		$\frac{1}{3}$									
4	$\frac{2}{4}$		$\frac{1}{4}$								
5				$\frac{1}{5}$							
6	$\frac{3}{6}$	$\frac{2}{6}$			$\frac{1}{6}$						
7						$\frac{1}{7}$					
8											
9											
10											
11											
12											
13											
14											
15											
16											
17											
18											
19											
20											
21											
22											
23											
24											

DENOMINATOR

CHAPTER REVIEW

What fraction is colored?

1.   parts colored
   ■ parts in all

2. 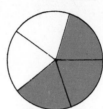   parts colored
   ■ parts in all

What fraction of the crayons are blue?

3. ⬤ blue crayons
   ■ crayons in all

4. ⬤ blue crayons
   ■ crayons in all

Complete.

5. $\frac{1}{4}$ of 8 = _?_

6. $\frac{2}{3}$ of 12 = _?_

Give the equivalent fraction.

7. $\frac{1}{2} = \frac{?}{?}$ ×3 ×3

8. $\frac{1}{3} = \frac{?}{?}$ ×2 ×2

9. $\frac{6}{8} = \frac{?}{?}$ ÷2 ÷2

$\longleftarrow\ \overset{\bullet}{\frac{0}{8}}\ \ \overset{\bullet}{\frac{1}{8}}\ \ \overset{\bullet}{\frac{2}{8}}\ \ \overset{\bullet}{\frac{3}{8}}\ \ \overset{\bullet}{\frac{4}{8}}\ \ \overset{\bullet}{\frac{5}{8}}\ \ \overset{\bullet}{\frac{6}{8}}\ \ \overset{\bullet}{\frac{7}{8}}\ \longrightarrow$

Use the number line to find these sums.

10. $\frac{1}{8} + \frac{2}{8}$

11. $\frac{3}{8} + \frac{2}{8}$

12. $\frac{4}{8} + \frac{3}{8}$

Use the number line to find these differences.

13. $\frac{5}{8} - \frac{2}{8}$

14. $\frac{6}{8} - \frac{5}{8}$

15. $\frac{7}{8} - \frac{2}{8}$

A **unit fraction** has a numerator of 1. Ancient Egyptians used only unit fractions, except for $\frac{2}{3}$. All other fractions were written as sums of unit fractions with no fraction repeated.

The fraction $\frac{3}{4}$ was written as $\frac{1}{2} + \frac{1}{4}$.

The fraction $\frac{2}{5}$ was written as $\frac{1}{4} + \frac{1}{10} + \frac{1}{20}$.

$$\frac{2}{5} = \frac{1}{5} + \frac{1}{5}$$

$$= \frac{1}{10} + \frac{1}{10} + \frac{1}{10} + \frac{1}{10}$$

$$= \underbrace{\frac{1}{20} + \frac{1}{20} + \frac{1}{20} + \frac{1}{20} + \frac{1}{20}} + \underbrace{\frac{1}{20} + \frac{1}{20}} + \frac{1}{20}$$

$$= \frac{1}{4} + \frac{1}{10} + \frac{1}{20}$$

Show how the ancient Egyptians would have written these fractions.

1. $\frac{3}{8}$ 2. $\frac{5}{8}$ 3. $\frac{7}{8}$ 4. $\frac{3}{5}$ 5. $\frac{4}{5}$ 6. $\frac{5}{6}$

7. $\frac{5}{9}$ 8. $\frac{7}{12}$ 9. $\frac{8}{10}$ 10. $\frac{5}{12}$ 11. $\frac{6}{10}$ 12. $\frac{9}{10}$

MAJOR CHECKUP
Standardized Format

Choose the correct letter.

1. 938 rounded to the nearest ten is

    a. 930
    b. 900
    c. 940
    d. none of these

2. Which digit in 58,267 is in the ten thousands place?

    a. 6
    b. 8
    c. 2
    d. 5

3. The standard numeral for six hundred eight thousand twenty-four is

    a. 608,240
    b. 608,024
    c. 680,024
    d. 608,204

4. Add.
    3675
    +2859

    a. 6534
    b. 6524
    c. 5424
    d. none of these

5. Add.
    35
    26
    58
    +29

    a. 147
    b. 138
    c. 148
    d. none of these

6. Subtract.
    524
    − 278

    a. 246
    b. 256
    c. 346
    d. none of these

7. Subtract.
    9702
    − 2358

    a. 7354
    b. 7444
    c. 7344
    d. none of these

8. What time is shown?

    a. quarter to eight
    b. quarter past nine
    c. quarter past eight
    d. quarter to nine

9. How many minutes from 8:30 P.M. to 9:20 P.M.?

    a. 10
    b. 40
    c. 50
    d. none of these

10. How much money?
    1 five-dollar bill
    3 one-dollar bills
    1 half-dollar
    2 dimes **a.** $4.80
    2 nickels **b.** $8.80
           c. $8.50
           d. none of these

11. In $9 \times 7 = 63$, the factors are

    a. 9 and 7
    b. 9 and 63
    c. 7 and 63
    d. none of these

12. Divide.
    8$)\overline{59}$

    a. 7 R7
    b. 8 R7
    c. 7 R3
    d. none of these

7 Measurement

Centimeter

The **centimeter** (**cm**) is a unit for measuring length in the metric system.

The length of the nail is between 5 and 6 centimeters. It is nearer to 6 centimeters. The length of the nail measured to the **nearest centimeter** is 6 centimeters.

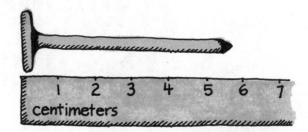

EXERCISES

Measure to the nearest centimeter.

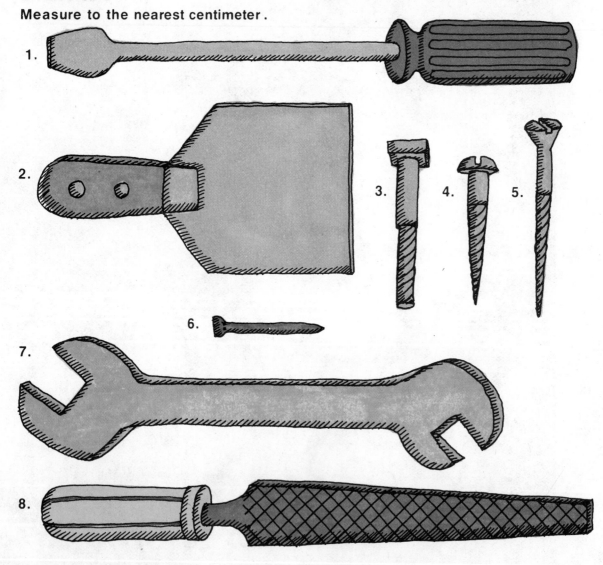

1.

2.

3.

4.

5.

6.

7.

8.

Draw segments of

9. 9 cm   10. 14 cm   11. 18 cm   12. 11 cm

Draw a segment that is between

13. 8 cm and 9 cm, but nearer 8 cm.

14. 6 cm and 7 cm, but nearer 7 cm.

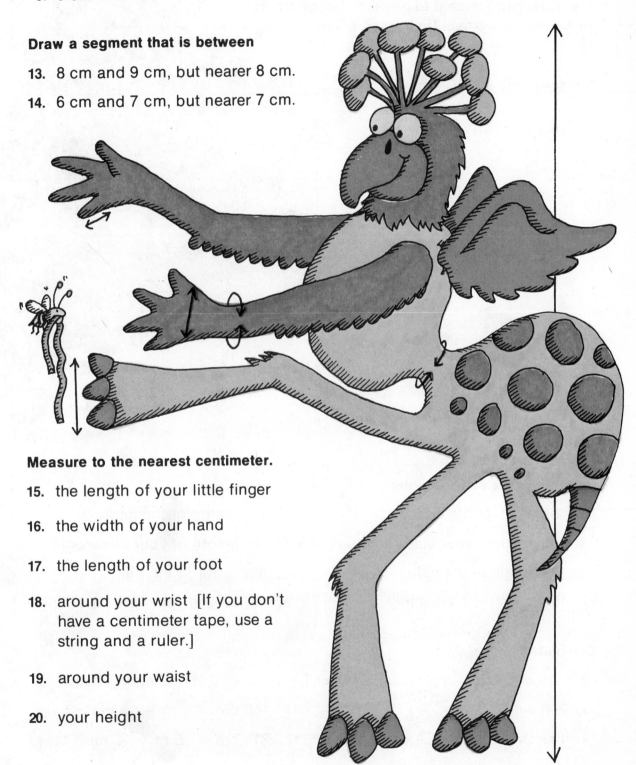

Measure to the nearest centimeter.

15. the length of your little finger

16. the width of your hand

17. the length of your foot

18. around your wrist [If you don't have a centimeter tape, use a string and a ruler.]

19. around your waist

20. your height

Meters and kilometers

The **meter** (**m**) is used to measure longer lengths in the metric system. If you took a "giant step," it would be close to 1 meter long.

1 meter (m) = 100 cm

OOPS.

EXERCISES
Measure to the nearest meter

1. the width of the door.

2. the height of the door.

3. the width of your classroom.

4. the length of your classroom.

5. the length of the hall.

6. the width of the hall.

7. the length of a chalktray.

8. the height from floor to ceiling.

Complete.

9. 1 m = _?_ cm

10. 3 m = _?_ cm

11. 5 m = _?_ cm

12. 200 cm = _?_ m

13. 150 cm = 1 m + _?_ cm

14. 135 cm = _?_ m + _?_ cm

15. 215 cm = _?_ m + _?_ cm

The **kilometer** (**km**) is used to measure long distances in the metric system. If you took 1000 giant steps, you would have walked about 1 kilometer.

1 kilometer (km) = 1000 m

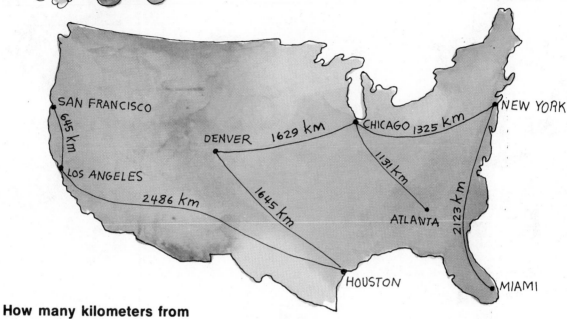

SAN FRANCISCO
645 km
LOS ANGELES
2486 km
DENVER
1629 km
CHICAGO 1325 km
NEW YORK
1131 km
ATLANTA
1645 km
2123 km
HOUSTON
MIAMI

How many kilometers from

16. New York to Miami?

17. Chicago to Atlanta?

18. Denver to Houston?

Give the total distance in kilometers for each of these road trips.

19. Denver–Chicago–New York

20. Houston–Los Angeles–San Francisco

Complete.

21. 1 km = _?_ m

22. 2 km = _?_ m

23. 4000 m = _?_ km

★24. 3800 m = _?_ km + _?_ m

 Project

Lay out a 50-meter course on the school grounds or in the gym. Find out how long it takes you to walk 1 kilometer.

Perimeter

The distance around a figure is called the **perimeter** of the figure.

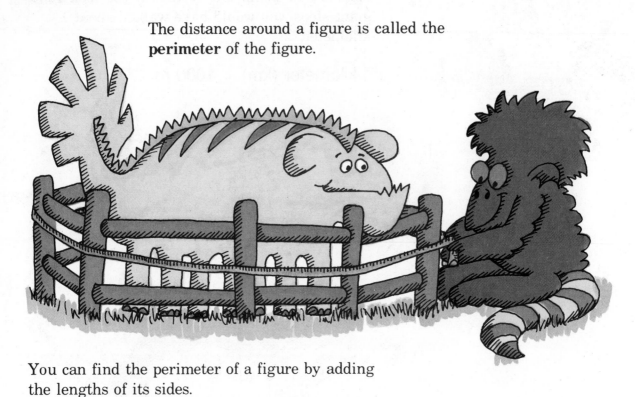

You can find the perimeter of a figure by adding the lengths of its sides.

EXERCISES

Give the perimeter of each figure.

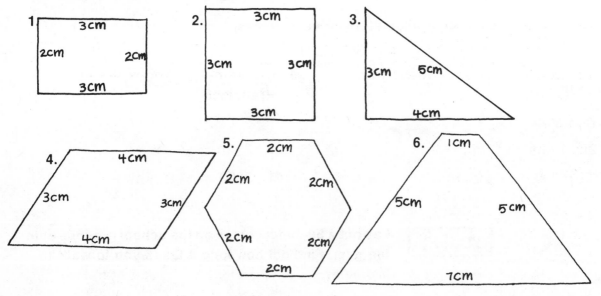

1. 3cm, 2cm, 2cm, 3cm

2. 3cm, 3cm, 3cm, 3cm

3. 3cm, 5cm, 4cm

4. 4cm, 3cm, 3cm, 4cm

5. 2cm, 2cm, 2cm, 2cm, 2cm, 2cm

6. 1cm, 5cm, 5cm, 7cm

7.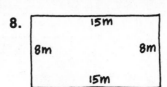

8.

9.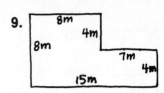

10. Measure the sides of a bulletin board to the nearest centimeter. Compute its perimeter.

11. Determine the perimeter of a table top in centimeters.

12. A yard is shaped like a rectangle. It is 42 m long and 26 m wide. How much fencing will be needed to enclose the yard?

13. Complete this table for squares.

Length of each side in cm	1	2	3	4	5	6	7	8	9
Perimeter in cm	?	?	?	?	?	?	?	?	?

14. A fourth-grade class made this scale drawing of their classroom.

a. How long is the wall with windows?

b. What is the perimeter of their classroom?

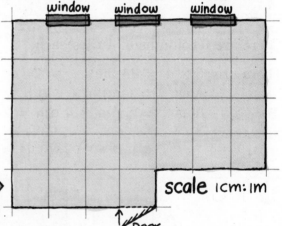

scale 1cm:1m

Keeping Skills Sharp

1. 98 − 24	**2.** 60 − 37	**3.** 81 − 46	**4.** 453 − 129	**5.** 325 − 172	**6.** 621 − 348
7. 907 − 229	**8.** 605 − 458	**9.** 2134 − 1715	**10.** 3964 − 1589	**11.** 5938 − 2659	**12.** 3023 − 1795

Area

To find the area of this region:
We pick a unit

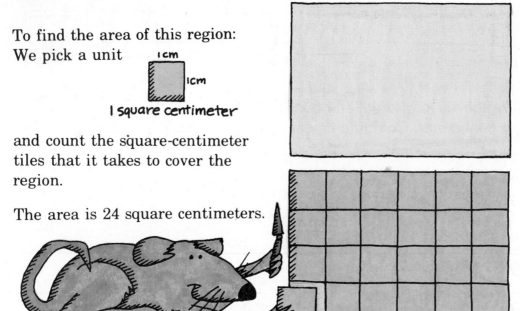

1 square centimeter

and count the square-centimeter tiles that it takes to cover the region.

The area is 24 square centimeters.

To find the area of squares and rectangles, you can multiply.

There are 6 columns of 4 tiles each.

There are $6 \times 4 = 24$ tiles.

Area = length × width

Area = 6 cm × 4 cm = 24 square centimeters

EXERCISES
Give each area.

1.
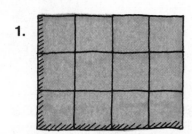

2.
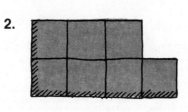

3.
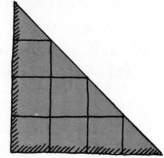

Give each area.

4.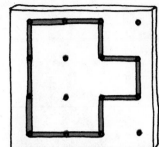

5.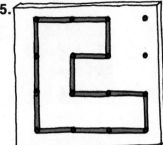

6.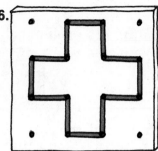

7. Copy and complete this table.

Figure

	A	B	C	D	E	F
Length in cm	3					
Width in cm	1					
Area in Square cm	3					

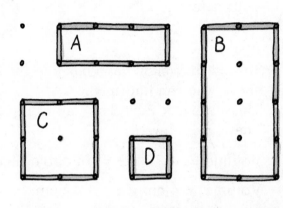

Solve.

8. A rectangular garden plot is 9 m long and 7 m wide. What is the area?

9. A square patio is 8 m on a side. What is its area?

10. A room has an area of 72 square m. Its length is 9 m. What is its width?

11. a. Get or draw a piece of square-centimeter graph paper.

    b. Draw some figures of different shapes that have an area of 12 square centimeters.

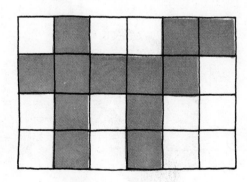

Volume

To find the volume of this box:
We pick a unit

and count the cubic centimeter blocks that will fill the box.

The volume is 16 cubic centimeters.

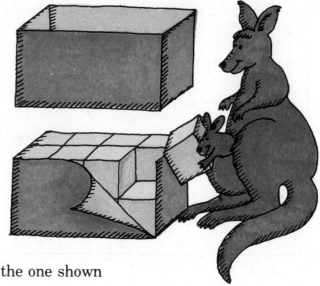

To find the volume of a box like the one shown above, you can multiply.
There are 4 × 2 blocks in a layer.
There are 2 layers.

Volume = 4 × 2 × 2 = 16 cubic blocks

Volume = 4 cm × 2 cm × 2 cm = 16 cubic cm

EXERCISES
Give each volume.

1.

2.

3.

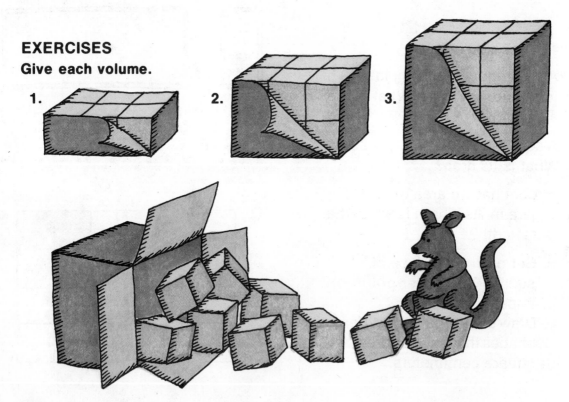

186

Give each volume.

4.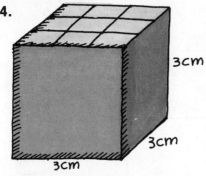

3 cm
3 cm
3 cm

5.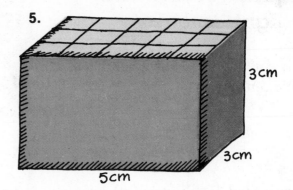

3 cm
3 cm
5 cm

Complete this table.

	Measurements of box in cm			
	Length cm	Width cm	Height cm	Volume cubic cm
6.	2	3	4	?
7.	3	2	5	?
8.	2	2	6	?
9.	5	2	4	?

TOYS

Is the question about length, area, or volume?

10. How much string do you have?

11. How much sand will the box hold?

12. How much paper is needed to cover the bulletin board?

✳ Solve.

13. A form 2 m long, 3 m wide, and 2 m deep is to be filled with concrete. How many cubic meters of concrete should be ordered?

14. A large aquarium is 4 m long, 2 m wide, and 3 m deep. How many cubic meters of water will it hold?

187

Liquid volume and weight—metric

This small tin box has a volume of 1 cubic centimeter.

It will hold 1 **milliliter** (**mL**) of water. The milliliter is used to measure small amounts of liquid.

For measuring greater amounts, the **liter** is used.

1 liter = 1000 mL

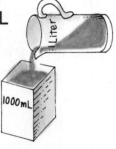

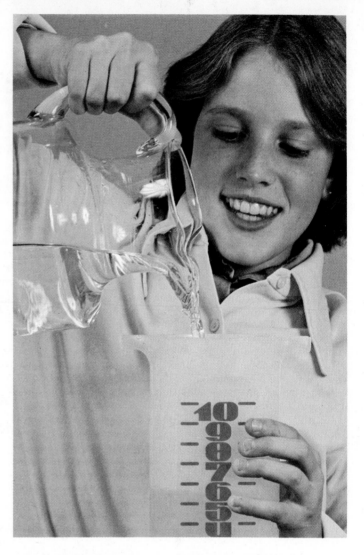

EXERCISES
Milliliter or liter?
Which unit would be used to measure

1. the amount of medicine in a bottle?

2. the amount of gasoline a tank holds?

3. the amount of water in an aquarium?

4. the juice of an orange?

Project 1 — Make a list of items that come in liter containers.

Project 2

1. Collect some containers and estimate how many liters they will hold.

2. Check your estimates by filling each container.

The weight of water that fills the same small tin box is about 1 **gram** (**g**). A mL of water weighs about 1 g.

For weighing heavier things, the **kilogram** is used.

1 kilogram (kg) = 1000 g

EXERCISES

Gram (g) or kilogram (kg)?
Which unit would be used to weigh

1. yourself?   2. a pencil?   3. a yo-yo?   4. a car?

Project 1   Weigh yourself in kilograms.

Project 2   Temperature is sometimes measured on the **Celsius** scale. Get a Celsius thermometer. Keep a record of the temperature at 12:00 noon each day for two weeks. Make a graph.

Inch

The customary system is another measurement system. The **inch** (**in.**) is a unit for measuring length in the customary system.

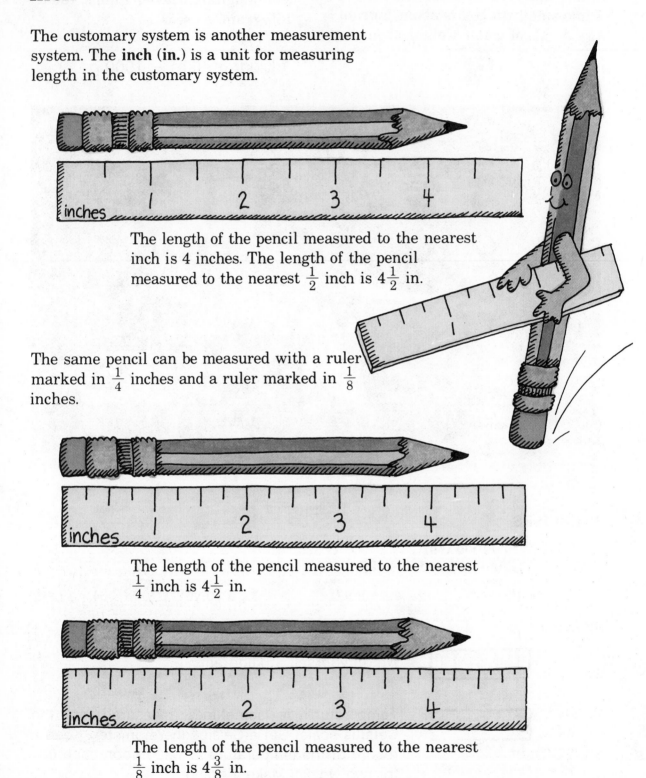

The length of the pencil measured to the nearest inch is 4 inches. The length of the pencil measured to the nearest $\frac{1}{2}$ inch is $4\frac{1}{2}$ in.

The same pencil can be measured with a ruler marked in $\frac{1}{4}$ inches and a ruler marked in $\frac{1}{8}$ inches.

The length of the pencil measured to the nearest $\frac{1}{4}$ inch is $4\frac{1}{2}$ in.

The length of the pencil measured to the nearest $\frac{1}{8}$ inch is $4\frac{3}{8}$ in.

EXERCISES

Draw segments of these lengths.

1. 3 in.   **2.** 4 in.   **3.** $2\frac{1}{2}$ in.   **4.** $3\frac{1}{2}$ in.

5. $2\frac{1}{4}$ in.   **6.** $2\frac{3}{4}$ in.   **7.** $3\frac{3}{8}$ in.   **8.** $2\frac{7}{8}$ in.

Measure the length of each rope to the nearest inch and $\frac{1}{2}$ inch.

9. **10.**

11. **12.**

13.

Measure the length of each rope to the nearest $\frac{1}{4}$ inch and $\frac{1}{8}$ inch.

14.

15.

16.

Project

Measure

1. the height of your desk top to the nearest inch.
2. the width of your desk top to the nearest $\frac{1}{2}$ inch.
3. the thickness of your desk top to the nearest $\frac{1}{4}$ inch.
4. the length of your pencil tray to the nearest $\frac{1}{8}$ inch.

191

Inch, foot, yard, and mile

In the customary system, the **foot**, **yard**, and **mile** are units used to measure longer lengths.

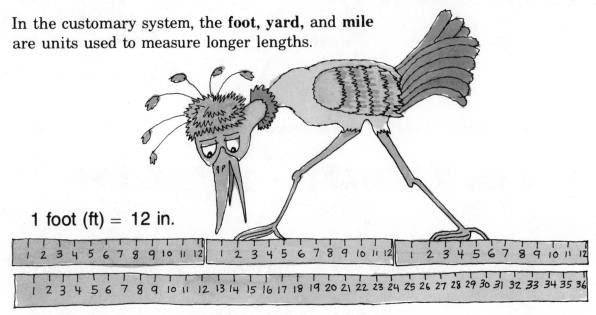

1 foot (ft) = 12 in.

1 yard (yd) = 3 ft

The mile is used to measure long distances.

1 mile (mi) = 5280 ft

1 mile (mi) = 1760 yd

You would have to take about 1800 giant steps to walk a mile.

EXERCISES

1. Measure the length of a chalkboard to the nearest foot.

2. Measure the width of a chalkboard to the nearest foot.

3. What is the perimeter of the chalkboard?

4. Measure the height of the door to the nearest foot.

5. Measure the length of your classroom to the nearest yard.

6. Measure the width of your classroom to the nearest yard.

7. Measure the height of the ceiling to the nearest yard.

Complete.

8.

Feet	Inches
1	12
2	
3	
4	
5	
6	

$$12$$
$$+12$$
$$\overline{24}$$

9.

Yards	Feet
1	3
2	
3	
4	
5	
6	

Inch, foot, or mile?
Tell which unit you would use to measure these lengths.

10. the length of a pencil

11. the width of a book

12. the height of a building

13. the length of a river

14. the perimeter of your classroom

15. the distance between two cities

Solve.

16. By automobile, it is 707 miles from Boston to Detroit and 269 miles from Detroit to Chicago. How many miles is a Boston–Detroit–Chicago trip?

17. It is 4931 miles from New York to Los Angeles by water. By air, it is 2451 miles. How many miles less is it by air?

Keeping Skills Sharp

1. 592 +378	**2.** 694 +258	**3.** 536 +377	**4.** 609 +958	**5.** 876 +876	**6.** 295 +786
7. 7281 +3465	**8.** 2229 +4068	**9.** 3156 +9588	**10.** 7645 +8369	**11.** 5648 +3782	**12.** 3782 +5648

Area and volume

Here is the floor plan of a kitchen. It is to be covered by tiles that are one-foot squares.

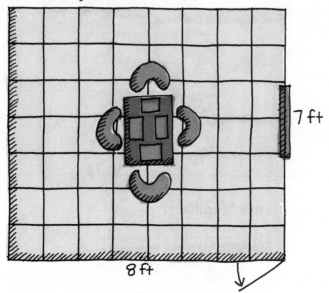

7 ft

8 ft

Area = length × width
Area = 8 ft × 7 ft = 56 square feet

So, 56 tiles will be needed.

Give each area.

1.
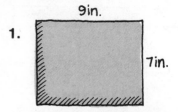
9in.

7in.

2.
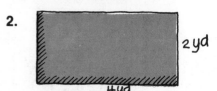
2yd

4yd

3.
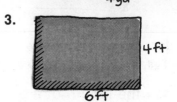
4ft

6ft

4. A room is 3 yards wide and 4 yards long. How many square yards of carpeting are needed to carpet the room?

5. Mrs. Johnson's living room is 12 feet wide and 18 feet long.
   a. How many yards wide is the room?
   b. How many yards long is the room?
   c. What is the area in square yards?

We can find the volume of this box by counting the cubic inches that fill the box.

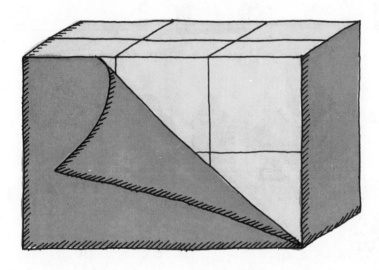

We can also find the volume by multiplying.

Volume = length × width × height
Volume = 3 in. × 2 in. × 2 in.
       = 12 cubic inches

Give each volume.

6.
3in.
3in.
3in.

7.
4ft
2ft
5ft

8.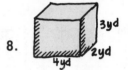
3yd
2yd
4yd

Is the question about length, area, or volume?

9. How deep is the aquarium?

10. How much water will it hold?

11. How much tin is needed to make a cover?

Solve.

12. How many cubic feet are there in one cubic yard?

13. Careful! How many cubic feet of concrete are needed for a walk that is 10 feet long and 3 feet wide if the concrete is to be 6 inches thick?

Liquid volume and weight—customary

These units are used to measure liquid volumes in the customary system.

2 cups (c) = 1 pint (pt)   2 pt = 1 quart (qt)

4 qt = 1 gallon (gal)

EXERCISES

Complete.

1. 2 pt = _?_ c

2. 2 pt = _?_ qt

3. 6 c = _?_ pt

4. 8 qt = _?_ gal

5. 3 qt = _?_ pt

6. 1 gal = _?_ pt

Complete.

7.

Quarts	1	2	3	4	5	6
Pints	?	?	?	?	?	?
Cups	?	?	?	?	?	?

Which is more?

8. 3 pints or 1 quart

9. 2 pints or 5 cups

10. 1 gallon or 3 quarts

11. 1 gallon or 9 cups

★12. Some things, such as milk, come in half-gallon containers. How many quarts are in one half-gallon? How many pints?

196

The ounce (oz) and the pound (lb)
are units used for measuring weight
in the customary system.

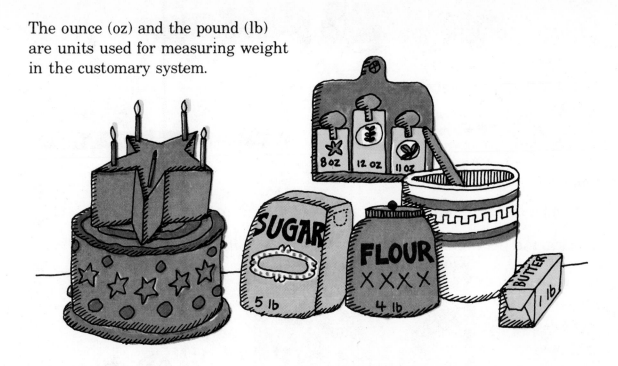

16 ounces (oz) = 1 pound (lb)

Complete.

13.

16 oz	? lb
18 oz	1 lb ? oz
24 oz	? lb ? oz
30 oz	? lb ? oz
32 oz	? lb
36 oz	? lb ? oz

Complete.

14. $\frac{1}{2}$ lb = ? oz

15. $\frac{1}{4}$ lb = ? oz

16. $\frac{3}{4}$ lb = ? oz

17. $\frac{5}{8}$ lb = ? oz

Project 1

Weigh yourself in
pounds.

Project 2

Temperature is some-
times measured on the
Fahrenheit scale. Study
a Fahrenheit thermom-
eter.
Graph the daily high
temperature for two
weeks in degrees
Fahrenheit. (You can
find this information in
a newspaper.)

Measure to the nearest centimeter. [pages 178–179]

1.

2.

Complete. [pages 180–181]

3. 1 meter = ? cm

4. 1 kilometer = ? meters

5. **Give the perimeter.** [pages 182–183]

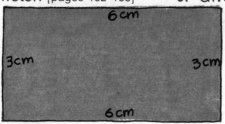

6cm
3cm
3cm
6cm

6. **Give the area.** [pages 184–185]

7. **Give the volume.** [pages 186–187]

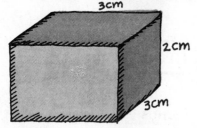

3cm
2cm
3cm

Complete. [pages 188–189]

8. 1 liter = ? milliliters

9. 1 kilogram = ? grams

Measure to the nearest $\frac{1}{4}$ inch. [pages 190–191]

10.

11.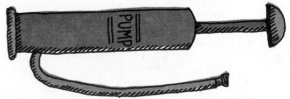

Complete. [pages 192–197]

12. 1 foot = ? inches

13. 1 yard = ? feet

14. 1 pint = ? cups

15. 1 quart = ? pints

16. 1 gallon = ? quarts

17. 1 pound = ? ounces

Project

1. Measure your arm span and your height to the nearest centimeter.

2. Compare your measurements.

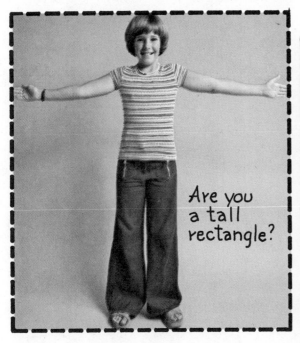

Are you a tall rectangle?

Are you a square?

3. Find the number of children in your class who are squares, tall rectangles, and short rectangles.

4. Make a bar graph of what you found.

5. Tell some things that your graph shows.

Are you a short rectangle?

CHAPTER REVIEW

1. Measure to the nearest centimeter.

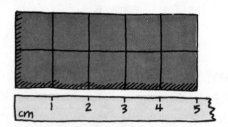

2. Give the perimeter.

3. Give the area.

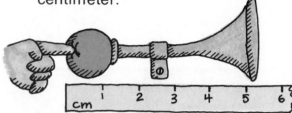

4. Give the volume.

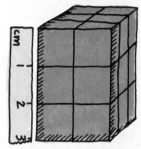

5. Measure to the nearest $\frac{1}{2}$ inch.

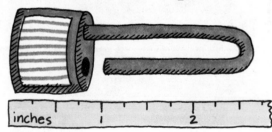

6. Measure to the nearest $\frac{1}{4}$ inch.

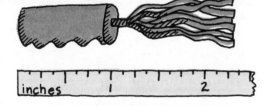

Complete.

7. 12 in. = _?_ ft

8. 1 yd = _?_ ft

This solid has been covered with centimeter graph paper.

If we add the areas of all six sides, we get the **surface area** of the solid.

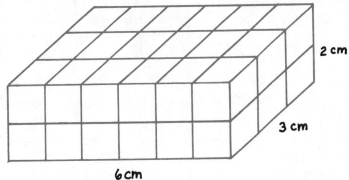

Top	18 square cm
Bottom	18 square cm
Front	12 square cm
Back	12 square cm
Right side	6 square cm
Left side	6 square cm
	72 square cm

Give the surface area of each solid.

1.

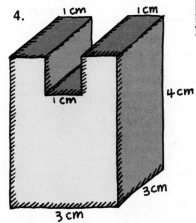

1 cm
4 cm
3 cm

2.

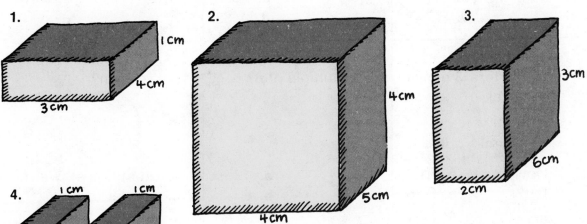

4 cm
5 cm
4 cm

3.

3 cm
6 cm
2 cm

4.

1 cm   1 cm
1 cm
4 cm
3 cm
3 cm

5. Complete this table for cubes (blocks).

Length of each side in cm	Volume in cubic cm	Surface area in square cm
1	1	6
2		
3		
4		

MAJOR CHECKUP
Standardized Format

Choose the correct letter.

---

1. 3568 rounded to the nearest hundred is

   a. 3500
   b. 4000
   c. 3570
   d. 3600

2. Which digit in 375,289 is in the hundred thousands place?

   a. 2
   b. 5
   c. 7
   d. 3

3. Add.

293
148
+256

   a. 687
   b. 597
   c. 697
   d. none of these

---

4. Subtract.

602
− 258

   a. 344
   b. 444
   c. 354
   d. none of these

5. Subtract.

5321
− 1783

   a. 4662
   b. 3538
   c. 4638
   d. 4538

6. Divide.

$6\overline{)46}$

   a. 4 R7
   b. 8 R2
   c. 7 R4
   d. none of these

---

7. You had:
3 quarters, 3 dimes, 1 nickel.

You buy:

 59¢

How much left?

   a. $1.69
   b. $.56
   c. $.51
   d. none of these

8. Which number is a multiple of 6?

   a. 12
   b. 9
   c. 3
   d. none of these

9. What time is shown?

   a. quarter past twelve
   b. quarter to one
   c. quarter to twelve
   d. quarter past one

---

10. Complete.

$\frac{2}{3}$ of 18 = ?

   a. 9
   b. 6
   c. 8
   d. none of these

11. Add.

$\frac{1}{4} + \frac{3}{8} = ?$

   a. $\frac{4}{12}$
   b. $\frac{5}{8}$
   c. $\frac{4}{8}$
   d. $\frac{4}{4}$

12. Subtract.

$\frac{5}{6} - \frac{1}{3} = ?$

   a. $\frac{4}{3}$
   b. $\frac{4}{6}$
   c. $\frac{4}{9}$
   d. $\frac{1}{2}$

8
Multiplication

READY OR NOT !

Multiply.

1. 2
   ×8

2. 7
   ×5

3. 3
   ×6

4. 6
   ×4

5. 7
   ×3

6. 3
   ×8

7. 5
   ×5

8. 6
   ×5

9. 4
   ×7

10. 8
    ×4

11. 9
    ×3

12. 7
    ×9

13. 9
    ×4

14. 8
    ×9

15. 5
    ×8

16. 9
    ×9

17. 6
    ×6

18. 7
    ×6

19. 6
    ×8

20. 9
    ×5

21. 7
    ×8

22. 7
    ×7

23. 6
    ×9

24. 8
    ×8

Multiplying a 2-digit number

The examples show how to multiply a 2-digit
number by a 1-digit number.

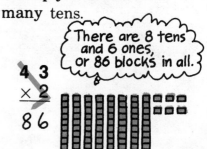

EXAMPLE 1.

4 3
× 2

Step 1.

Multiply to find
how many ones.

4 3
× 2
___
  6

Step 2.

Multiply to find how
many tens.

There are 8 tens
and 6 ones,
or 86 blocks in all.

4 3
× 2
___
8 6

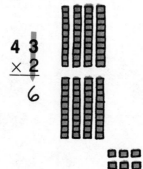

204

EXAMPLE 2.   **Step 1.** Multiply to find how many ones.   **Step 2.** Multiply to find how many tens.

31
×3

31
×3
 3

31
×3
9 3

EXERCISES
Multiply.

1. 32
  ×3

2. 23
  ×2

3. 43
  ×2

4. 20
  ×4

5. 22
  ×2

6. 10
  ×6

7. 12
  ×3

8. 10
  ×8

9. 32
  ×2

10. 21
  ×4

11. 34
  ×2

12. 11
  ×5

13. 22
  ×3

14. 20
  ×3

15. 12
  ×2

16. 12
  ×4

17. 11
  ×6

18. 22
  ×4

19. 42
  ×2

20. 23
  ×3

How many?

21. 1 dozen = _?_

22. 2 dozen = _?_

23. 3 dozen = _?_

24. 4 dozen = _?_

Solve.

25. 11 weeks
   How many days?

26. 21 gallons
   How many quarts?

27. 23 yards
   How many feet?

28. 11 nickels
   How many cents?

29. 32 quarts
   How many pints?

30. 4 feet
   How many inches?

More about multiplying

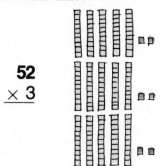

$$\begin{array}{r} 52 \\ \times 3 \end{array}$$

Step 1. Multiply to find how many ones.

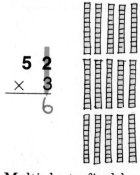

$$\begin{array}{r} 5\ 2 \\ \times\quad 3 \\ \hline 6 \end{array}$$

Step 2. Multiply to find how many tens.

15 tens or 1 hundred and 5 tens.

$$\begin{array}{r} 5\ 2 \\ \times\quad 3 \\ \hline 156 \end{array}$$

There are 156 blocks in all.

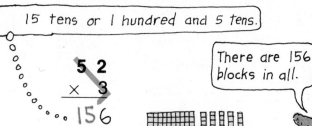

EXERCISES
Multiply.

1. 42
   ×3

2. 21
   ×5

3. 52
   ×4

4. 43
   ×3

5. 64
   ×2

6. 41
   ×4

7. 50
   ×3

8. 54
   ×2

9. 62
   ×4

10. 31
    ×5

11. 31 ×7	12. 64 ×2	13. 21 ×5	14. 50 ×8	15. 40 ×6
16. 53 ×2	17. 83 ×3	18. 60 ×5	19. 73 ×2	20. 43 ×3
21. 60 ×6	22. 50 ×5	23. 40 ×8	24. 80 ×7	25. 70 ×4

Give each product.

26. 52×4 27. 40×7 28. 63×3

29. 72×2 30. 31×8 31. 50×2

Complete the table.

	Bottles	Refund
32.	22	88¢
33.	12	?
34.	31	?
35.	42	?
36.	50	?
37.	61	?

Keeping Skills Sharp

1. 58 +21	2. 72 +19	3. 85 +28	4. 761 +385	5. 297 +378
6. 1859 +376	7. 2485 +999	8. 2618 +3596	9. 8421 +3678	10. 5214 +3786

Multiplying with regrouping

EXAMPLE 1.

$$\begin{array}{r} 24 \\ \times\ 3 \end{array}$$

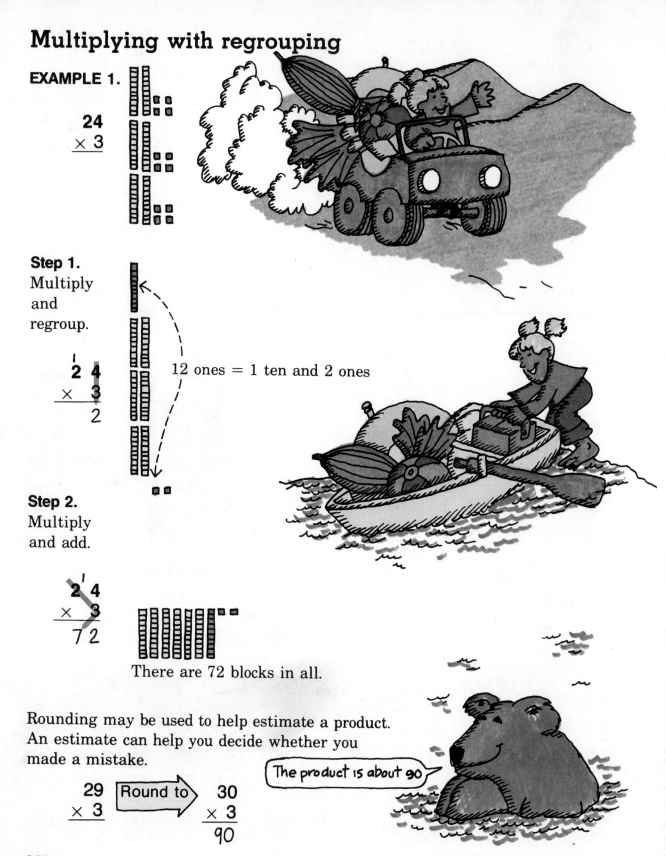

Step 1.
Multiply and regroup.

$$\begin{array}{r} \overset{1}{2}\,4 \\ \times\ 3 \\ \hline 2 \end{array}$$

12 ones = 1 ten and 2 ones

Step 2.
Multiply and add.

$$\begin{array}{r} \overset{1}{2}\,4 \\ \times\ 3 \\ \hline 72 \end{array}$$

There are 72 blocks in all.

Rounding may be used to help estimate a product.
An estimate can help you decide whether you
made a mistake.

$$\begin{array}{r} 29 \\ \times\ 3 \end{array}$$ Round to $$\begin{array}{r} 30 \\ \times\ 3 \\ \hline 90 \end{array}$$

The product is about 90

208

EXERCISES

Multiply. Then estimate the product to see if your answer makes sense.

1. 46
   ×2

2. 81
   ×4

3. 37
   ×5

4. 92
   ×7

5. 54
   ×5

6. 61
   ×6

7. 38
   ×4

8. 31
   ×9

9. 75
   ×6

10. 86
    ×7

11. 78
    ×3

12. 65
    ×7

13. 73
    ×6

14. 48
    ×3

15. 68
    ×7

16. $.63
    ×8

17. $.56
    ×2

18. $.62
    ×4

19. $.54
    ×9

20. $.83
    ×5

21.

How many eggs?

22.

How many cents?

Solve.

23. 4 days
    How many hours?

24. 8 hours
    How many minutes?

25. 24 weeks
    How many days?

26. 7 minutes
    How many seconds?

Use the shortcut to find each product.

27. 54 × 3

To find this product I add 50×3 and 4×3.

SHORTCUT

60+3

28. 63 × 5

29. 48 × 4

30. 72 × 6

31. 87 × 3

Problem solving

Julie and Matt set up a vegetable stand.

1. They had 72 tomatoes in one basket and 59 in another. How many tomatoes in all?

2. One day they sold 39 green peppers and 28 red peppers. How many peppers were sold?

3. A customer bought 3 dozen tomatoes. Matt took them out of the basket that contained 72 tomatoes. How many were left in the basket?

4. One week they sold an average of 75 tomatoes a day. How many tomatoes did they sell that week?

5. Mrs. Ross bought 3 pounds of peas for 65¢ a pound. How much did the peas cost?

6. Mrs. Ross paid with a $5 bill. How much change did she get?
[See exercise 5.]

7. Mr. Martinez bought 4 dozen ears of corn for $.95 a dozen. How much did he owe?

8. Miss Peck bought a dozen ears of corn for $.95, 2 pounds of peas for $.65 each, and 3 peppers for $.13 each. How much did she owe?

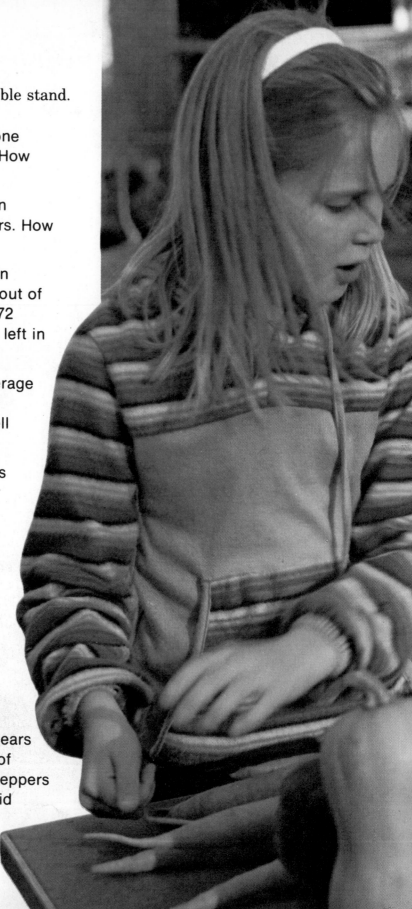

9. Miss Peck gave Julie $3.00. How much change did she get? [See exercise 8.]

★10. Matt and Julie sold bunches of beets in two sizes. The large bunches had 9 beets; the small ones had 5 beets. If they had 15 large bunches and 21 small bunches, how many beets were there in all?

Multiplying a 3-digit number

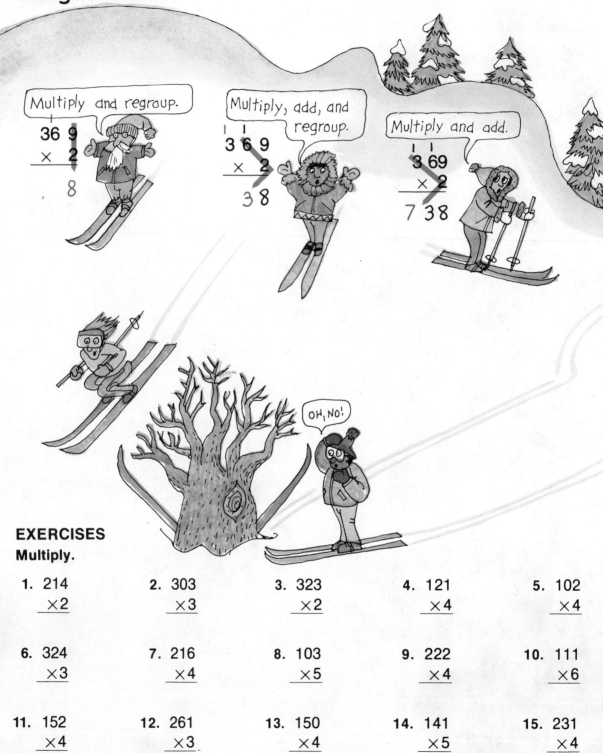

Multiply and regroup.

$$\begin{array}{r} 36\overset{\downarrow}{9} \\ \times\ 2 \\ \hline 8 \end{array}$$

Multiply, add, and regroup.

$$\begin{array}{r} {}^{1\ 1}\\ 3\overset{\downarrow}{6}9 \\ \times\ 2 \\ \hline 3\ 8 \end{array}$$

Multiply and add.

$$\begin{array}{r} {}^{1\ 1}\\ 3\overset{\downarrow}{69} \\ \times\ 2 \\ \hline 7\ 38 \end{array}$$

OH, NO!

EXERCISES
Multiply.

1. 214
   ×2

2. 303
   ×3

3. 323
   ×2

4. 121
   ×4

5. 102
   ×4

6. 324
   ×3

7. 216
   ×4

8. 103
   ×5

9. 222
   ×4

10. 111
    ×6

11. 152
    ×4

12. 261
    ×3

13. 150
    ×4

14. 141
    ×5

15. 231
    ×4

16. 126 ×4	17. 196 ×5	18. 178 ×6	19. 159 ×8	20. 138 ×4
21. 168 ×5	22. 167 ×5	23. 126 ×3	24. 284 ×3	25. 296 ×3
26. 157 ×5	27. 287 ×3	28. 175 ×4	29. 359 ×2	30. 248 ×3
31. 375 ×2	32. 146 ×6	33. 129 ×3	34. 137 ×8	35. 159 ×7

Solve.

36.

How much will 5 cost?

37.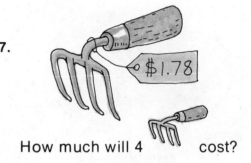

How much will 4 cost?

38. Had:

Bought: 2

How much money left?

39. Had:

Bought: 3

How much money left?

Keeping Skills Sharp

1. 68 − 24	2. 83 − 36	3. 90 − 47	4. 494 − 216	5. 501 − 375
6. 500 − 178	7. 7268 − 179	8. 3895 − 1978	9. 8114 − 2609	10. 8004 − 2769

More about multiplying 3-digit numbers

Multiply and regroup.

$$\begin{array}{r} 4 \\ 53\,8 \\ \times\quad 6 \\ \hline 8 \end{array}$$

Multiply, add, and regroup.

$$\begin{array}{r} 2\quad4 \\ 5\,3\,8 \\ \times\quad 6 \\ \hline 2\,8 \end{array}$$

Multiply and add.

$$\begin{array}{r} 2\quad4 \\ 5\,38 \\ \times\quad 6 \\ \hline 32\,2\,8 \end{array}$$

32 hundreds, or 3 thousands and 2 hundreds

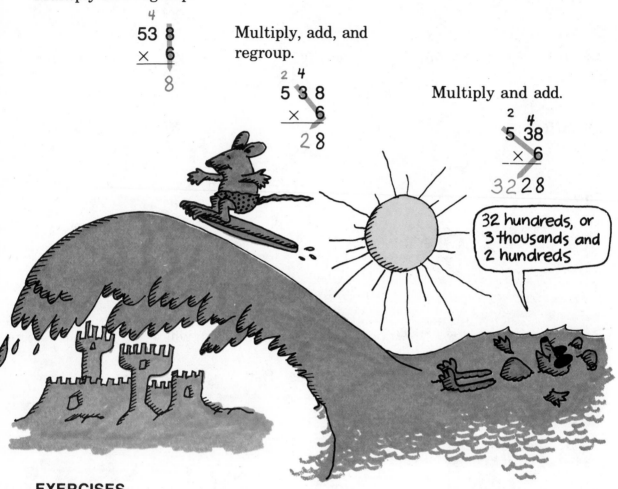

EXERCISES
Multiply.

1. 358 ×5	2. 643 ×4	3. 482 ×6	4. 952 ×3	5. 554 ×2
6. 683 ×7	7. 397 ×8	8. 749 ×5	9. 376 ×7	10. 874 ×9
11. 755 ×8	12. 576 ×5	13. 892 ×3	14. 675 ×6	15. 453 ×8

16. 556	17. 653	18. 759	19. 914	20. 371
×5	×6	×3	×6	×4

21. 853	22. 493	23. 942	24. 784	25. 256
×4	×9	×3	×7	×8

26. 300	27. 800	28. 900	29. 700	30. 800
×5	×9	×6	×7	×4

Give each product.

31. 264 × 3   32. 526 × 5   33. 387 × 4

34. 468 × 6   35. 706 × 7   36. 257 × 9

Multiply across. Multiply down.

37.
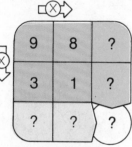

9	8	?
3	1	?
?	?	?

38.
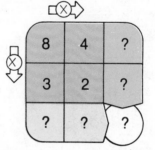

8	4	?
3	2	?
?	?	?

39.
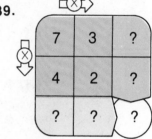

7	3	?
4	2	?
?	?	?

Find the missing digits.

40.

```
  72
 × 8
————
2976
```

★41.
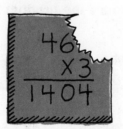
```
  46
 × 3
————
1404
```

★42.
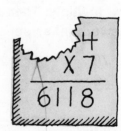
```
    4
 × 7
————
6118
```

215

Multiplying a 4-digit number

Larger numbers are multiplied in the same way as smaller numbers. Study this example.

$$\begin{array}{r} 4178 \\ \times\ 7 \\ \hline 29{,}246 \end{array}$$

Remember that we can use rounding to estimate a product. An estimate can tell us whether our answer makes sense.

$$\begin{array}{r} 4178 \\ \times\ 7 \end{array}$$

Round to

$$\begin{array}{r} 4000 \\ \times\ 7 \\ \hline 28{,}000 \end{array}$$

SHORTCUT

So the product is about 28,000.

Since 29,246 (our answer) is close to 28,000 (our estimate), our answer makes sense.

EXERCISES

First multiply. Then estimate the product to see if your answer makes sense.

1. $\begin{array}{r} 78 \\ \times 9 \end{array}$
2. $\begin{array}{r} 94 \\ \times 8 \end{array}$
3. $\begin{array}{r} 766 \\ \times 5 \end{array}$
4. $\begin{array}{r} 911 \\ \times 7 \end{array}$
5. $\begin{array}{r} 835 \\ \times 6 \end{array}$

6. $\begin{array}{r} 2130 \\ \times 4 \end{array}$
7. $\begin{array}{r} 3896 \\ \times 7 \end{array}$
8. $\begin{array}{r} 5235 \\ \times 6 \end{array}$
9. $\begin{array}{r} 7869 \\ \times 5 \end{array}$
10. $\begin{array}{r} 8350 \\ \times 8 \end{array}$

Multiply.

11. 4328 ×2	12. 5210 ×4	13. 6348 ×3	14. 2065 ×6	15. 3154 ×5
16. 5281 ×7	17. 7306 ×8	18. 5829 ×5	19. 7465 ×6	20. 3842 ×9

21. 396 × 5   22. 784 × 6   23. 923 × 8

24. 7124 × 2   25. 5638 × 4   26. 6341 × 5

Solve.

27. How much for 4 kg?

HILLSIDE FARMS

APPLES 99¢ per kg

28. How much for 3 tickets?

MOVIE $3.50 TOWN THEATER

29. A dozen doughnuts cost $1.12. How much do 6 dozen cost?

30. A jet airplane averaged 916 kilometers per hour for a 3-hour flight. How many kilometers was the flight?

31. A rectangular lot is 9 meters wide and 27 meters long. What is its area?

32. A certain style of jeans costs $12.79. How much do 3 pairs cost?

★ **Multiply.**

33. 12345679
×9

34. Can you guess this product?

12345679
×18

Hint: Compare Exercises 33 and and 34.

Addition, subtraction, multiplication, and division

Remember to work inside the grouping symbols first.

$$(158 \times 3) + 174 = 648$$

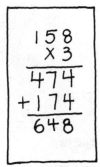

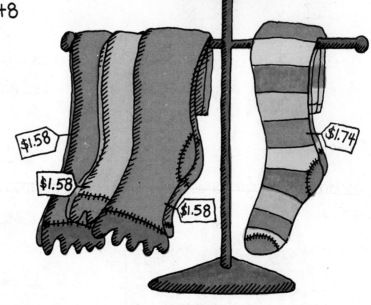

EXERCISES
Compute.

1. $(58 \times 3) + 4$

2. $58 \times (3 + 4)$

3. $(167 \times 5) - 2$

4. $167 \times (5 - 2)$

5. $(532 - 4) \times 2$

6. $532 - (4 \times 2)$

7. $(3821 \times 5) + 253$

8. $(4816 \times 2) - 4816$

9. $(5621 - 387) \times 6$

10. $(7135 + 2816) \times 8$

Tell what you would do to solve each problem.
Hint: **Each problem has two steps.**

11. Mary bought 2 blouses for $■ each and a pair of jeans for $■. What was the total cost?

12. Al bought a sweater for $■ and a pair of jeans for $■. He gave the clerk $■. How much change did he get back?

13. Steve could buy 3 pairs of socks for $■ and a sweater for $■. How much would 1 pair of socks and a sweater cost?

14. Susan bought 3 shirts for $■ each. She gave the clerk $■. How much change did she get back?

218

Build the Greatest Product

$$
\begin{array}{r}
\overset{6\ 5\ 3}{7764} \\
\times\ 8 \\
\hline
62{,}112
\end{array}
\qquad
\begin{array}{r}
\overset{3\ 5\ 5}{6478} \\
\times\ 7 \\
\hline
45{,}346
\end{array}
$$

Which product is greater?

1.
$$
\begin{array}{r} 3504 \\ \times\ 8 \\ \hline \end{array}
\qquad
\begin{array}{r} 4830 \\ \times\ 5 \\ \hline \end{array}
$$

2.
$$
\begin{array}{r} 5768 \\ \times\ 9 \\ \hline \end{array}
\qquad
\begin{array}{r} 7985 \\ \times\ 6 \\ \hline \end{array}
$$

3.
$$
\begin{array}{r} 7385 \\ \times\ 4 \\ \hline \end{array}
\qquad
\begin{array}{r} 4538 \\ \times\ 7 \\ \hline \end{array}
$$

4.
$$
\begin{array}{r} 9473 \\ \times\ 6 \\ \hline \end{array}
\qquad
\begin{array}{r} 6347 \\ \times\ 9 \\ \hline \end{array}
$$

Play the game.

1. Choose a leader.

2. Make two cards for each digit.

3. Each player draws a table.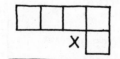

4. As the leader picks a digit, write it in your table.

5. Repeat step 4 until your table is filled in.

6. Multiply. The player who builds the greatest product wins the game.

Problem solving

1. Jan rode the roller coaster 3 times. How much did she spend for roller-coaster tickets?
2. How much do 5 merry-go-round tickets cost?
3. What is the total cost of 2 rides on the whip and 2 rides on the bumper cars?
4. What is the total cost of 3 Ferris wheel rides and 2 flying-saucer rides?

TICKETS

Merry-Go-Round	45¢
Roller Coaster	85¢
Ferris Wheel	55¢
Whip	60¢
Flying Saucer	40¢
Bumper Cars	75¢
Monster House	35¢
Speedboat	45¢

5. Which costs more, 4 monster-house tickets or 3 speedboat tickets?

6. Ruth had $3.40. She bought 2 bumper-car tickets. How much money did she have left?

7. John bought 3 roller-coaster tickets. He gave the ticket seller $3.00. How much change did he get back?

8. Maria had $5.00. She bought 2 speedboat tickets and a roller-coaster ticket. How much money did she have left?

★9. Alan got $5 for his birthday. He wanted to go on each ride once. Did he have enough money?

★10. Juan had $2.05. He rode the merry-go-round twice and the bumper cars once. What other rides could he take?

CHAPTER CHECKUP

Multiply. [pages 204–209]

1. 34 ×2	**2.** 23 ×3	**3.** 41 ×2	**4.** 52 ×4	**5.** 60 ×3
6. 38 ×3	**7.** 49 ×2	**8.** 76 ×4	**9.** 57 ×6	**10.** 89 ×8

Multiply. [pages 212–217]

11. 329 ×2	**12.** 438 ×3	**13.** 219 ×2	**14.** 178 ×4	**15.** 159 ×6
16. 553 ×9	**17.** 734 ×6	**18.** 692 ×4	**19.** 5938 ×5	**20.** 2167 ×8

Complete. [pages 218–219]

21. $68 \times 4 = \underline{?}$ **22.** $459 \times 7 = \underline{?}$ **23.** $2314 \times 5 = \underline{?}$

24. $(329 + 61) \times 2 = \underline{?}$ **25.** $429 \times (9 - 6) = \underline{?}$ **26.** $(429 \times 9) - 6 = \underline{?}$

Solve. [pages 210–211, 218, 220–221]

27. What is the cost of 4 loaves of bread?

28. What is the cost of 5 cartons of milk?

29. How much do 3 dozen eggs and 1 carton of milk cost?

30. Jill bought 2 cartons of milk, a loaf of bread, and 2 dozen eggs. What was the total price?

Project

Napier's rods (named after John Napier, 1550–1617) can be used to multiply.

1. Get some graph paper and make a set of Napier's rods as shown. Notice that the numbers listed on each rod are the first 9 multiples of the "red" number.

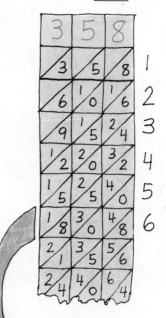

2. The example shows how to use your Napier's rods to find this product:

$$\begin{array}{r} 358 \\ \times\ 6 \\ \hline \end{array}$$

To find the product, add as shown.

2 1 4 8

3. Use your set of rods to find these products.

	a.	**b.**	**c.**	**d.**	**e.**
	529	738	509	6831	5874
	×4	×3	×7	×6	×5

223

CHAPTER REVIEW

Multiply.

$$\begin{array}{r} 21 \\ \times 4 \\ \hline 84 \end{array}$$

1. $\begin{array}{r} 20 \\ \times 3 \end{array}$ **2.** $\begin{array}{r} 12 \\ \times 4 \end{array}$ **3.** $\begin{array}{r} 32 \\ \times 2 \end{array}$

$$\begin{array}{r} 52 \\ \times 3 \\ \hline 156 \end{array}$$

Regroup 10 tens for 1 hundred.

4. $\begin{array}{r} 72 \\ \times 3 \end{array}$ **5.** $\begin{array}{r} 81 \\ \times 5 \end{array}$ **6.** $\begin{array}{r} 60 \\ \times 4 \end{array}$

$$\begin{array}{r} \overset{2}{5}9 \\ \times 3 \\ \hline 177 \end{array}$$

Regroup two times.

7. $\begin{array}{r} 68 \\ \times 7 \end{array}$ **8.** $\begin{array}{r} 56 \\ \times 8 \end{array}$ **9.** $\begin{array}{r} 95 \\ \times 6 \end{array}$

$$\begin{array}{r} \overset{12}{2}58 \\ \times 3 \\ \hline 774 \end{array}$$

Regroup two times.

10. $\begin{array}{r} 398 \\ \times 2 \end{array}$ **11.** $\begin{array}{r} 148 \\ \times 5 \end{array}$ **12.** $\begin{array}{r} 276 \\ \times 3 \end{array}$

$$\begin{array}{r} \overset{32}{5}86 \\ \times 4 \\ \hline 2344 \end{array}$$

Regroup three times.

13. $\begin{array}{r} 765 \\ \times 3 \end{array}$ **14.** $\begin{array}{r} 529 \\ \times 8 \end{array}$ **15.** $\begin{array}{r} 477 \\ \times 6 \end{array}$

$$\begin{array}{r} \overset{152}{5}284 \\ \times 6 \\ \hline 31{,}704 \end{array}$$

Regroup three or more times.

16. $\begin{array}{r} 2568 \\ \times 3 \end{array}$ **17.** $\begin{array}{r} 4563 \\ \times 5 \end{array}$ **18.** $\begin{array}{r} 3829 \\ \times 7 \end{array}$

CHAPTER CHALLENGE

A story of long ago tells of a man whose horse needed shoes. He asked a blacksmith how much it would cost. The blacksmith explained that he had two ways of charging—either $1000 for the whole job or 2¢ for the first nail, 4¢ for the second nail, 8¢ for the third nail, and so on for the 16 nails needed to shoe the horse. The man decided to pay the second way.

1. How much did he have to pay for each nail to shoe his horse? To answer the question, copy and complete this table.

Nail	1	2	3	4	5	6	7	8	9	10	11	12	13	14	15	16
Charge	2¢	4¢	8¢	16¢	32¢	?	?	?	?	?	?	?	?	?	?	?

2. What was the total charge?

3. Did he pay more or less than $1000?

4. How much more or less?

Form W

	a	b	c	d		a	b	c	d		a	b	c	d		a	b	c	d		a	b	c	d
14					34					14					4					30				
15	a	b	c	d													c	d		31		a		

MAJOR CHECKUP
Standardized Format

Choose the correct letter.

1. 78,521 rounded to the nearest thousand is
    a. 78,000
    b. 78,500
    c. 79,000
    d. 80,000

2. Add.
    2653
   +8797
    a. 11,340
    b. 11,450
    c. 10,450
    d. none of these

3. Subtract.
    3205
   − 1678
    a. 2473
    b. 1537
    c. 1627
    d. 1527

4. What time is it?

    a. quarter to nine
    b. quarter past nine
    c. quarter to eight
    d. quarter past eight

5. How many minutes from 9:45 A.M. to 10:25 A.M.?
    a. 50
    b. 30
    c. 70
    d. none of these

6. What is the value of 1 half-dollar, 1 quarter, 3 dimes, and 2 nickels?
    a. $1.10
    b. $1.15
    c. $1.05
    d. none of these

7. Complete.
$\frac{3}{4}$ of 12 =
    a. 9
    b. 8
    c. 3
    d. none of these

8. Add.
$\frac{2}{3} + \frac{5}{6}$
    a. $\frac{3}{2}$
    b. $\frac{7}{6}$
    c. $\frac{7}{3}$
    d. none of these

9. Change to a fraction.
$2\frac{3}{4}$
    a. $\frac{5}{4}$
    b. $\frac{11}{4}$
    c. $\frac{10}{4}$
    d. none of these

10. What is the perimeter?

2 cm
3 cm
    a. 5 cm
    b. 6 cm
    c. 10 cm
    d. none of these

11. What is the area?

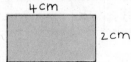

4 cm
2 cm
    a. 8 cm
    b. 6 square cm
    c. 8 square cm
    d. none of these

12. What is the volume?

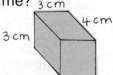

3 cm
4 cm
3 cm
    a. 10 cubic cm
    b. 36 cubic cm
    c. 36 square cm
    d. none of these

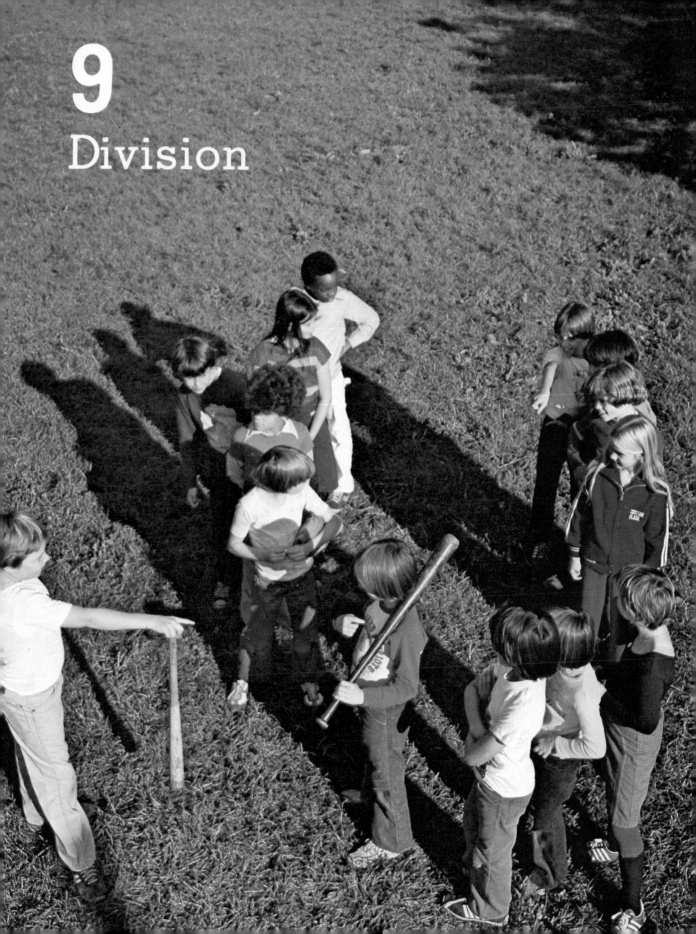

9
Division

READY OR NOT !

1. $8\overline{)32}$ 2. $6\overline{)30}$ 3. $4\overline{)32}$ 4. $4\overline{)36}$ 5. $6\overline{)36}$

6. $8\overline{)40}$ 7. $9\overline{)36}$ 8. $9\overline{)45}$ 9. $5\overline{)40}$ 10. $7\overline{)42}$

11. $5\overline{)45}$ 12. $8\overline{)56}$ 13. $6\overline{)42}$ 14. $7\overline{)56}$ 15. $9\overline{)72}$

16. $8\overline{)48}$ 17. $7\overline{)63}$ 18. $6\overline{)48}$ 19. $9\overline{)81}$ 20. $9\overline{)54}$

Dividing a 2-digit number

The examples show how to divide a 2-digit number by a 1-digit number.

EXAMPLE 1. Think about dividing up the blocks.

$3\overline{)69}$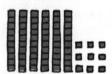

Step 1. Divide tens.

$3\overline{)69}$ with quotient 2

Step 2. Divide ones.

Number in each set →
Number of sets → $3\overline{)69}$ quotient 23

EXAMPLE 2.

$2\overline{)80}$

Step 1. Divide tens.

$2\overline{)80}$ with quotient 4

Step 2. Divide ones.

$2\overline{)80}$ with quotient 40

The answer, 40, is called the **quotient**. Why is it important to write the 0 in the quotient?

228

EXERCISES
Divide.

1. $2\overline{)42}$ 2. $4\overline{)40}$ 3. $2\overline{)68}$ 4. $5\overline{)55}$ 5. $2\overline{)62}$

6. $6\overline{)66}$ 7. $3\overline{)33}$ 8. $4\overline{)88}$ 9. $2\overline{)86}$ 10. $4\overline{)44}$

11. $2\overline{)80}$ 12. $3\overline{)63}$ 13. $2\overline{)44}$ 14. $3\overline{)36}$ 15. $2\overline{)88}$

16. $4\overline{)84}$ 17. $4\overline{)48}$ 18. $3\overline{)66}$ 19. $2\overline{)84}$ 20. $2\overline{)46}$

21. $3\overline{)30}$ 22. $2\overline{)64}$ 23. $3\overline{)39}$ 24. $4\overline{)80}$ 25. $3\overline{)99}$

26. What problem did Beth get wrong? What mistake did she make?

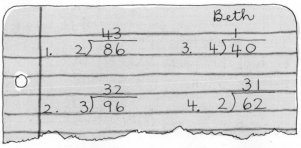

Complete.

27.

How many pencils can you buy?

28.

How many erasers can you buy?

Solve.

29. Bill divided up 48 marbles. He put the same number of marbles in each of 2 boxes. How many marbles did he put in each box?

30. Sandy found 66 seashells. She shared them equally with her 2 sisters. How many seashells did each child get?

Division with regrouping

Sometimes you will need to regroup when dividing.
In Example 1, 2 tens are regrouped for 20 ones.

EXAMPLE 1.

$$3\overline{)81}$$

Step 1. Divide tens.

$$3\overline{)81}$$ with 2 on top, -6, 2

There are 2 tens in
each of the 3 sets. We
used up 6 tens.

2 tens and 1 one left.

Step 2. Regroup 2 tens for 20
ones.

$$3\overline{)81}$$ with 2 on top, -6, 21

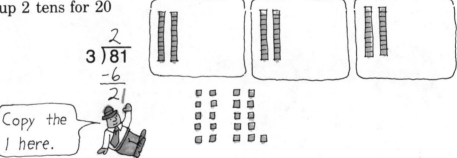

Copy the 1 here.

Step 3. Divide ones.

$$3\overline{)81}$$ with 27 on top, -6, 21, -21, 0

There are 7 ones in
each of the 3 sets. We
used up 21 ones.

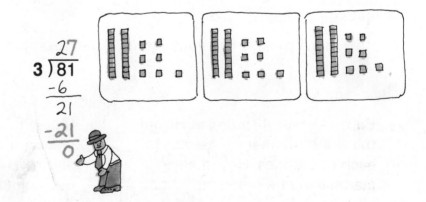

EXERCISES
Copy and complete.

$$\begin{array}{r} 15 \\ 3\overline{)45} \\ -\ 3 \\ \hline 15 \\ -\ 15 \\ \hline ? \end{array}$$
1.

$$\begin{array}{r} 26 \\ 2\overline{)52} \\ -\ 4 \\ \hline 12 \\ -\ ?? \\ \hline ? \end{array}$$
2.

$$\begin{array}{r} 1? \\ 4\overline{)72} \\ -\ 4 \\ \hline 32 \\ -\ ?? \\ \hline ? \end{array}$$
3.

$$\begin{array}{r} 1? \\ 5\overline{)75} \\ -\ 5 \\ \hline ?? \\ -\ ?? \\ \hline ? \end{array}$$
4.

$$\begin{array}{r} ?? \\ 7\overline{)84} \\ -\ ? \\ \hline ?? \\ -\ ?? \\ \hline ? \end{array}$$
5.

Divide.

6. $6\overline{)84}$ 7. $2\overline{)64}$ 8. $3\overline{)57}$ 9. $7\overline{)84}$ 10. $6\overline{)90}$

11. $3\overline{)48}$ 12. $2\overline{)74}$ 13. $5\overline{)70}$ 14. $3\overline{)87}$ 15. $8\overline{)96}$

16. $7\overline{)91}$ 17. $5\overline{)60}$ 18. $4\overline{)88}$ 19. $3\overline{)54}$ 20. $5\overline{)65}$

21. $4\overline{)80}$ 22. $3\overline{)42}$ 23. $6\overline{)96}$ 24. $5\overline{)75}$ 25. $2\overline{)58}$

26. $2\overline{)96}$ 27. $5\overline{)90}$ 28. $7\overline{)98}$ 29. $5\overline{)80}$ 30. $6\overline{)78}$

Solve.

31. 84 days
How many weeks?

32. 96 quarts
How many gallons?

33. 77 feet
How many yards?
How many feet left over?

34. 43 cups
How many pints?
How many cups left over?

Find the end number.

35.

36.

Division with remainder

EXAMPLE.

$3\overline{)58}$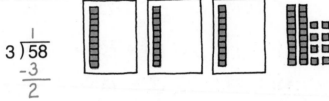

Step 1. Divide tens. Subtract.

$$3\overline{)58} \\ \,\underline{-3} \\ \,2$$

with quotient digit 1

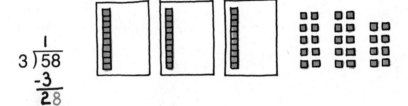

Step 2. Regroup.

$$3\overline{)58} \\ \,\underline{-3} \\ \,28$$

with quotient digit 1

Step 3. Divide ones. Subtract.

$$3\overline{)58} \\ \,\underline{-3} \\ \,28 \\ \,\underline{-27} \\ \,1$$

with quotient 19

This number is called the remainder.

Step 4. Write the remainder.

$$3\overline{)58} \\ \,\underline{-3} \\ \,28 \\ \,\underline{-27} \\ \,1$$

with quotient 19 R1

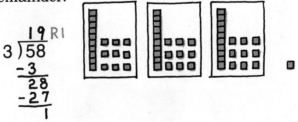

232

EXERCISES

First divide. Then estimate the quotient to see if your answer makes sense.

1. 3)68
2. 5)58
3. 4)58
4. 3)38
5. 6)82

6. 4)72
7. 5)74
8. 7)79
9. 8)86
10. 5)68

11. 6)60
12. 3)78
13. 6)84
14. 3)71
15. 4)81

16. 4)69
17. 7)89
18. 5)72
19. 8)95
20. 6)75

21. 3)92
22. 5)73
23. 4)53
24. 3)95
25. 7)85

26. 5)97
27. 6)91
28. 3)68
29. 4)98
30. 4)92

31. How much for each child?

32. How much for each child?

33. 82 bottles in all.
Put in 6-bottle cartons.
How many cartons are needed?
How many bottles are left over?

34. 95 bottles in all.
Put in 8-bottle cartons.
How many cartons are needed?
How many bottles are left over?

Keeping Skills Sharp

1. $\frac{2}{9} + \frac{4}{9}$
2. $\frac{3}{8} + \frac{1}{8}$
3. $\frac{1}{4} + \frac{1}{4}$
4. $\frac{2}{3} + \frac{2}{3}$

5. $\frac{1}{2} + \frac{3}{6}$
6. $\frac{1}{2} + \frac{1}{4}$
7. $\frac{2}{9} + \frac{1}{3}$
8. $\frac{3}{4} + \frac{1}{8}$

9. $\frac{5}{8} + \frac{1}{4}$
10. $\frac{5}{6} + \frac{1}{3}$
11. $\frac{1}{3} + \frac{1}{6}$
12. $\frac{1}{3} + \frac{1}{2}$

Finding an average

The PTA of Clark Elementary School had a school carnival to raise money. The students sold tickets for one week. The table shown below was kept on the school bulletin board. It shows how many tickets each class sold every day.

Ticket Sales

	Monday	Tuesday	Wednesday	Thursday	Friday
Kindergarten	5	8	5	6	6
First Grade	7	5	6	3	9
Second Grade	7	6	5	3	9
Third Grade	8	8	9	10	10
Fourth Grade	9	8	9	7	12
Fifth Grade	11	8	14	17	15
Sixth Grade	9	7	8	12	9

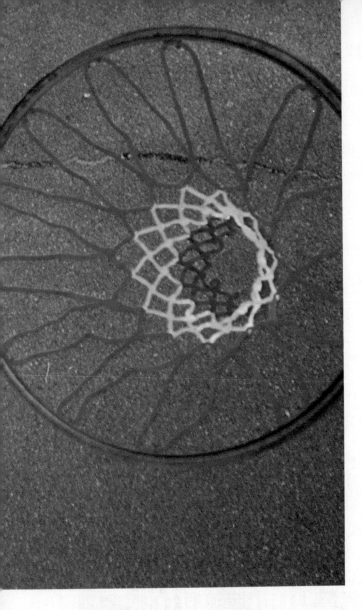

EXERCISES

1. Find the average number of tickets sold each day by the second grade.

2. Find the average number of tickets sold each day by the fifth grade.

3. Find the average number of tickets sold by each class on Monday.

4. Find the average number of tickets sold by each class on Friday.

5. At the carnival, David threw darts 3 times. His scores were 28, 23, and 21. What was his average score?

6. Alice won the basketball free-throw contest for sixth graders. Four times she took 20 shots. She made 11, 12, 14, and 15 baskets. What was her average?

7. **a.** Bill won the baseball-throwing contest. In his 6 throws, he knocked over 8, 6, 3, 1, 5, and 7 bottles. What was his average?

   b. How many times did he knock down fewer bottles than his average? More bottles than his average?

8. Six students sold 84 chances on a radio. What was the average number of chances sold by each student?

The kindergarten class sold 30 tickets altogether. Suppose that they had sold the same number of tickets each day. How many tickets would they have sold each day?

$$\begin{array}{r} 5 \\ 8 \\ 5 \\ 6 \\ + 6 \\ \hline 30 \end{array}$$

$$5 \overline{)30}^{\,6}$$

6 is the *average* number of tickets sold each day.

Dividing a 3-digit number

The example shows how to divide a 3-digit number by a 1-digit number.

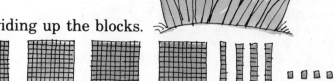

GRRRR

EXAMPLE. Think about dividing up the blocks.

$3\overline{)448}$

Step 1. Divide hundreds. Subtract.

$$3\overline{)448} \\ \underline{-3} \\ 1$$

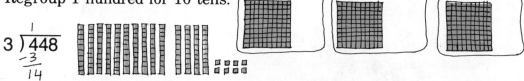

Step 2. Regroup 1 hundred for 10 tens.

$$3\overline{)448} \\ \underline{-3} \\ 14$$

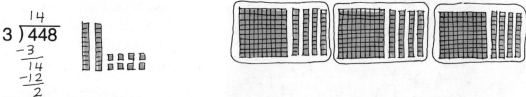

Step 3. Divide tens. Subtract.

$$3\overline{)\overset{14}{448}} \\ \underline{-3} \\ 14 \\ \underline{-12} \\ 2$$

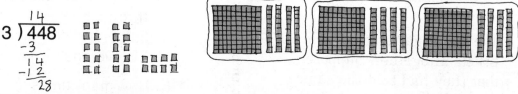

Step 4. Regroup 2 tens for 20 ones.

$$3\overline{)\overset{14}{448}} \\ \underline{-3} \\ 14 \\ \underline{-12} \\ 28$$

Step 5. Divide ones. Subtract.

$$3\overline{)\overset{149\,R1}{448}} \\ \underline{-3} \\ 14 \\ \underline{-12} \\ 28 \\ \underline{-27} \\ 1$$

236

EXERCISES

Divide.

1. $3\overline{)527}$ 2. $4\overline{)952}$ 3. $2\overline{)504}$ 4. $5\overline{)745}$ 5. $2\overline{)963}$

6. $2\overline{)856}$ 7. $5\overline{)742}$ 8. $6\overline{)629}$ 9. $4\overline{)859}$ 10. $3\overline{)398}$

11. $7\overline{)749}$ 12. $8\overline{)900}$ 13. $2\overline{)378}$ 14. $6\overline{)842}$ 15. $4\overline{)726}$

16. $4\overline{)953}$ 17. $9\overline{)974}$ 18. $3\overline{)627}$ 19. $2\overline{)700}$ 20. $9\overline{)958}$

21. $2\overline{)\$4.76}$ 22. $7\overline{)\$8.96}$ 23. $8\overline{)\$8.08}$ 24. $3\overline{)\$5.34}$ 25. $5\overline{)\$8.85}$

26. The Adams family drove 360 kilometers in 5 hours. How many kilometers did they average each hour?

27. The Adamses' car averaged 8 kilometers per liter of gasoline. How many liters of gasoline did they use on the 360-kilometer trip?

Copy and complete these division problems.

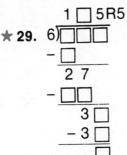

28.
```
     □68 R1
  2)□3□
   -4
    13
   -12
     1□
    -□□
      □
```

★ 29.
```
     1□5R5
  6)□□□
   -□
    27
   -□□
    3□
   -3□
     □
```

237

More about division

Sometimes you have to regroup before you start dividing.

"Not enough hundreds." 3)268

"Think about 26 tens." 3)268

"All finished!"

$$3\overline{)268} \quad 89\,R1$$
$$-24$$
$$28$$
$$-27$$
$$1$$

You can check your work.
Multiply the quotient by the divisor:

$$\begin{array}{r} 89 \\ \times\ 3 \\ \hline 267 \end{array}$$

Then add the remainder:

$$\begin{array}{r} 267 \\ +\ 1 \\ \hline \end{array}$$

It checks. $268 \leftarrow$ Dividend

EXERCISES
Check each answer.

1. $4\overline{)158}$ → 39 R2

2. $5\overline{)261}$ → 50 R1

3. $3\overline{)174}$ → 57 R2

4. $4\overline{)229}$ → 57 R1

5. $6\overline{)361}$ → 6 R1

6. $5\overline{)278}$ → 53 R3

7. $3\overline{)258}$ → 86

8. $5\overline{)227}$ → 45 R1

238

Divide.

9. $6\overline{)312}$

10. $4\overline{)407}$

11. $3\overline{)148}$

12. $2\overline{)642}$

13. $6\overline{)357}$

14. $4\overline{)349}$

15. $5\overline{)409}$

16. $8\overline{)839}$

17. $3\overline{)745}$

18. $4\overline{)392}$

19. $7\overline{)314}$

20. $5\overline{)517}$

21. $6\overline{)236}$

22. $7\overline{)432}$

23. $5\overline{)819}$

24. $2\overline{)248}$

25. $3\overline{)731}$

26. $3\overline{)557}$

27. $7\overline{)603}$

28. $8\overline{)548}$

29. $2\overline{)726}$

30. $3\overline{)225}$

31. $7\overline{)837}$

32. $4\overline{)453}$

33. $9\overline{)329}$

34. $8\overline{)951}$

35. $8\overline{)626}$

36. $5\overline{)961}$

37. $5\overline{)969}$

38. $6\overline{)624}$

Solve.

39. Frank bought 3 records for $4.35 each. What was the total cost?

40. Sarah had $8.72. She spent $3.79 for a record. How much money did she have left?

41. Al bought 2 records for $2.85 each. He gave the clerk a $10 bill. How much change did he receive?

42. Ann bought 4 records that cost $2.85, $3.74, $2.94, and $4.35. What was the average cost of each record?

Who am I?

★ 43. I am between 20 and 50. If you divide me by 6, you get a remainder of 3. If you divide me by 8, you get a remainder of 7.

★ 44. I am between 30 and 55. If you divide me by 3, you get a remainder of 2. If you divide me by 7, you get a remainder of 1.

Dividing a 4-digit number

Large numbers are divided in the same way as
small numbers.
Remember that you can check division by
multiplying.

The division tells us that there are
1776 blocks in each of 3 sets. So,
we can multiply to see if we get 5328
blocks in all.

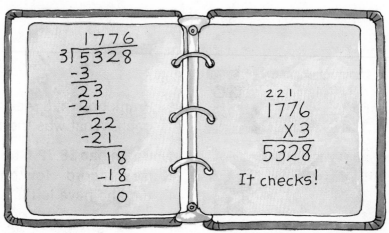

To check a division problem,
multiply the quotient by the divisor.
Then add the remainder. Your final
answer should be the dividend.

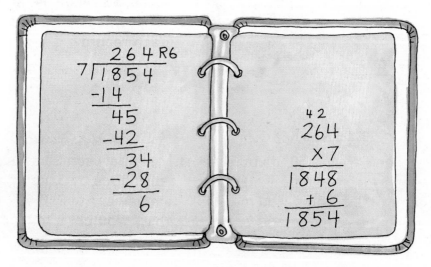

EXERCISES

First divide. Then check your answer.

1. 4)2248
2. 5)1335
3. 3)1506
4. 6)4374

5. 7)3821
6. 6)7342
7. 9)5000
8. 8)3967

Divide.

9. 3)75
10. 2)54
11. 5)78
12. 6)93

13. 4)361
14. 6)742
15. 7)396
16. 6)125

17. 9)2358
18. 8)4695
19. 5)7803
20. 9)3016

21. 7)7213
22. 4)4246
23. 4)6381
24. 4)5000

25. 8)4382
26. 8)3005
27. 9)2000
28. 7)5378

29. 7)3999
30. 5)2916
31. 6)3742
32. 5)9465

Who am I?

33. If you divide me by 6, you get a quotient of 248 and a remainder of 0.

34. If you divide me by 8, you get a quotient of 429 and a remainder of 5.

Keeping Skills Sharp

1. $\frac{5}{6} - \frac{1}{6}$
2. $\frac{5}{3} - \frac{2}{3}$
3. $\frac{3}{6} - \frac{1}{6}$
4. $\frac{3}{4} - \frac{1}{4}$

5. $\frac{3}{8} - \frac{0}{8}$
6. $\frac{5}{8} - \frac{1}{4}$
7. $\frac{9}{16} - \frac{1}{8}$
8. $\frac{5}{6} - \frac{1}{2}$

9. $\frac{5}{6} - \frac{2}{3}$
10. $\frac{5}{6} - \frac{1}{3}$
11. $\frac{4}{3} - \frac{5}{6}$
12. $\frac{5}{4} - \frac{1}{2}$

Addition, subtraction, multiplication, and division

Work inside the grouping symbols first.

EXAMPLE. $242 + (756 \div 4) = 431$

```
    189
  4)756
   -4
   ‾‾
    35
   -32
   ‾‾‾
    36        242
   -36       +189
   ‾‾‾       ‾‾‾‾
     0        431
```

EXERCISES

Compute.

1. $(252 \div 2) - 28$

2. $681 + (396 \div 3)$

3. $753 - (400 \div 4)$

4. $(385 \div 5) - 19$

5. $(462 \div 3) \times 4$

6. $(507 - 287) \div 5$

7. $(246 \times 7) \div 7$

8. $(836 + 259) - 259$

Less than (<), equal to (=), or greater than (>)?

9. $382 + 167 \quad \bullet \quad 275 \times 2$

10. $974 - 395 \quad \bullet \quad 4504 \div 8$

11. $68 \times 4 \quad \bullet \quad 1664 \div 6$

12. $143 \times 6 \quad \bullet \quad 1001 - 143$

PROBLEM SOLVING   **Make up a story.**

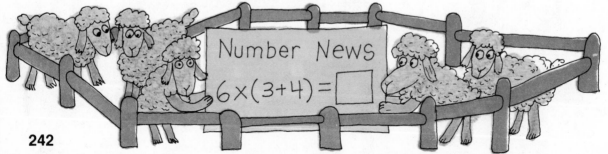

Number News

$6 \times (3 + 4) = \Box$

242

BUILD THE GREATEST QUOTIENT

Which quotient is greater?

1. $2\overline{)4\ 5\ 8\ 3}$ $3\overline{)8\ 2\ 5\ 4}$ 2. $6\overline{)5\ 8\ 7\ 2}$ $8\overline{)7\ 6\ 2\ 5}$

3. $4\overline{)7\ 8\ 5\ 0}$ $5\overline{)8\ 4\ 0\ 7}$ 4. $6\overline{)8\ 3\ 6\ 4}$ $4\overline{)6\ 6\ 3\ 8}$

Play the game.

1. Choose a leader.

2. Make two cards for each of the digits.

3. Each player draws a table.

4. As the leader picks a digit, fill in your table.

5. Repeat step 4 until your table is filled in.

6. The player who builds the greatest quotient wins.
   Later you may wish to play least quotient wins.

Problem solving

Clerks have to know how to operate a cash register and make change. Sometimes they have to solve a problem like this.

How much should the customer be charged for 1 can of soup?

To find the cost of 1 can, the clerk can divide:

$$
\begin{array}{r}
26 \\
3\overline{)79} \\
-6 \\
\hline
19 \\
-18 \\
\hline
1
\end{array}
$$

Since there is a remainder, the clerk knows that the cost of 1 can is between 26¢ and 27¢. The rule used by stores is always to round up to the next cent. Is this the same as rounding to the nearest cent?

EXERCISES

1. How much will 1 jar cost?

2. What is the cost of 1 grapefruit?

3. How much will 1 cost?

4. What will be the cost of 3 bunches?

   Hint: Add the costs of 2 bunches and 1 bunch.

5. If two boxes of prunes cost $1.89, what is the cost of 1 box?

6. If pudding is 4 packages for $.79, how much will 5 packages cost?

7. Terry took $1 to the store. He wanted 1 can of orange juice. The juice was 3 cans for $1.17. How much money did Terry have left?

8. Bread was on sale, 3 loaves for $1.89. Craig bought a carton of milk for $.73 and 4 loaves of bread. What was the total cost?

9. Jam is on sale: 2 jars of grape for $1.75 and 3 jars of strawberry for $2.00. What is the cost of 3 jars of grape jam and 4 jars of strawberry jam?

Divide. [pages 228–233]

1. $3\overline{)69}$ 　　 2. $4\overline{)52}$ 　　 3. $2\overline{)38}$ 　　 4. $5\overline{)95}$ 　　 5. $6\overline{)84}$

6. $4\overline{)79}$ 　　 7. $8\overline{)94}$ 　　 8. $5\overline{)76}$ 　　 9. $9\overline{)93}$ 　　 10. $7\overline{)80}$

Divide. [pages 236–241]

11. $4\overline{)944}$ 　　 12. $3\overline{)741}$ 　　 13. $5\overline{)940}$ 　　 14. $6\overline{)804}$ 　　 15. $8\overline{)960}$

16. $6\overline{)282}$ 　　 17. $8\overline{)392}$ 　　 18. $9\overline{)538}$ 　　 19. $4\overline{)796}$ 　　 20. $7\overline{)451}$

21. $3\overline{)2941}$ 　　 22. $6\overline{)8536}$ 　　 23. $5\overline{)9478}$ 　　 24. $8\overline{)2000}$ 　　 25. $7\overline{)9163}$

Solve. [pages 234–235, 244–245]

Each week Mr. Allison gives a review test of 25 problems. In each exercise, find the average score.

26.

27.

28. Eight members of a youth group were going on a backpacking trip. Together they planned to take 96 kilograms of gear. They wanted to divide the weight equally. How much should each carry?

29. The group planned to hike up a mountain trail in 3 hours. The trail is 4926 meters long. How many meters per hour would they average?

Project

Round each average to the nearest centimeter.

1. From a line, take 3 standing long jumps. What is your average?

2. Find the average standing long jump of each classmate. Make a graph.

3. Take 3 standing backward jumps. Find your average.

4. From a line, take 3 running long jumps. What is your average?

247

CHAPTER REVIEW

$$2\overline{)42}$$ with quotient 21

Divide.

1. $2\overline{)86}$ quotient 43

2. $3\overline{)93}$

3. $4\overline{)80}$

4. $3\overline{)78}$ quotient 26, -6, 18, -18, 0

5. $5\overline{)85}$

6. $4\overline{)96}$

7. $2\overline{)75}$ quotient 37 R1, -6, 15, -14, 1

8. $7\overline{)95}$

9. $6\overline{)98}$

10. $3\overline{)765}$ quotient 255, -6, 16, -15, 15, -15, 0

11. $7\overline{)958}$

12. $4\overline{)729}$

13. $5\overline{)287}$ quotient 57 R2, -25, 37, -35, 2

14. $6\overline{)460}$

15. $8\overline{)632}$

16. $5\overline{)4937}$ quotient 987 R2, -45, 43, -40, 37, -35, 2

17. $9\overline{)4539}$

18. $7\overline{)6000}$

248

CHAPTER CHALLENGE

If the remainder is 0 when you divide a number by 2, the number is divisible by 2.

If this number is divisible by 2, what can you say about the last digit of the number?

Can it be 0? 2? 4? 6? 8?

A number is divisible by 2 if its last digit is divisible by 2.

Which of these numbers are divisible by 2?

| 1. 578 | 2. 639 | 3. 507 |
| 4. 7405 | 5. 6384 | 6. 3310 |

A number is divisible by 3 if the sum of its digits is divisible by 3.

Which of these numbers are divisible by 3?

1 + 4 + 7 = 12

| 7. 147 | 8. 352 | 9. 601 |
| 10. 723 | 11. 537 | 12. 888 |

A number is divisible by 4 if its last two digits are divisible by 4.

Which of these numbers are divisible by 4?

| 13. 7132 | 14. 8404 | 15. 3915 |
| 16. 7726 | 17. 5384 | 18. 6032 |

19. See if you can find a rule to tell whether a number is divisible by 5.

MAJOR CHECKUP
Standardized Format

Choose the correct letter.

1. Which number is greater than 58,163?

    a. 58,171
    b. 6999
    c. 57,238
    d. none of these

2. Add.

    5387
    +2694

    a. 7971
    b. 7981
    c. 7071
    d. none of these

3. Subtract.

    5285
    − 3436

    a. 2251
    b. 2859
    c. 1849
    d. none of these

---

4. What time is it?

    a. half past twelve
    b. thirty minutes after twelve
    c. half past eleven
    d. none of these

5. $\frac{6}{8}$ reduced to lowest terms is

    a. $\frac{6}{4}$
    b. $\frac{3}{8}$
    c. $\frac{5}{7}$
    d. none of these

6. Add.

$$\frac{1}{4}$$
$$+\frac{3}{8}$$

    a. $\frac{5}{4}$
    b. $\frac{5}{8}$
    c. $\frac{5}{12}$
    d. none of these

---

7. Subtract.

$$\frac{5}{6}$$
$$-\frac{1}{3}$$

    a. $\frac{1}{2}$
    b. $\frac{1}{3}$
    c. $\frac{2}{3}$
    d. none of these

8. Write $\frac{9}{4}$ as a mixed number.

    a. $2\frac{1}{4}$
    b. $3\frac{1}{4}$
    c. $1\frac{3}{4}$
    d. none of these

9. What is the area?

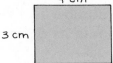

4 cm
3 cm

    a. 7 square cm
    b. 12 square cm
    c. 14 square cm
    d. none of these

---

10. What is the volume?

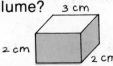

3 cm
2 cm
2 cm

    a. 7 cubic cm
    b. 8 cubic cm
    c. 12 cubic cm
    d. none of these

11. Multiply.

    87
    ×6

    a. 482
    b. 402
    c. 522
    d. none of these

12. Multiply.

    597
    ×8

    a. 4776
    b. 4026
    c. 4076
    d. none of these

10
Geometry

Solids

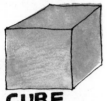

CUBE

RECTANGULAR SOLID

SPHERE

CYLINDER

CONE

PYRAMID

EXERCISES
Name the shape of each numbered item.

GARAGE SALE

OLD JARS 25¢ each

A cube has 8 vertices (the plural of vertex is vertices), 12 edges, and 6 flat surfaces.

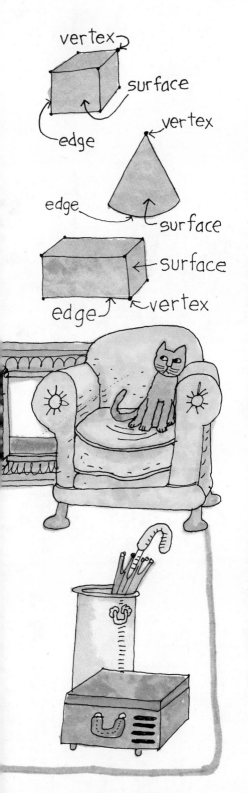

Complete this table.

Solid	Number of vertices	Number of edges	Number of flat surfaces	Number of curved surfaces
Cube	7.	8.	9.	10.
Rectangular Solid	11.	12.	13.	14.
Sphere	15.	16.	17.	18.
Cylinder	19.	20.	21.	22.
Cone	23.	24.	25.	26.
Pyramid	27.	28.	29.	30.

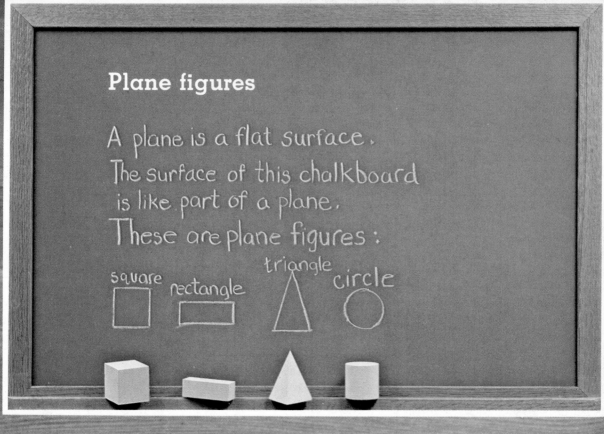

Plane figures

A plane is a flat surface.
The surface of this chalkboard
is like part of a plane.
These are plane figures:

square   rectangle   triangle   circle

EXERCISES

1. Name each shape. If it is not a
square, rectangle, triangle, or
circle, write "something else."

a.

b.

c.

d.

e.

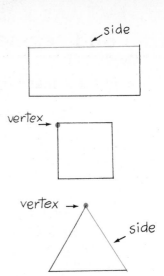

side

vertex →

vertex →

side

2. How many sides does a square have?

3. How many vertices (plural of vertex) does a rectangle have?

4. How many vertices does a triangle have?

5. Does a circle have a vertex?

★ **6.** How many triangles are shown here?

★ **7.** How many squares?

Points and segments

The sides of these plane figures are **segments**.

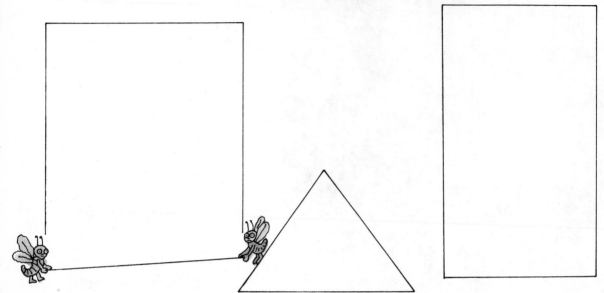

You can think of a segment as a straight path between two points.

Here is another segment.
A •—————————————————————————• B

The endpoints are A and B.

You can call it either segment AB or segment BA.
For short we write $\overline{AB}$ or $\overline{BA}$.

($\overline{AB}$ is read as "segment AB.")

EXERCISES
Which are segments?

1.    2.   3.

4. What are the endpoints of this segment?

5. What are two ways to name this segment?

6. $\overline{AB}$ crosses $\overline{RS}$ at what point?

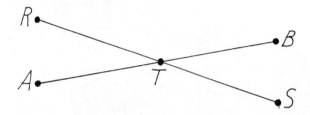

7. Give 4 segments that have point V as an endpoint.

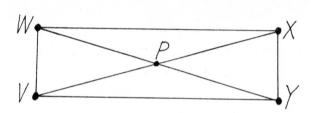

8. How many segments are shown?

Draw a figure to go with each sentence. Be sure to write the letters for the endpoints and crossing points.

9. $\overline{RS}$ crosses $\overline{CD}$ at point P.

10. $\overline{AB}$ crosses $\overline{XY}$ at point X.

You can draw 6 segments using 4 points.
Draw segments to complete the table.

	11.	12.	13.	14.	15.
Number of points	2	3	4	5	6
Number of segments			6		

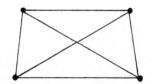

Lines

A segment is part of a **line**. The arrows remind you that a line goes on and on in both directions. You can call it either line *RS* or line *SR*.

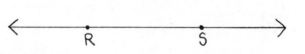

Line *XY* and line *AB* cross at point *P*. Lines that cross are called **intersecting lines**.

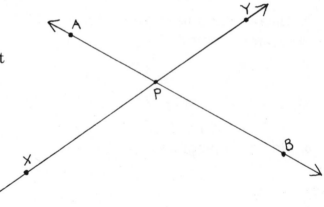

Line *CD* and line *EF* do not cross. Lines in a plane that do not cross are called **parallel lines**.

EXERCISES

The lines shown in each exercise were torn from a piece of paper. Do you think that the lines are intersecting or parallel?

1.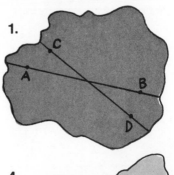

2.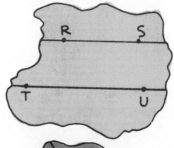

3.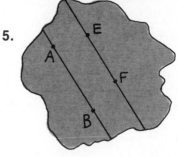

4.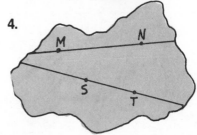

5.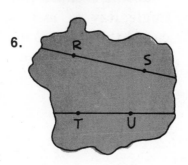

6.

7. Trace these four points.

8. Draw $\overleftrightarrow{AB}$.

9. Draw $\overleftrightarrow{DC}$.

10. Do you think that line AB is parallel to line DC?

A •   •B

•D   •C

Draw a figure to go with each sentence.

11. $\overleftrightarrow{CD}$ intersects $\overleftrightarrow{RS}$ at point T.

12. $\overleftrightarrow{AB}$ is parallel to $\overleftrightarrow{UV}$, $\overleftrightarrow{RS}$ intersects $\overleftrightarrow{AB}$ at point Y, and $\overleftrightarrow{RS}$ intersects $\overleftrightarrow{UV}$ at point Z.

Keeping Skills Sharp

1. 32 ×3	2. 46 ×2	3. 78 ×5	4. 153 ×4	5. 378 ×6	6. 528 ×9
7. 846 ×6	8. 935 ×8	9. 706 ×5	10. 931 ×9	11. 812 ×7	12. 777 ×9

Rays and angles

A **ray** is part of a line. The arrow reminds you that a ray goes on and on in one direction. The red ray is called ray *RS*.

Two rays having the same endpoint form an **angle**. The common endpoint is called the **vertex** of the angle. Ray *AC* and ray *AB* are called the **sides** of the angle. This angle is called angle *A*.

An angle that forms a square corner is called a **right angle**.

Angle *Y* is a right angle.

The part shown in blue is called angle *A* of the square. Which part is angle *D*?

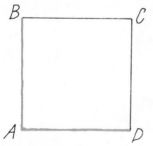

260

EXERCISES

How many endpoints does each figure have?

1. segment

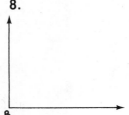

2. line

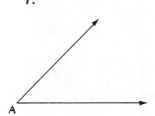

3. ray

4. Name the angle shown.

5. Give the vertex of the angle.

6. Give the sides.

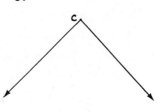

Which of these angles are right angles?

7.

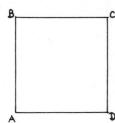

8.

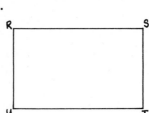

9.

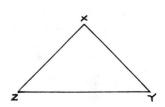

How many right angles does each of these figures have?

10.

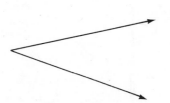

11.

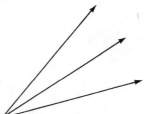

12.

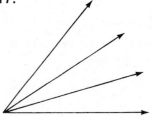

13. List some things in your classroom that form right angles.

14. Name two figures that have four right angles.

How many angles can you find in each figure?

15. 16. ★17.

261

Congruent figures

Figures that are the same size and shape are **congruent figures**.

Tom found this Hippy the Hippo pattern in his box of cereal. He used the pattern to draw this picture.

EXERCISES
Which of these pictures could have been made with Tom's Hippy the Hippo pattern?

1.

2.

3.

4.

5.

6.

Which figure is congruent to the blue figure?

Step 1. Trace the blue figure.

Step 2. See which red figure your tracing fits.

7.
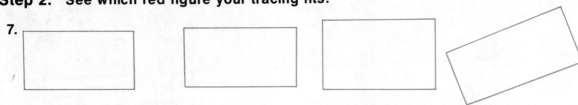

8.

9.

10.
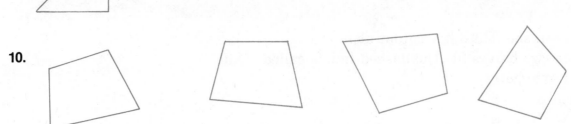

11. **a.** Is figure A the same shape as figure B?
   b. Is figure A the same size as figure B?
   c. Are they congruent?

12. **a.** Is figure A the same shape as figure C?
   b. Is figure A the same size as figure C?
   c. Are they congruent?

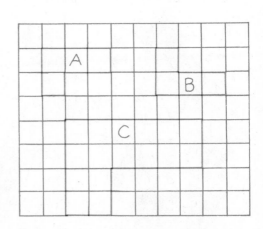

Line of symmetry

Sandy made this cutout from a folded piece of paper.

When she folded her cutout along the dashed line, the two halves fit. The dashed line is called a **line of symmetry.**

EXERCISES
Is the dashed line a line of symmetry?

1.

2.

3.

4.
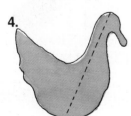

5.
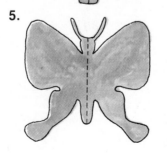

6.
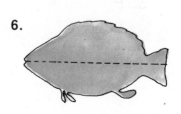

264

How many lines of symmetry?

7.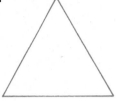

8.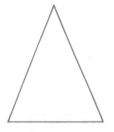

9.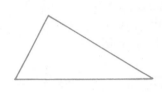

10.

11.

12.

13.

14.

15.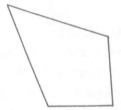

16. Fold a piece of paper. Cut out a figure from the folded edge. Draw the line of symmetry.

17. Can you draw a triangle that has only 2 lines of symmetry?

18. Can you draw a 6-sided figure that has only 1 line of symmetry?

Keeping Skills Sharp

1. $2\overline{)68}$ 2. $5\overline{)55}$ 3. $3\overline{)72}$ 4. $5\overline{)85}$ 5. $4\overline{)92}$

6. $8\overline{)256}$ 7. $6\overline{)390}$ 8. $5\overline{)335}$ 9. $8\overline{)742}$ 10. $9\overline{)683}$

11. $7\overline{)9161}$ 12. $8\overline{)3824}$ 13. $6\overline{)6351}$ 14. $9\overline{)7881}$ 15. $7\overline{)5298}$

Points on a grid

You can use a **number pair** to locate a point on a grid.

To locate point *A*, you start at 0 and count 7 units to the right and then count 5 units up.

The number pair (7, 5) gives the location of point *A*.

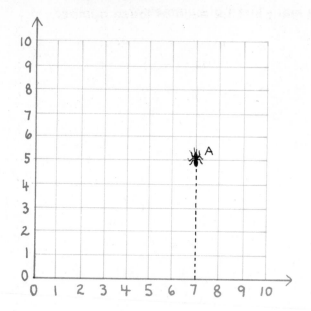

Give the number pair for each point. *Remember:* The first number is the number of units to the right. The second number is the number of units up.

1. D (8,5)

2. H   **3.** A   **4.** G

5. C   **6.** I   **7.** F

8. E   **9.** J   **10.** B

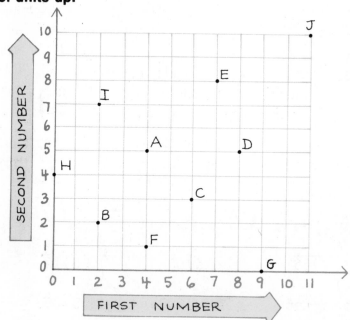

266

Give the point for each of these number pairs.

11. (2, 3)   12. (3, 2)

13. (5, 1)   14. (1, 7)

15. (8, 0)   16. (0, 8)

17. (6, 4)   18. (4, 6)

19. (4, 5)   20. (7, 3)

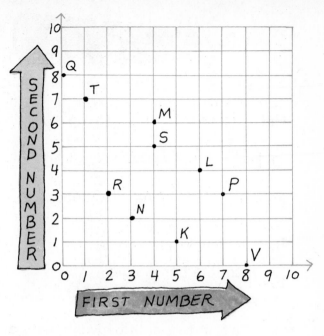

FIRST NUMBER

SECOND NUMBER

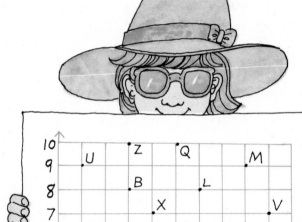

21. Jerry belonged to a secret club. Each member had a copy of this grid with all the letters of the alphabet. They used it to send secret messages. Here is a message that the president sent to each member. Use the grid to decode the message.

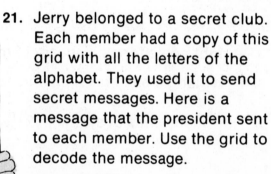

(8,9) (6,2) (6,2) (8,2) / (1,6) (8,2)

(8,2) (5,4) (6,2) / (2,2) (6,8) (1,9) (3,8)

(5,4) (9,3) (1,9) (5,1) (6,2) / (1,6) (8,2)

(2,5) (9,3) (9,3) (2,5)

(5,1) (1,6) (8,2) (1,9) (1,3) (3,1) (1,6) (10,5)

22. Use the grid to write a message of your own.

267

CHAPTER CHECKUP

Match. [pages 252–253]

1.   2.   3.   4.   5.   6.

a. sphere **b.** cone **c.** cube **d.** cylinder **e.** pyramid **f.** rectangular solid

True or false? [pages 254–263]

7. A square has 4 sides.

8. A triangle has 4 vertices.

9. The shortest path between two points is a segment.

10. A line has two endpoints.

11. Parallel lines can intersect.

12. Any two rays form an angle.

13. A right angle forms a square corner.

14. A rectangle has four right angles.

15. How many lines of symmetry? [pages 264–265]

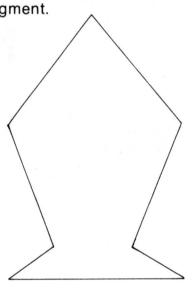

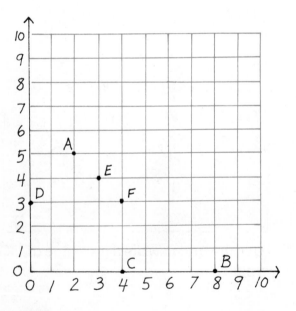

[pages 266–267]

16. Give the number pair for point *A*.

17. Give the number pair for point *B*.

18. What point is at (4, 3)?

Project

1. Get a compass and practice drawing some circles.

2. The distance from the center of the circle to the circle is called the *radius*. Get a centimeter ruler and draw a circle with a radius of 3 cm. Of 4 cm.

3. The distance across a circle through its center is the *diameter*. Draw a circle with a diameter of 4 cm. Of 6 cm.

4. Two designs are shown above. The pictures below show how the first one was made.

   Make the design.

5. Make some designs of your own.

CHAPTER REVIEW

Match.

1.   2.   3.   4.   5.   6.

a. pyramid   **b.** cube   **c.** cone   **d.** rectangular solid   **e.** sphere   **f.** cylinder

Match.

7.   8.   9.   10.

g. rectangle   **h.** triangle   **i.** square   **j.** circle

True or false?

11. Point *A* and point *B* are called endpoints of segment AB.

12. Line *RS* and line *UV* intersect at point *P*.

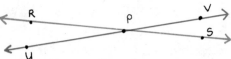

13. Point *D* is an endpoint of ray *CD*.

14. Point *A* is called the vertex.

15. Angle *A* is a right angle.

16. Use a tracing to tell which triangle is congruent to the red triangle.

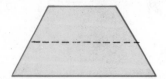

17. Is the dashed line a line of symmetry?

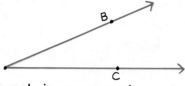

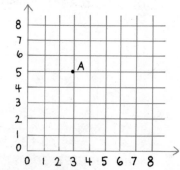

18. Give the number pair for point *A*.

CHAPTER CHALLENGE

This is Carla's computing machine. She gives it a rule and some starting numbers. The machine computes number pairs for her and prints out a card. When she gave the computer the rule *Add 2* and the numbers 0 through 4, the card looked like this:

Add 2

0	2
1	3
2	4
3	5
4	6

0 + 2 = 2
1 + 2 = 3

Here is how Carla graphed the number pairs printed on the card.

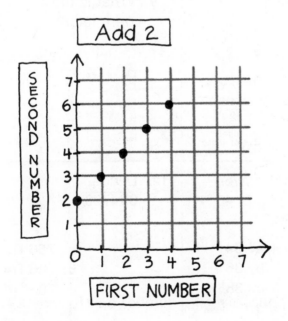

Add 2

SECOND NUMBER

FIRST NUMBER

Complete the cards. Then graph the number pairs.

1. ### Add 1

0	1
1	2
2	3
3	
4	

2. ### Subtract 2

2	0
3	1
4	
5	
6	

3. ### Multiply by 2

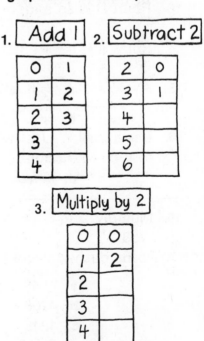

0	0
1	2
2	
3	
4	

Form W

a b c d   a b c d   a b c d   a b c d   a b c d
14   34   14   4   30
a b c d   a b c d   c d   c d   a b c d
15   31
a b c   Standardized Format   a b c   a b c d

MAJOR CHECKUP

Choose the correct letter.

1. 65,381 rounded to the nearest hundred is

    a. 65,000
    b. 65,400
    c. 65,300
    d. none of these

2. Which is the smallest number?

    a. 86,521
    b. 769,431
    c. 86,397
    d. 86,400

3. Subtract.
$$8204 - 3569$$

    a. 3365
    b. 4745
    c. 4635
    d. none of these

4. What time is shown?

    a. quarter past one
    b. quarter to one
    c. quarter to two
    d. quarter past two

5. How many minutes from 11:50 A.M. to 12:30 P.M.?

    a. 80
    b. 40
    c. 50
    d. none of these

6. Complete.
$\frac{2}{3}$ of $18 = \underline{\ ?\ }$

    a. 27
    b. 12
    c. 15
    d. none of these

7. Add.
$\frac{1}{2} + \frac{1}{6}$

    a. $\frac{2}{3}$
    b. $\frac{1}{3}$
    c. $\frac{1}{4}$
    d. none of these

8. Subtract.
$\frac{3}{8} - \frac{1}{4}$

    a. $\frac{1}{8}$
    b. $\frac{1}{4}$
    c. $\frac{1}{2}$
    d. none of these

9. What is the perimeter?

2 cm, 3 cm

    a. 6 cm
    b. 5 cm
    c. 10 cm
    d. none of these

10. Multiply.
$$758 \times 6$$

    a. 4548
    b. 4208
    c. 4248
    d. none of these

11. What is the average of 26, 38, 45, and 31?

    a. 34
    b. 36
    c. 38
    d. none of these

12. Divide.
$6\overline{)4720}$

    a. 786 R2
    b. 786 R4
    c. 783 R4
    d. none of these

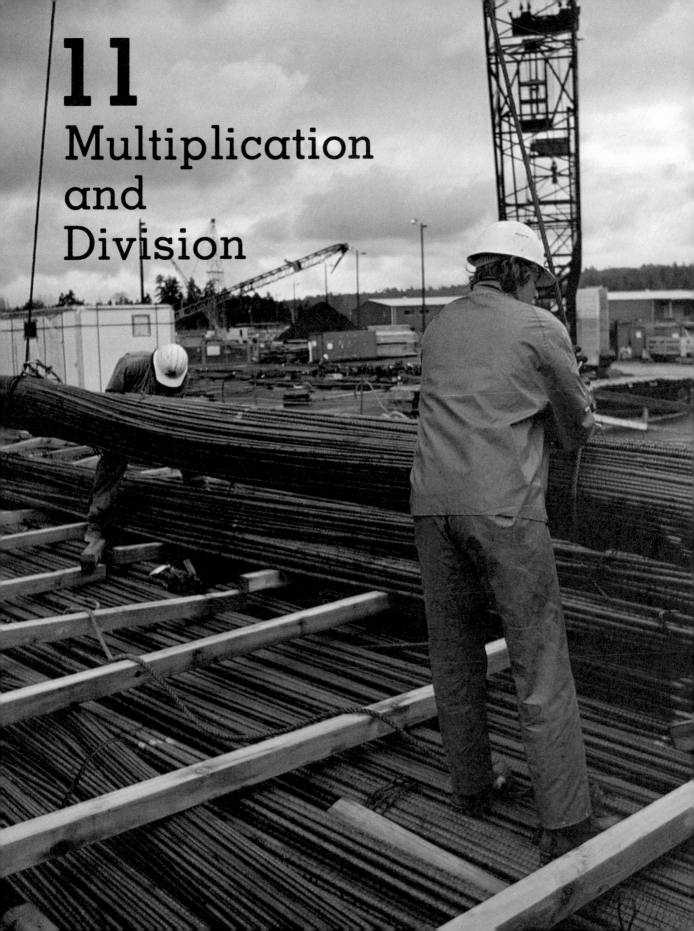

11
Multiplication and Division

Multiply.

1. 8
  ×4

2. 7
  ×7

3. 9
  ×7

4. 7
  ×6

5. 8
  ×9

6. 9
  ×6

7. 9
  ×8

8. 6
  ×8

9. 4
  ×9

10. 6
  ×9

Divide.

11. 7)28

12. 3)27

13. 8)32

14. 8)48

15. 6)36

16. 5)40

17. 9)63

18. 6)54

19. 6)42

20. 9)72

Multiplying by 10

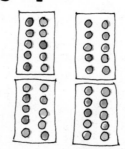

To find the total number of marbles, you can multiply.

10
×6
——
60

6 （6 tens）
×10
——
60

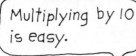

Multiplying by 10 is easy.

SHORTCUT

MARBLES

9
×10
——
90

12
×10
——
120

18
×10
——
180

25
×10
——
250

Do you see an easy way to multiply a number by 10?

EXERCISES

Multiply.

1. 13
  ×10

2. 15
  ×10

3. 19
  ×10

4. 22
  ×10

5. 26
  ×10

6. 34
  ×10

7. 53
  ×10

8. 58
  ×10

9. 62
  ×10

10. 92
  ×10

Multiply.

11. 124 ×10	12. 156 ×10	13. 132 ×10	14. 175 ×10	15. 190 ×10
16. 210 ×10	17. 234 ×10	18. 353 ×10	19. 482 ×10	20. 526 ×10
21. 672 ×10	22. 684 ×10	23. 792 ×10	24. 800 ×10	25. 943 ×10

Complete.

26. 5 dimes are worth _?_ pennies.

27. 16 dimes are worth _?_ pennies.

28. 3 dollars are worth _?_ dimes.

29. 36 dollars are worth _?_ dimes.

Solve.

30.

How many oranges in 10 packages?

31.

How many apples in 10 packages?

32. Jack puts 10 pictures on each page of his picture album. How many pictures can he put on 36 pages?

33. June has 43 pieces of track for her electric train. Each piece is 10 cm long. How long is the longest track she can build?

Multiplying by tens

How would you find the number of chocolates in all?

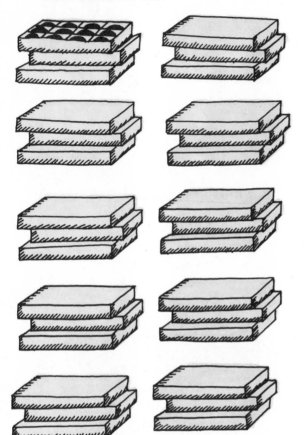

Here is how Jeff found the number of chocolates.

> Jeff
>
> 12 in each box
> × 3
> ────────
> 36 in each stack
>
> 36 in each stack
> × 10 stacks
> ────────
> 360 chocolates

To find this product,
$$\begin{array}{r} 12 \\ \times\, 30 \\ \hline \end{array}$$
chocolates in each box
boxes of chocolates

he first multiplied 12 by 3. Then he multiplied that answer by 10.

He could have shortened his work by doing this:

> Jeff
>
> 12
> × 30
> ────
> 360

To multiply by 30, first multiply by 3 and then multiply by 10.

EXERCISES
Multiply.

1. 42
   ×20   *Multiply by 2 and then by 10.*

2. 31
   ×30   *Multiply by 3 and then by 10.*

3. 43
   ×20   *Multiply by 2 and then by 10.*

4. 16
   ×40   *Multiply by 4 and then by 10.*

You can write the 0 first and then mutiply by 4.

```
   1
  53
×40
----
2120
```

SHORTCUT

Multiply. Write the 0 first.

5. 34
   ×20

6. 21
   ×30

7. 23
   ×30

8. 36
   ×20

9. 30
   ×30

10. 48
    ×50

11. 46
    ×40

12. 68
    ×50

13. 93
    ×60

14. 82
    ×70

15. 84
    ×50

16. 318
    ×20

17. 284
    ×30

18. 358
    ×40

19. 472
    ×30

20. 529
    ×50

21. 603
    ×60

22. 381
    ×80

23. 749
    ×70

24. 600
    ×60

25. 745
    ×50

Solve.

26.

13¢

How much will 20 stamps cost?

27.

36 COOKIES

How many cookies in 30 boxes?

28. Mark earns $4.50 each week. How much will he earn in 40 weeks?

29. Sally earns $1.25 an hour for baby-sitting. One month she baby-sat 5 hours each Saturday. There were 4 Saturdays in the month. How much did she earn?

Multiplying by a 2-digit number

There are 24 sardines in each can.
There are 23 cans. The total number
of sardines is this product:

$$
\begin{array}{r}
24 \\
\times\ 23 \\
\end{array}
$$

Here is how to find the product.

Step 1. Multiply by 3.

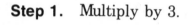

$$
\begin{array}{r}
\overset{\scriptstyle 1}{24} \\
\times\ 23 \\
\hline
72 \\
\end{array}
$$
sardines in 3 cans

Step 2. Multiply by 20.

$$
\begin{array}{r}
\overset{\scriptstyle 1}{24} \\
\times\ 23 \\
\hline
72 \\
480 \\
\end{array}
$$
sardines in 20 cans

Step 3. Add.

$$
\begin{array}{r}
\overset{\scriptstyle 1}{24} \\
\times\ 23 \\
\hline
72 \\
480 \\
\hline
552 \\
\end{array}
$$
sardines in all 23 cans

EXERCISES
Multiply.

1.
```
   42
 × 23
  126
  840
  966
```
3×42
20×42
23×42

2.
```
   43
 × 32
   86
 1290
```
2×43
30×43

3.
```
   32
 × 26
  192
```
6×32
20×32

4.
```
   54
 × 43
```

5.
```
   78
 × 53
```

6.
```
   65
 × 48
```

7.
```
   53
 × 49
```

8.
```
   49
 × 53
```

9.
```
   54
 × 32
```

10.
```
   58
 × 42
```

11.
```
   79
 × 19
```

12.
```
   65
 × 25
```

13.
```
   80
 × 52
```

14.
```
   74
 × 29
```

15.
```
   93
 × 50
```

16.
```
   76
 × 43
```

17.
```
   85
 × 74
```

18.
```
   96
 × 44
```

19.
```
   54
 × 63
```

20.
```
   63
 × 63
```

21.
```
   69
 × 41
```

22.
```
   77
 × 55
```

23.
```
   86
 × 48
```

24.
```
   52
 × 37
```

25.
```
   78
 × 58
```

26.
```
   65
 × 49
```

27.
```
   79
 × 27
```

28.
```
   95
 × 63
```

Solve.

29. 28 days
How many hours?

30. 54 dozen eggs
How many eggs?

Copy and complete.

31.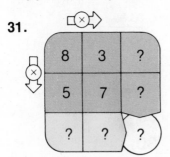

32.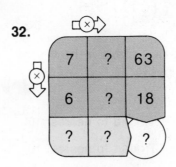

33.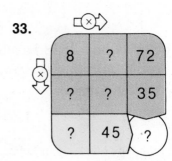

Multiplying by a 2-digit number

Sylvia had 28 boxes of baseball cards. There were 126 cards in each box. How many cards did she have?

Step 1. Multiply by 8.

$$
\begin{array}{r}
\overset{2\,4}{126} \\
\times\ 28 \\
\hline
1008
\end{array}
$$

Step 2. Multiply by 20.

$$
\begin{array}{r}
\overset{1}{}\overset{2\,4}{126} \\
\times\ 28 \\
\hline
1008 \\
2520
\end{array}
$$

Step 3. Add.

$$
\begin{array}{r}
\overset{1}{}\overset{2\,4}{126} \\
\times\ 28 \\
\hline
1008 \\
2520 \\
\hline
3528
\end{array}
$$

Sylvia had 3528 baseball cards. Here is how you could estimate the product to see if the answer makes sense.

126	Round to nearest 100	100
× 28	Round to nearest 10	× 30
		3000

280

EXERCISES

Estimate each product.

1. 89 → 90
   ×52   ×50
             ?

2. 73 → 70
   ×41   ×40
             ?

3. 68 → 70
   ×56   ×60
             ?

4. 112 → 100
   ×46   ×50
              ?

5. 283 → 300
   ×34   ×30
              ?

6. 419 → 400
   ×85   ×90
              ?

First multiply. Then estimate to see if the answer makes sense.

7. 72   8. 82   9. 59   10. 76   11. 93
   ×40   ×36   ×54   ×18   ×27

12. 48   13. 92   14. 78   15. 65   16. 49
    ×86   ×52   ×23   ×49   ×65

17. 115   18. 782   19. 592   20. 435   21. 673
    ×36   ×40   ×36   ×48   ×25

22. 806   23. 291   24. 746   25. 926   26. 824
    ×54   ×38   ×45   ×30   ×42

Who am I?

27. I am the product of 427 and 83.

28. I am 54 greater than the product of 226 and 36.

29. I am 137 less than the product of 483 and 29.

Keeping Skills Sharp

1. $\frac{1}{4}$
   $+\frac{1}{2}$

2. $\frac{5}{8}$
   $+\frac{1}{2}$

3. $\frac{4}{5}$
   $+\frac{3}{10}$

4. $\frac{2}{3}$
   $+\frac{1}{6}$

5. $\frac{7}{8}$
   $+\frac{1}{2}$

6. $\frac{2}{9}$
   $+\frac{1}{3}$

Multiplication practice

Multiply.

1. 26
    ×12

2. 84
    ×19

3. 53
    ×27

4. 48
    ×39

5. 68
    ×50

6. 58
    ×26

7. 67
    ×35

8. 49
    ×48

9. 76
    ×19

10. 85
    ×92

11. 48
    ×75

12. 93
    ×68

13. 68
    ×93

14. 56
    ×74

15. 74
    ×56

16. 374
    ×65

17. 281
    ×56

18. 519
    ×74

19. 650
    ×32

20. 942
    ×60

21. 321
    ×31

22. 746
    ×92

23. 883
    ×48

24. 609
    ×85

25. 619
    ×73

26. 344
    ×76

27. 551
    ×88

28. 668
    ×26

29. 748
    ×15

30. 526
    ×65

31. $2.53
    ×24
    10.12
    50.60
    $60.72

32. $.25
    ×32

33. $.69
    ×50

34. $6.20
    ×26

35. $8.62
    ×68

36. $2.74
    ×62

37. $3.58
    ×79

38. $5.06
    ×82

39. $9.53
    ×91

40. $6.27
    ×34

41. $8.36
    ×15

42. $4.98
    ×25

43. $5.08
    ×42

44. $7.69
    ×83

45. $2.96
    ×39

46. $7.09
    ×64

47. $8.81
    ×69

48. $9.20
    ×53

49. $2.37
    ×68

One day a fourth-grade class kept a record of the number of people in each car that passed their school. They made this **picture graph** of what they found.

NUMBER OF PEOPLE IN CARS

1 person	(cars)
2 people	(cars)
3 people	(cars)
4 people	(cars)

Each 🚗 stands for 12 cars

EXERCISES

1. How many cars does each 🚗 stand for?

2. How many cars had only 1 person?

3. How many had 2 people?

4. Can you tell exactly how many cars had 3 people? If not, estimate the number.

5. Estimate the number of cars that had 4 people.

6. About how many cars passed the school?

Problem solving

The Criser family is planning a
camping vacation. They need to
order some supplies from the
Camp-Away Supply Company.
Kent filled out the order shown on
the next page.

284

Campaway SUPPLIES

ITEM NO.	SIZE	COLOR	DESCRIPTION	QUANTITY	PRICE EACH	TOTAL PRICE
42318	—	green	Alpine Tent	2	$72.46	
37942	large	blue	Sleeping Bag	4	61.75	
29005	small	blue	Air Mattress	4	8.96	
12003	small	—	Pancake Mix	12	1.39	
13216	small	—	Freeze-Dried Dinner	24	2.65	
13242	small	—	Freeze-Dried Soup	16	1.78	
32617	small	—	Can of Heat	20	1.25	
32654	—	—	Cooking Pot	1	12.50	
SIGNATURE				TOTAL AMOUNT ENCLOSED		

1. **a.** How many tents did they order?
   b. How much for each?
   c. What is the total price of the tents?

2. What is the total price of the sleeping bags?

3. What is the total price of the air mattresses?

4. Find the total price of the
   a. pancake mix.   **b.** freeze-dried dinners.
   c. freeze-dried soup.   **d.** can of heat.
   e. cooking pots.

5. What is the total of the order?

Dividing by a 2-digit number

Dividing by a number greater than 10 is easy when you know the multiplication facts. Here are the multiplication facts for 23.

23 x0 ― 0	23 x1 ― 23	23 x2 ― 46	23 x3 ― 69	23 x4 ― 92
23 x5 ― 115	23 x6 ― 138	23 x7 ― 161	23 x8 ― 184	23 x9 ― 207

We will use them to do this division.

$$23\overline{)558}$$

Step 1. Not enough hundreds.

$$23\overline{)5\,5\,8}$$

Step 2. Regroup and divide. Think 55 tens.

$$23\overline{)55\,8}$$
$$\underline{-46}$$
$$9$$

23
x2
―
46

Step 3. Regroup and divide.

$$24 \quad R6$$
$$23\overline{)558}$$
$$\underline{-46}$$
$$98$$
$$\underline{-92}$$
$$6$$

23
x4
―
92

EXERCISES

Use the given multiplication facts to help you divide.

18 ×0 — 0	18 ×1 — 18	18 ×2 — 36	18 ×3 — 54	18 ×4 — 72
18 ×5 — 90	18 ×6 — 108	18 ×7 — 126	18 ×8 — 144	18 ×9 — 162

1. $18\overline{)72}$ 2. $18\overline{)162}$ 3. $18\overline{)720}$

4. $18\overline{)882}$ 5. $18\overline{)990}$ 6. $18\overline{)342}$

7. $18\overline{)702}$ 8. $18\overline{)684}$ 9. $18\overline{)738}$

24 ×0 — 0	24 ×1 — 24	24 ×2 — 48	24 ×3 — 72	24 ×4 — 96
24 ×5 — 120	24 ×6 — 144	24 ×7 — 168	24 ×8 — 192	24 ×9 — 216

10. $24\overline{)853}$ 11. $24\overline{)675}$ 12. $24\overline{)842}$

13. $24\overline{)921}$ 14. $24\overline{)792}$ 15. $24\overline{)296}$

16. $24\overline{)578}$ 17. $24\overline{)868}$ 18. $24\overline{)907}$

First list the multiplication facts for 32. Then divide.

32 ×0 — 0	32 ×1 — 32	32 ×2 — 64	32 ×3 — 96	32 ×4 — 128
32 ×5 — 160	32 ×6 — 192	32 ×7 — 224	32 ×8 — 258	32 ×9 — 288

19. $32\overline{)674}$ 20. $32\overline{)829}$ 21. $32\overline{)767}$

22. $32\overline{)981}$ 23. $32\overline{)569}$ 24. $32\overline{)994}$

25. $32\overline{)482}$ 26. $32\overline{)873}$ 27. $32\overline{)296}$

Division practice

Use these multiplication facts to help you divide.

47 x0 0	47 x1 47
47 x2 94	47 x3 141
47 x4 188	

1. 47)145   2. 47)275   3. 47)388

4. 47)958   5. 47)1964   6. 47)1735

7. 47)2817   8. 47)4263   9. 47)4917

47 x5 235	47 x6 282	47 x7 329	47 x8 376	47 x9 423

83 x0 0	83 x1 83	83 x2 166	83 x3 249	83 x4 332

10. 83)356   11. 83)621   12. 83)700

13. 83)1467   14. 83)2844   15. 83)3581

83 x5 415	83 x6 498	83 x7 581	83 x8 664	83 x9 747

16. 83)5442   17. 83)2148   18. 83)966

Compute these multiplication facts.
Divide.

68 x0	68 x1	68 x2	68 x3	68 x4

19. 68)408   20. 68)612   21. 68)251

22. 68)540   23. 68)1700   24. 68)2856

25. 68)3411   26. 68)2131   27. 68)8224

68 x5	68 x6	68 x7	68 x8	68 x9

Keeping Skills Sharp

Can you do each set in less than 1 minute?

A.

1. 5 ×6	2. 3 ×8	3. 7 ×4	4. 9 ×1	5. 0 ×6	6. 3 ×5
7. 8 ×9	8. 7 ×6	9. 5 ×5	10. 9 ×6	11. 8 ×7	12. 9 ×9
13. 7 ×3	14. 3 ×3	15. 2 ×2	16. 4 ×4	17. 7 ×5	18. 6 ×6
19. 8 ×6	20. 7 ×7	21. 3 ×4	22. 8 ×8	23. 8 ×5	24. 8 ×4

B.

1. 7 ×3	2. 7 ×9	3. 5 ×4	4. 7 ×8	5. 3 ×5	6. 6 ×2
7. 8 ×5	8. 7 ×5	9. 5 ×2	10. 3 ×4	11. 3 ×3	12. 4 ×8
13. 6 ×6	14. 3 ×2	15. 9 ×3	16. 5 ×1	17. 5 ×6	18. 9 ×5
19. 6 ×7	20. 4 ×4	21. 6 ×5	22. 8 ×4	23. 9 ×3	24. 6 ×4

C.

1. 2 ×6	2. 8 ×3	3. 6 ×5	4. 9 ×6	5. 8 ×6	6. 9 ×9
7. 2 ×4	8. 3 ×3	9. 3 ×6	10. 9 ×4	11. 5 ×3	12. 8 ×7
13. 6 ×7	14. 7 ×7	15. 7 ×6	16. 5 ×6	17. 9 ×8	18. 9 ×6
19. 7 ×8	20. 6 ×3	21. 4 ×9	22. 8 ×4	23. 4 ×3	24. 8 ×9

Dividing by a 2-digit number

In this lesson you will not be given the
multiplication facts. You can guess which
multiplication facts you will need by rounding the
divisor to the nearest ten.

EXAMPLE 1. $23 \overline{)947}$

Step 1. Think about dividing by 20.

$$23 \overline{)94\,7}$$

Step 2. Think: $20 \times 3 = 60$
$20 \times 4 = 80$
$20 \times 5 = 100$ Too big!
So try 4.

$$
\begin{array}{r}
4 \\
23 \overline{)94\,7} \\
-92 \\
\hline
2
\end{array}
\qquad
\begin{array}{r}
23 \\
\times 4 \\
\hline
92
\end{array}
$$

It works!

Step 3. Regroup and divide.

$$
\begin{array}{r}
41 \\
23 \overline{)947} \\
-92 \\
\hline
27 \\
-23 \\
\hline
4
\end{array}
$$

EXAMPLE 2. $27 \overline{)866}$

Step 1. Think about dividing by 30.

$$30 \quad 27 \overline{)86\,6}$$

Step 2. Think: $30 \times 2 = 60$
$30 \times 3 = 90$ Too big!

Remainder is greater than 27.

$$
\begin{array}{r}
2 \\
27 \overline{)86\,6} \\
-54 \\
\hline
32
\end{array}
\qquad
\begin{array}{r}
27 \\
\times 2 \\
\hline
54
\end{array}
$$

Step 3. Try 3.

$$
\begin{array}{r}
3 \\
27 \overline{)86\,6} \\
-81 \\
\hline
5
\end{array}
$$

Step 4. Regroup and divide.

$$
\begin{array}{r}
32 \\
27 \overline{)866} \\
-81 \\
\hline
56 \\
-54 \\
\hline
2
\end{array}
$$

EXERCISES
Divide.

1. 30 (thought bubble)
   $31\overline{)175}$
   $\begin{array}{r} 31 \\ \times 5 \\ \hline 155 \end{array}$

2. 20 (thought bubble)
   $18\overline{)685}$
   $\begin{array}{r} 18 \\ \times 3 \\ \hline 54 \end{array}$

3. 20 (thought bubble)
   $22\overline{)700}$
   $\begin{array}{r} 22 \\ \times 3 \\ \hline 66 \end{array}$

4. 20 (thought bubble)
   $24\overline{)596}$

5. 30 (thought bubble)
   $32\overline{)943}$

6. 20 (thought bubble)
   $15\overline{)682}$

7. 30 (thought bubble)
   $28\overline{)974}$

8. 40 (thought bubble)
   $41\overline{)867}$

9. 30 (thought bubble)
   $34\overline{)593}$

Divide.

10. $18\overline{)784}$
11. $31\overline{)968}$
12. $29\overline{)742}$
13. $42\overline{)942}$
14. $20\overline{)860}$

15. $35\overline{)596}$
16. $21\overline{)873}$
17. $43\overline{)895}$
18. $34\overline{)906}$
19. $26\overline{)593}$

20. $38\overline{)940}$
21. $32\overline{)592}$
22. $19\overline{)678}$
23. $33\overline{)793}$
24. $22\overline{)666}$

Solve.

25. 988 books in all.
    38 books on each shelf.
    How many shelves?

26. 8306 books in all.
    2548 are checked out.
    How many are left?

27. Had 8306 books.
    Bought 458 more.
    How many books in all?

28. One dictionary costs $9.78.
    Ordered 12.
    What was the total cost?

Problem solving

Sometimes you don't have enough facts to solve a problem. Other times you have more facts than you really need.

EXERCISES

What else do you need to know?

1. Robert earned $1.25 an hour for raking leaves. How much did he earn altogether?

2. Jan found some buttons she liked for her new coat. There were 5 buttons on a card. How many cards did she need?

3. Jeff bought a record. He gave the clerk a $5 bill. How much change should he have gotten back?

4. Eric returned 143 bottles. How much did he get for the bottles?

5. Sonya's class sold 126 tickets one week. How many tickets did they sell during both weeks?

6. One hundred eighty students were going on a field trip. How many buses did they need?

Solve.

7. Jan filled a 42-page album with photos. She put 12 photos on each page. How many photos was that?

8. For two weeks, Bill kept a record of the minutes he watched television. He watched for a total of 630 minutes. How many minutes did he average each day?

9. Make up a problem.

10. Make up a problem.

Keeping Skills Sharp

1. $\frac{3}{8}$ $-\frac{1}{4}$	**2.** $\frac{1}{3}$ $-\frac{1}{6}$	**3.** $\frac{1}{2}$ $-\frac{1}{4}$	**4.** $\frac{7}{8}$ $-\frac{3}{4}$	**5.** $\frac{5}{6}$ $-\frac{1}{2}$	**6.** $\frac{1}{2}$ $-\frac{1}{8}$
7. $\frac{7}{6}$ $-\frac{2}{3}$	**8.** $\frac{5}{8}$ $-\frac{1}{2}$	**9.** $\frac{7}{10}$ $-\frac{1}{5}$	**10.** $\frac{5}{8}$ $-\frac{1}{4}$	**11.** $\frac{4}{5}$ $-\frac{3}{10}$	**12.** $\frac{3}{4}$ $-\frac{5}{8}$

Checking division

Study the example to review how to check a division problem.

```
       26 R12
37 ) 974
    -74
     234
    -222
      12
```

```
       1
       4
      26
    × 37
     182
     780
     962
    + 12
     974  }  It checks!
```

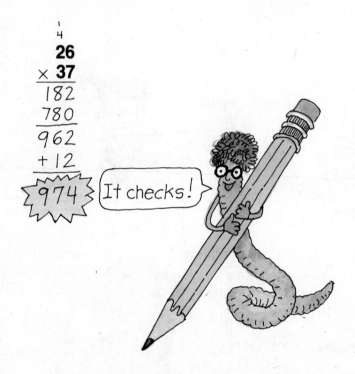

EXERCISES
Divide. Then check your answer.

1. 23)873
2. 42)749
3. 36)963
4. 43)805
5. 18)542

6. 18)784
7. 24)862
8. 15)705
9. 29)690
10. 32)800

Divide.

```
        $ .28
11. 16)$4.48
      -32
       128
      -128
         0
```

12. 30)$9.60
13. 26)$9.88
14. 21)$9.87
15. 18)$9.00

16. 38)596
17. 17)809
18. 40)999
19. 24)862

20. 19)832
21. 37)782
22. 20)593
23. 45)900

24. 17)783
25. 41)865
26. 33)875
27. 28)965

Some children in a fourth-grade class weighed themselves on a kilogram scale. They wrote their names and weights on slips of paper.

Mary 21 kg
Sue 27 kg
Marty 24 kg
Dave 28 kg
Ann 24 kg
Jack 24 kg
John 23 kg
Craig 27 kg
Julie 24 kg
Jose 22 kg
Al 26 kg
Mark 27 kg
Terry 28 kg

28. How many weigh 24 kg?

29. How many weigh more than 25 kg?

30. Who weighs the least?

31. Who weighs the same as Terry?

32. What is their total weight?

33. What is their average weight?

34. How many weigh more than the average?

35. How many weigh less than the average?

Multiply. [pages 274–282]

1. 58 ×10	2. 63 ×10	3. 254 ×10	4. 821 ×10	5. 760 ×10
6. 65 ×20	7. 78 ×30	8. 349 ×40	9. 567 ×60	10. 725 ×80
11. 841 ×32	12. 725 ×27	13. 395 ×58	14. 942 ×85	15. 658 ×64

Divide. [pages 286–288, 290–291, 294]

16. 24)576   17. 42)966   18. 22)990   19. 38)950   20. 25)875

21. 19)834   22. 24)729   23. 16)683   24. 37)955   25. 38)900

Solve. [pages 283–285, 292–293, 295]

$4.65

26. How much will 12 boxes of apples cost?

27. Mr. Butler ordered 468 apple trees. He wants to plant them in 18 rows. How many should he plant in each row?

28. In one orchard Mr. Butler has 124 rows of trees with 38 trees in each row. How many trees does he have in that orchard?

Project

1. Find out how to take your pulse.

2. Count the number of times your heart beats in a minute.

3. How many times does it beat in an hour?

4. How many times in a day?

5. How many times does your heart beat in 30 days?

6. About how many times does it beat in a year?

CHAPTER REVIEW

Multiply.

1. 52
    ×10
    520

2. 83
    ×10

3. 246
    ×10

4. 48
    ×20
    960

5. 175
    ×30

6. 314
    ×50

7. 256
    ×32
    512
    7680
    8192

8. 468
    ×68

9. 729
    ×59

Divide.

10. 24)432
        18
       -24
       192
      -192
        0

11. 24)936

12. 24)648

13. 33)597

14. 22)784

15. 38)936

16. 43)543

17. 27)781

18. 39)960

CHAPTER CHALLENGE

The ancient Egyptians multiplied by doubling and adding. Here is how they would find this product:

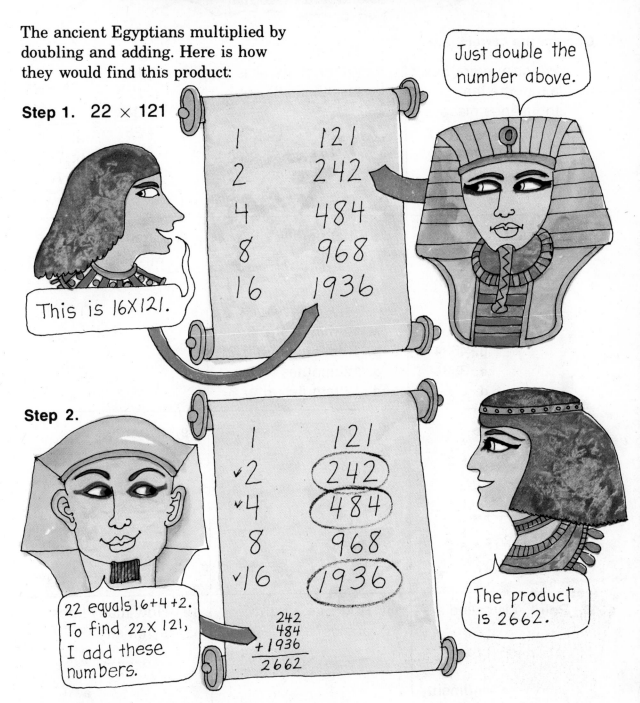

Step 1. 22 × 121

Just double the number above.

This is 16 × 121.

1	121
2	242
4	484
8	968
16	1936

Step 2.

22 equals 16 + 4 + 2. To find 22 × 121, I add these numbers.

The product is 2662.

1	121
✓2	(242)
✓4	(484)
8	968
✓16	(1936)

```
  242
  484
+1936
─────
 2662
```

Use the Egyptian method to find these products.

1. 24 × 120   2. 19 × 112   3. 26 × 126   4. 30 × 235   5. 27 × 364

Form W

| | a | b | c | d | | a | b | c | d | | a | b | c | d | | a | b | c | d | | a | b | c | d |
14 | | | | | 34 | | | | | 14 | | | | | 4 | | | | | 30 | | | | |

| | a | b | c | d | | a | b | c | d | | | | c | d | | a | b | c | d |
15 | | | | | | | | | | | | | | | | 31 | | | |

MAJOR CHECKUP
Standardized Format

Choose the correct letter.

1. Which numeral has a 6 in the ten thousands place?
   - **a.** 596,037
   - **b.** 763,842
   - **c.** 615,274
   - **d.** none of these

2. Which number is less than 283,465?
   - **a.** 284,465
   - **b.** 283,500
   - **c.** 300,000
   - **d.** none of these

3. Add.

   263
   348
   + 257
   - **a.** 868
   - **b.** 758
   - **c.** 768
   - **d.** none of these

4. Subtract.

   6413
   − 2879
   - **a.** 4466
   - **b.** 4634
   - **c.** 3534
   - **d.** none of these

5. What time is shown?
   - **a.** 12 minutes to 3
   - **b.** 12 minutes after 2
   - **c.** 12 minutes to 2
   - **d.** 12 minutes after 3

6. Change $\frac{10}{3}$ to a mixed number.
   - **a.** $2\frac{2}{3}$
   - **b.** 30
   - **c.** $3\frac{1}{3}$
   - **d.** none of these

7. Reduce $\frac{6}{9}$ to lowest terms.
   - **a.** $\frac{1}{4}$
   - **b.** $\frac{2}{3}$
   - **c.** $\frac{3}{6}$
   - **d.** none of these

8. Add.

   $\frac{5}{8}$
   $+ \frac{1}{4}$
   - **a.** $\frac{3}{4}$
   - **b.** $\frac{3}{8}$
   - **c.** $\frac{7}{8}$
   - **d.** none of these

9. Subtract.

   $\frac{2}{3}$
   $- \frac{5}{9}$
   - **a.** $\frac{1}{3}$
   - **b.** $\frac{1}{9}$
   - **c.** $\frac{2}{9}$
   - **d.** none of these

10. Point A is called a
    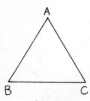
    - **a.** segment
    - **b.** side
    - **c.** vertex
    - **d.** none of these

11. How many right angles?
    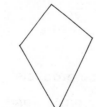
    - **a.** 1
    - **b.** 2
    - **c.** 3
    - **d.** 4

12. How many lines of symmetry?

    - **a.** 1
    - **b.** 2
    - **c.** 4
    - **d.** none of these

300

NET WT.	PRICE FOR THIS PACKAGE	PRICE PER LB.
1.25	$1.36	1.09

CHICKEN LEGS

OCT 29

SELL BY ↑   KEEP REFRIGERATED

FRESH YOUNG CHICKEN

OR MONEY BACK
KEEP REFRIGERATED

NET WT.	PRICE FOR THIS PACKAGE	PRICE PER LB.
0.80	$1.35	1.69

GROUND BEEF

OCT 29

SELL BY ↑   KEEP REFRIGERATED

simply super!

NOT MORE THAN 14% FAT

Extra Lean

Tenths

How many squares are painted?

$1\frac{4}{10}$ squares have been painted.

We can write the number in
a place-value table like this:

Ones	Tenths
1	**4**

or without a table
like this: **1.4**

This is a decimal point.

Such a numeral is called a **decimal fraction** or
just a **decimal**. Read "1.4" as "one and four
tenths."

EXERCISES
How many squares are painted?
Give answers as decimals.

1.

2.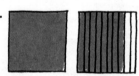

3.

4.

5.

6.

Give a decimal for the number of painted squares.

7.

8.

9.

10.

Match.

11. 2.1   **a.** two and three tenths

12. 1.2   **b.** three and two tenths

13. 3.2   **c.** two and one tenth

14. 2.3   **d.** one and two tenths

Read these decimals.

15. 3.6	16. 4.8	17. 2.9	18. 5.0	19. 6.8
20. 5.9	21. 10.3	22. 15.4	23. 18.6	24. 21.8

Give a decimal that is between the two numbers.

25. 3, 4	26. 5, 6	27. 9, 10
28. 14, 15	29. 25, 26	30. 28, 29

Hundredths

How many squares are shaded?

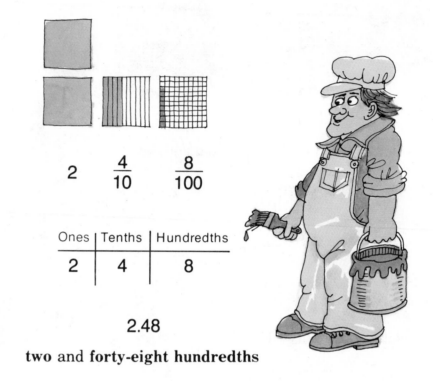

$$2 \qquad \frac{4}{10} \qquad \frac{8}{100}$$

Ones	Tenths	Hundredths
2	4	8

2.48

two and **forty-eight hundredths**

EXERCISES
How many squares are painted?
Give answers as decimals.

1.

2.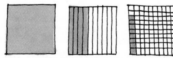

3.

4.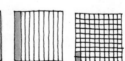

Match.

5. 1.2

6. 1.02

7. 2.1

8. 2.01

a.

b.

c.

d.

Give the next three numbers.

9. 2.3, 2.4, 2.5, _?_, _?_, _?_

10. 15.8, 15.9, 16.0, _?_, _?_, _?_

11. 8.6, 8.7, 8.8, _?_, _?_, _?_

12. 6.02, 6.03, 6.04, _?_, _?_, _?_

13. 5.95, 5.96, 5.97, _?_, _?_, _?_

14. 9.96, 9.97, 9.98, _?_, _?_, _?_

Give a decimal that is between the two numbers.

15. 0.1, 0.3

16. 15.4, 15.6

17. 17.8, 18.0

18. 12.3, 12.4

19. 16.2, 16.3

20. 19.5, 19.6

21. 23.9, 24.0

22. 25.37, 25.40

23. 28.99, 29.01

★ 24. 40.98, 40.99

305

Decimal practice

586.34

Which digit is in the

1. tens place?

2. hundredths place?

3. hundreds place?

4. tenths place?

Build a decimal.

5. **4** in the **tenths** place

   2 in the **ones** place

6. **3** in the **tens** place

   6 in the **tenths** place

   0 in the **ones** place

7. **5** in the **tens** place

   2 in the **ones** place

   1 in the **tenths** place

   4 in the **hundreds** place

   3 in the **hundredths** place

8. **9** in the **tenths** place

   3 in the **ones** place

   8 in the **hundreds** place

   7 in the **tens** place

   1 in the **hundredths** place

Complete.

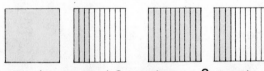

9. 1 one and 3 tenths = _?_ tenths

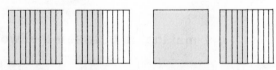

10. 15 tenths = _?_ one and _?_ tenths

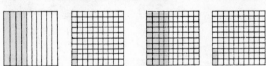

11. 4 tenths and 3 hundredths = _?_ hundredths

Less than (<) or greater than (>)?

12. 1 ⬤ .1

13. .3 ⬤ .7

14. .8 ⬤ .81

15. .9 ⬤ 1

16. 2 ⬤ 2.1

17. .2 ⬤ 2

18. 2.35 ⬤ 2.36

19. 3.46 ⬤ 3.4

20. 5.37 ⬤ 5.4

Forgetful Freddie, a fourth-grade student, wrote these "facts" about himself. Of course he forgot the decimal points. Copy each numeral, and place the decimal point so the "fact" makes sense.

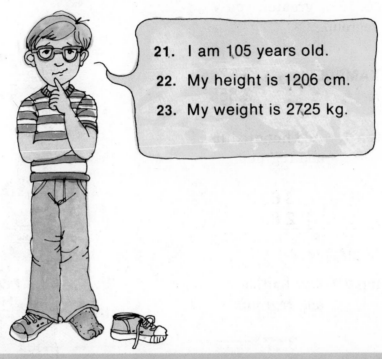

21. I am 105 years old.

22. My height is 1206 cm.

23. My weight is 2725 kg.

Keeping Skills Sharp

1. 62
   ×28

2. 59
   ×42

3. 74
   ×29

4. 68
   ×50

5. 93
   ×39

6. 118
   ×16

7. 205
   ×24

8. 400
   ×48

9. 326
   ×39

10. 742
    ×26

11. 811
    ×57

12. 653
    ×46

13. 925
    ×93

14. 820
    ×47

15. 762
    ×38

Adding decimals

You can find the sum of two decimals by adding in columns just as you did with whole numbers.

Notice that the decimal points are lined up. You line up the decimal points so that numerals in the same place will be lined up.

When a sum is 10 or greater, you will need to regroup.

EXAMPLE 1.

$$2.13$$
$$+ 1.43$$
$$\overline{3.56}$$

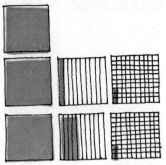

EXAMPLE 2.

$$3.67$$
$$+ 2.85$$

Step 1. Add hundredths and regroup.

$$\overset{1}{}$$
$$3.67$$
$$+ 2.85$$
$$\overline{2}$$

Step 2. Add tenths and regroup.

$$\overset{1\ \ 1}{}$$
$$3.67$$
$$+ 2.85$$
$$\overline{.52}$$

Step 3. Add ones.

$$\overset{1\ \ 1}{}$$
$$3.67$$
$$+ 2.85$$
$$\overline{6.52}$$

Be sure to put a decimal point in the sum.

EXERCISES
Add.

1. 2.6
    +3.1

2. 5.3
    +2.5

3. .74
    +.21

4. .53
    +.42

5. 1.5
    +0.4

6. 3.5
    +2.8

7. .39
    +.67

8. .48
    +.75

9. 9.2
    +6.3

10. 4.8
     +7.6

11. 32.8
     +53.6

12. 2.95
     +4.83

13. 69.1
     +78.2

14. 5.76
     +2.18

15. 3.49
     +2.38

16. 58.4
     +26.8

17. 3.95
     +3.17

18. 76.2
     +29.8

19. 9.43
     +1.57

20. 75.1
     +85.9

21. 7.59
     +5.38

22. 6.55
     +1.34

23. 88.8
     +21.6

24. 3.74
     +7.43

25. 92.1
     +56.9

Solve.

26. Ms. Weaver drove 236.8 km before lunch and 348.5 km after lunch. How far did she drive that day?

Copy and complete.

27.
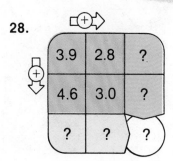

2.4	3.5	?
5.1	4.6	?
?	?	?

28.

3.9	2.8	?
4.6	3.0	?
?	?	?

29.
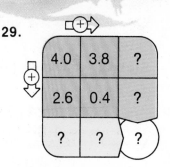

4.0	3.8	?
2.6	0.4	?
?	?	?

309

Subtracting decimals

You can find the difference of two decimals by subtracting in columns just as you did with whole numbers.

EXAMPLE 1.

$$\begin{array}{r} 2.49 \\ - 1.13 \\ \hline 1.36 \end{array}$$

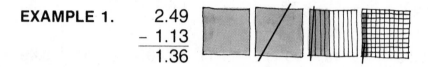

Remember to line up the decimal points.

EXAMPLE 2.

$$\begin{array}{r} 3.24 \\ - 1.86 \end{array}$$

Step 1. Regroup, and subtract hundredths.

$$\begin{array}{r} \overset{1\ 1}{3.\cancel{2}4} \\ - 1.86 \\ \hline 8 \end{array}$$

Step 2. Regroup, and subtract tenths.

$$\begin{array}{r} \overset{2\ 11}{\cancel{3}.\cancel{2}4} \\ - 1.86 \\ \hline .38 \end{array}$$

Step 3. Subtract ones.

$$\begin{array}{r} \overset{2\ 11}{\cancel{3}.\cancel{2}4} \\ - 1.86 \\ \hline 1.38 \end{array}$$

310

EXERCISES
Subtract.

1. .83
  − .21

2. 7.5
  − 6.2

3. .98
  − .15

4. 6.9
  − 2.4

5. .87
  − .33

6. 7.2
  − 3.7

7. .81
  − .39

8. 6.3
  − 2.8

9. 9.2
  − 4.7

10. .54
  − .23

11. 42.5
  − 23.8

12. 93.1
  − 45.6

13. 30.7
  − 21.8

14. 5.43
  − 1.97

15. 7.85
  − 1.39

16. 65.2
  − 28.0

17. 3.12
  − 1.26

18. 89.6
  − 24.8

19. 3.25
  − 1.46

20. 37.2
  − 29.7

21. 3.51
  − 1.79

22. 43.1
  − 28.6

23. 8.31
  − 4.79

24. 52.6
  − 28.4

25. 3.91
  − 1.40

Solve.

26. One boat completed a lap in 13.42 seconds.
The next lap took 13.91 seconds.
How much slower was the second lap?

27. The winning boat averaged 57.2 km per hour.
The second-place boat averaged 56.9 km per hour.
How much faster was the winning boat?

Copy and complete.

28.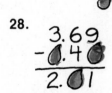
```
   3.69
 − 1.48
 ──────
   2.01
```

★ 29.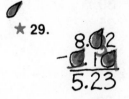
```
   8.02
 − 2.79
 ──────
   5.23
```

★ 30.
```
   6.20
 − 1.07
 ──────
   4.74
```

More about adding and subtracting decimals

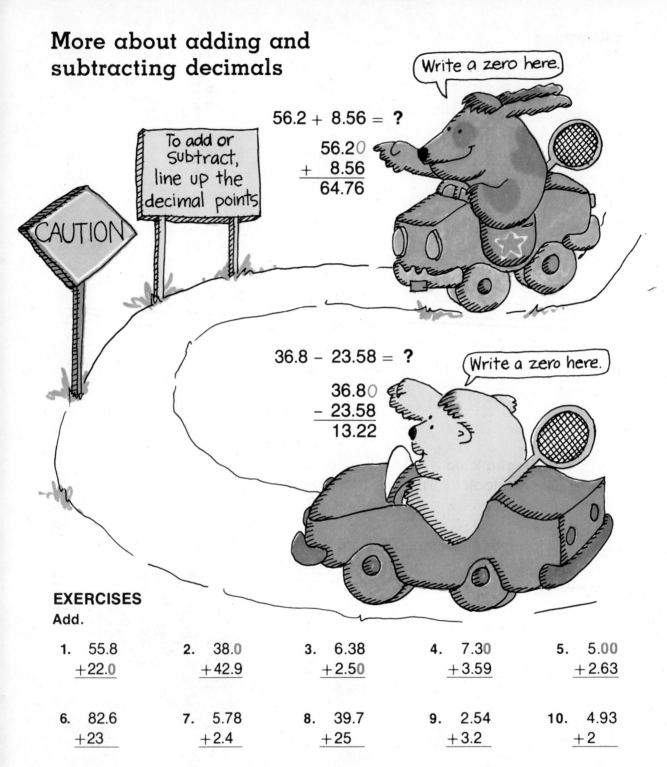

To add or subtract, line up the decimal points

CAUTION

Write a zero here.

$56.2 + 8.56 = ?$

$$\begin{array}{r} 56.20 \\ +\ 8.56 \\ \hline 64.76 \end{array}$$

$36.8 - 23.58 = ?$

$$\begin{array}{r} 36.80 \\ -\ 23.58 \\ \hline 13.22 \end{array}$$

Write a zero here.

EXERCISES
Add.

1. $\begin{array}{r} 55.8 \\ +22.0 \\ \hline \end{array}$
2. $\begin{array}{r} 38.0 \\ +42.9 \\ \hline \end{array}$
3. $\begin{array}{r} 6.38 \\ +2.50 \\ \hline \end{array}$
4. $\begin{array}{r} 7.30 \\ +3.59 \\ \hline \end{array}$
5. $\begin{array}{r} 5.00 \\ +2.63 \\ \hline \end{array}$

6. $\begin{array}{r} 82.6 \\ +23 \\ \hline \end{array}$
7. $\begin{array}{r} 5.78 \\ +2.4 \\ \hline \end{array}$
8. $\begin{array}{r} 39.7 \\ +25 \\ \hline \end{array}$
9. $\begin{array}{r} 2.54 \\ +3.2 \\ \hline \end{array}$
10. $\begin{array}{r} 4.93 \\ +2 \\ \hline \end{array}$

11. $38.6 + 22$
12. $1.8 + 2.54$
13. $34.9 + 26$
14. $27 + 5.08$
15. $32.6 + .38$
16. $.06 + 24.5$

Subtract.

17. 9.80
    − 5.27

18. 6.50
    − 2.74

19. 3.34
    − 1.60

20. 82.0
    − 14.5

21. 25.9
    − 19.0

22. 37
    − 24.6

23. 21
    − 17.3

24. 48.1
    − 26.35

25. 75.32
    − 35.8

26. 93
    − 25.3

27. 53.2 − 27

28. 78 − 21.6

29. 42 − 38.5

30. 2.36 − 1.5

31. 5.28 − 2.6

32. 9.3 − .05

Solve.

33. A tennis racket is on sale for $13.
    A can of balls is on sale for $2.79.
    How much will both cost?

34. Mary had a ten-dollar bill. She
    bought a baseball glove for $8.67.
    How much money was left?

Keeping Skills Sharp

1. 20)‾400‾

2. 21)‾903‾

3. 19)‾912‾

4. 32)‾992‾

5. 29)‾725‾

6. 33)‾853‾

7. 24)‾964‾

8. 34)‾755‾

9. 25)‾800‾

10. 23)‾776‾

11. 42)‾803‾

12. 30)‾900‾

13. 22)‾599‾

14. 18)‾653‾

15. 41)‾943‾

Problem solving

Mary and her father went to the auto races. The results of the race are shown in the table.

	Place	Driver	Time, in minutes	Average speed, in km per hour.
RESULTS OF LAST RACE	1	DAVIS	53.93	222.35
	2	ADAMS	54.04	222.06
	3	GARCIA	54.21	221.38
	4	THOMAS	54.27	221.12
	5	WEAVER	54.44	220.42
	6	ROGERS	54.65	219.56
	7	BENDER	54.86	218.75
	8	PRIDE	55.60	215.84

1. Who was the winner?

2. How many minutes did it take the winning car to run the race?

3. What was the average speed of the fourth-place car?

4. The last-place car took how much longer than the first-place car?

5. What was the difference in the average speed of the first- and last-place cars?

6. How many minutes behind the winning car was Adams?

7. Which driver averaged 1.82 km per hour less than Garcia?

8. Which driver took .4 min longer than Adams?

CHAPTER CHECKUP

[pages 302–307]

In 534.27, what digit is in the

1. tens place?

2. hundredths place?

3. ones place?

4. tenths place?

5. hundreds place?

534.27

Add. [pages 308–309]

6. 3.8 +2.1	7. .46 +.23	8. 7.8 +1.4	9. 5.9 +6.8	10. .34 +.68
11. 35.2 +16.5	12. 7.58 +2.97	13. 52.6 +39.4	14. 78.84 +34.2	15. 5.9 +3.09

Subtract. [pages 310–311]

16. 5.8 − 2.4	17. .76 − .33	18. 8.2 − 5.8	19. 7.0 − 5.3	20. .92 − .84
21. 76.3 − 48.5	22. 9.02 − 3.75	23. 5.72 − 2.8	24. 32 − 16.5	25. 5.8 − 2.37

Solve. [pages 314–315]

Record Sale

26.

$4 $3.69

How much for both?

27.

$4 $1.29

How much more does the large record cost?

Project

Work with a group of classmates.

1. Measure off 40 meters on the playground.
2. Get a stopwatch.
3. Have each classmate run a 40-meter dash twice. Record the better time.
4. Show the times on a graph.
5. Tell some things that your graph shows.

CHAPTER REVIEW

What digit is in the

1. ones place?

2. hundredths place?

3. tenths place?

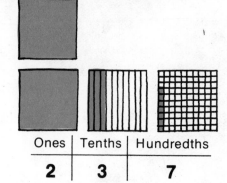

Ones	Tenths	Hundredths
2	3	7

2.37

Use a decimal to tell how many squares are painted.

4.

5.

6.

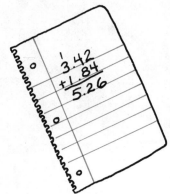

Add.

7. 2.3
   +4.2

8. 6.8
   +2.6

9. .57
   +.69

10. 5.38
   +4.95

11. 2.5
   +9.75

12. 65.4
   +32

Subtract.

13. 5.9
   - 2.6

14. .74
   - .28

15. 8.4
   - 3.7

16. 4.26
   - 1.59

17. 6.2
   - 1.75

18. 8.
   - 7.65

CHAPTER CHALLENGE

**Build the sum or difference. Use each
red symbol once.**

1.
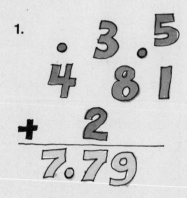

$$
\begin{array}{r}
.\ 3\ .5 \\
4\quad 8\ 1 \\
+\ 2 \\
\hline
7.79
\end{array}
$$

2.
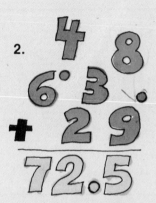

$$
\begin{array}{r}
4\qquad 8 \\
6\ 3\ . \\
+\ 2\quad 9 \\
\hline
72.5
\end{array}
$$

3.

$$
\begin{array}{r}
9\ 2\ 7 \\
\ 1\ . \\
+5\ .\ 6 \\
\hline
8.67
\end{array}
$$

4.
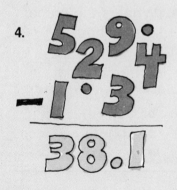

$$
\begin{array}{r}
5\ 2\ 9\ 4 \\
-1\ .\ 3 \\
\hline
38.1
\end{array}
$$

5.
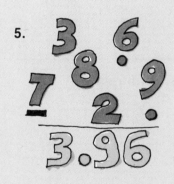

$$
\begin{array}{r}
3\qquad 6 \\
8\ .\ 9 \\
7\quad 2\ . \\
\hline
3.96
\end{array}
$$

6.
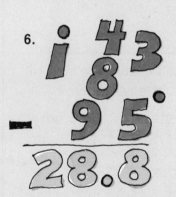

$$
\begin{array}{r}
1\ 4\ 3 \\
8 \\
-\ 9\ 5\ . \\
\hline
28.8
\end{array}
$$

Form W

14 | a b c d
15 | a b c d

34 | a b c d

14 | a b c d

4 | a b c d

30 | a b c d
31 | a b c d

MAJOR CHECKUP
Standardized Format

Choose the correct letter.

1. 752,831 rounded to the nearest thousand is

   a. 750,000
   b. 752,000
   c. 753,000
   d. none of these

2. Add.

   26
   34
   52
   87
  +54

   a. 253
   b. 233
   c. 243
   d. none of these

3. Subtract.

   90563
  − 27890

   a. 62,573
   b. 63,573
   c. 62,673
   d. none of these

4. Reduce $\frac{6}{12}$ to lowest terms.

   a. $\frac{3}{6}$
   b. $\frac{2}{4}$
   c. $\frac{1}{2}$
   d. none of these

5. Add.

$$\frac{1}{3} + \frac{2}{9}$$

   a. $\frac{5}{9}$
   b. $\frac{1}{4}$
   c. $\frac{1}{3}$
   d. none of these

6. Subtract.

$$\frac{3}{4} - \frac{3}{8}$$

   a. $\frac{0}{8}$
   b. $\frac{0}{4}$
   c. $\frac{3}{8}$
   d. none of these

7. What is the area of the rectangle?

2 cm
5 cm

   a. 7 cm
   b. 10 cm
   c. 10 square cm
   d. none of these

8. What is the average of these numbers?
78, 65, 74, and 75

   a. 73
   b. 74
   c. 75
   d. none of these

9. What is the name of this figure?

   a. rectangular solid
   b. cone
   c. sphere
   d. none of these

10. Which triangle is congruent to the red triangle?

A
B
C

   a. A
   b. B
   c. C
   d. none of these

11. Multiply.

   726
  ×48

   a. 34,848
   b. 34,648
   c. 34,508
   d. none of these

12. What is the remainder?
$32 \overline{)583}$

   a. 18
   b. 9
   c. 7
   d. none of these

SKILL TEST

1	Basic addition facts, sums through 18	$\begin{array}{r} 3 \\ +4 \\ \hline \end{array}$	$\begin{array}{r} 5 \\ +6 \\ \hline \end{array}$	$\begin{array}{r} 8 \\ +5 \\ \hline \end{array}$	$\begin{array}{r} 9 \\ +8 \\ \hline \end{array}$	$\begin{array}{r} 6 \\ +9 \\ \hline \end{array}$
2	Basic subtraction facts, sums through 18	$\begin{array}{r} 8 \\ -3 \\ \hline \end{array}$	$\begin{array}{r} 12 \\ -4 \\ \hline \end{array}$	$\begin{array}{r} 9 \\ -7 \\ \hline \end{array}$	$\begin{array}{r} 16 \\ -7 \\ \hline \end{array}$	$\begin{array}{r} 14 \\ -5 \\ \hline \end{array}$
3	Addition, no regrouping	$\begin{array}{r} 52 \\ +21 \\ \hline \end{array}$	$\begin{array}{r} 38 \\ +40 \\ \hline \end{array}$	$\begin{array}{r} 226 \\ +143 \\ \hline \end{array}$	$\begin{array}{r} 190 \\ +406 \\ \hline \end{array}$	
4	Addition, one regrouping	$\begin{array}{r} 47 \\ +29 \\ \hline \end{array}$	$\begin{array}{r} 38 \\ +53 \\ \hline \end{array}$	$\begin{array}{r} 282 \\ +154 \\ \hline \end{array}$	$\begin{array}{r} 352 \\ +165 \\ \hline \end{array}$	
5	Addition, two regroupings	$\begin{array}{r} 78 \\ +46 \\ \hline \end{array}$	$\begin{array}{r} 95 \\ +68 \\ \hline \end{array}$	$\begin{array}{r} 426 \\ +285 \\ \hline \end{array}$	$\begin{array}{r} 763 \\ +159 \\ \hline \end{array}$	
6	Addition, more than two regroupings	$\begin{array}{r} 3821 \\ +1689 \\ \hline \end{array}$	$\begin{array}{r} 7468 \\ +1563 \\ \hline \end{array}$	$\begin{array}{r} 9354 \\ +2897 \\ \hline \end{array}$	$\begin{array}{r} 6827 \\ +3578 \\ \hline \end{array}$	
7	Subtraction, no regrouping	$\begin{array}{r} 58 \\ -22 \\ \hline \end{array}$	$\begin{array}{r} 79 \\ -14 \\ \hline \end{array}$	$\begin{array}{r} 526 \\ -103 \\ \hline \end{array}$	$\begin{array}{r} 958 \\ -325 \\ \hline \end{array}$	
8	Subtraction, one regrouping	$\begin{array}{r} 80 \\ -26 \\ \hline \end{array}$	$\begin{array}{r} 93 \\ -25 \\ \hline \end{array}$	$\begin{array}{r} 538 \\ -153 \\ \hline \end{array}$	$\begin{array}{r} 746 \\ -492 \\ \hline \end{array}$	

9	Subtraction, two regroupings	625 − 456	431 − 238	758 − 269	906 − 358
10	Subtraction, more than two regroupings	5263 − 1884	8174 − 3698	9203 − 4735	5374 − 2896

11	Basic multiplication facts, products through 9 × 9	8 ×6	7 ×9	6 ×8	9 ×6	8 ×7

12	Division facts, quotients through 81 ÷ 9	6)42	8)40	7)56	9)72

13	Division with remainder	7)40	9)35	5)48	6)50

14	Multiplication, no regrouping	23 ×3	12 ×4	42 ×2	20 ×4

15	Multiplication, regrouping tens to hundreds	83 ×2	40 ×5	32 ×4	74 ×2

16	Multiplication, two regroupings	59 ×4	78 ×6	65 ×7	94 ×3

17	Multiplication, more than two regroupings	356 ×4	282 ×8	7465 ×6	5698 ×4

18	Division, no regrouping	2⟌46	3⟌96	4⟌48	3⟌60
19	Division, one regrouping	6⟌84	5⟌95	3⟌81	4⟌56
20	Division with remainder	5⟌74	4⟌81	6⟌93	3⟌59
21	Division, two regroupings	4⟌362	6⟌753	5⟌394	8⟌742
22	Division, more than two regroupings	5⟌3658	6⟌2174	8⟌5974	4⟌6081

23	Multiplying by 10	$\begin{array}{r}43\\ \times 10\end{array}$	$\begin{array}{r}26\\ \times 10\end{array}$	$\begin{array}{r}226\\ \times 10\end{array}$	$\begin{array}{r}438\\ \times 10\end{array}$
24	Multiplying by tens	$\begin{array}{r}36\\ \times 20\end{array}$	$\begin{array}{r}28\\ \times 40\end{array}$	$\begin{array}{r}152\\ \times 60\end{array}$	$\begin{array}{r}248\\ \times 80\end{array}$
25	Multiplying by a 2-digit number	$\begin{array}{r}58\\ \times 24\end{array}$	$\begin{array}{r}63\\ \times 37\end{array}$	$\begin{array}{r}268\\ \times 82\end{array}$	$\begin{array}{r}472\\ \times 56\end{array}$
26	Dividing by a 2-digit number	13⟌583	22⟌792	18⟌964	33⟌829

27 Fraction of a number $\frac{1}{2}$ of 18 = ? $\frac{2}{3}$ of 12 = ? $\frac{3}{4}$ of 20 = ?

28 Reducing to lowest terms $\frac{6}{8}$ = ? $\frac{5}{10}$ = ? $\frac{6}{9}$ = ? $\frac{3}{12}$ = ?

29 Adding fractions

$$\begin{array}{c}\frac{3}{5}\\[4pt]+\frac{1}{5}\\\hline\end{array}\qquad\begin{array}{c}\frac{5}{12}\\[4pt]+\frac{1}{3}\\\hline\end{array}\qquad\begin{array}{c}\frac{2}{5}\\[4pt]+\frac{3}{10}\\\hline\end{array}\qquad\begin{array}{c}\frac{1}{2}\\[4pt]+\frac{3}{4}\\\hline\end{array}\qquad\begin{array}{c}\frac{3}{8}\\[4pt]+\frac{1}{2}\\\hline\end{array}$$

30 Subtracting fractions

$$\begin{array}{c}\frac{5}{9}\\[4pt]-\frac{1}{9}\\\hline\end{array}\qquad\begin{array}{c}\frac{3}{4}\\[4pt]-\frac{1}{8}\\\hline\end{array}\qquad\begin{array}{c}\frac{5}{8}\\[4pt]-\frac{1}{2}\\\hline\end{array}\qquad\begin{array}{c}\frac{5}{12}\\[4pt]-\frac{1}{3}\\\hline\end{array}\qquad\begin{array}{c}\frac{5}{9}\\[4pt]-\frac{1}{3}\\\hline\end{array}$$

31 Changing mixed numbers to fractions $2\frac{1}{2}$ $1\frac{2}{3}$ $3\frac{1}{4}$ $2\frac{3}{4}$

32 Changing fractions to mixed numbers $\frac{7}{3}$ $\frac{9}{2}$ $\frac{7}{4}$ $\frac{11}{3}$

33 Adding decimals

$$\begin{array}{c}7.2\\+1.4\\\hline\end{array}\qquad\begin{array}{c}3.8\\+2.9\\\hline\end{array}\qquad\begin{array}{c}.65\\+.34\\\hline\end{array}\qquad\begin{array}{c}.83\\+.57\\\hline\end{array}$$

34 Subtracting decimals

$$\begin{array}{c}6.8\\-2.4\\\hline\end{array}\qquad\begin{array}{c}.86\\-.29\\\hline\end{array}\qquad\begin{array}{c}6.0\\-2.8\\\hline\end{array}\qquad\begin{array}{c}.52\\-.48\\\hline\end{array}$$

EXTRA PRACTICE

Set 1

1. 4 +4	**2.** 2 +4	**3.** 8 +2	**4.** 2 +5	**5.** 9 +1	**6.** 0 +0	**7.** 2 +6
8. 3 +2	**9.** 2 +7	**10.** 0 +4	**11.** 6 +3	**12.** 0 +6	**13.** 7 +3	**14.** 3 +4
15. 3 +5	**16.** 1 +4	**17.** 3 +3	**18.** 4 +6	**19.** 1 +6	**20.** 2 +8	**21.** 4 +5

Set 2

1. $3 + 8$ **2.** $6 + 8$ **3.** $5 + 8$ **4.** $9 + 7$

5. $6 + 6$ **6.** $9 + 6$ **7.** $9 + 8$ **8.** $7 + 6$

9. $8 + 8$ **10.** $5 + 9$ **11.** $9 + 4$ **12.** $8 + 3$

13. $3 + 9$ **14.** $6 + 5$ **15.** $7 + 8$ **16.** $8 + 9$

17. $7 + 7$ **18.** $9 + 9$ **19.** $6 + 9$ **20.** $8 + 7$

Set 3

1. 3 2 7 +4	**2.** 6 5 4 +2	**3.** 4 6 5 +1	**4.** 8 1 3 +7	**5.** 3 4 7 +6	**6.** 2 6 5 +5	**7.** 2 4 8 +3
8. 3 1 5 +7	**9.** 6 3 4 +5	**10.** 5 5 2 +7	**11.** 3 6 2 +8	**12.** 1 4 5 +9	**13.** 3 8 7 +0	**14.** 5 5 5 +5

Set 4

1. $8 + \underline{?} = 10$ **2.** $6 + \underline{?} = 9$ **3.** $9 + \underline{?} = 13$ **4.** $7 + \underline{?} = 15$

5. $9 + \underline{?} = 9$ **6.** $9 + \underline{?} = 15$ **7.** $2 + \underline{?} = 10$ **8.** $5 + \underline{?} = 14$

9. $5 + \underline{?} = 13$ **10.** $2 + \underline{?} = 9$ **11.** $9 + \underline{?} = 18$ **12.** $6 + \underline{?} = 13$

13. $5 + \underline{?} = 10$ **14.** $8 + \underline{?} = 17$ **15.** $3 + \underline{?} = 10$ **16.** $7 + \underline{?} = 16$

17. $8 + \underline{?} = 16$ **18.** $5 + \underline{?} = 11$ **19.** $7 + \underline{?} = 14$ **20.** $3 + \underline{?} = 12$

Set 5

1. 8 − 3	2. 13 − 8	3. 9 − 5	4. 10 − 4	5. 8 − 4	6. 18 − 9
7. 4 − 4	8. 10 − 8	9. 0 − 0	10. 17 − 9	11. 6 − 3	12. 10 − 5
13. 15 − 8	14. 12 − 7	15. 15 − 7	16. 17 − 8	17. 14 − 9	18. 15 − 9

Set 6 How many?

1.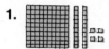

2.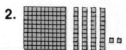

3.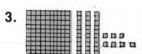

4.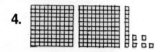

5.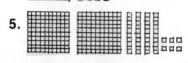

6.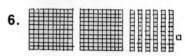

7.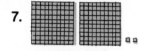

8.

9.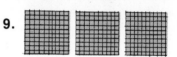

Set 7 Round to the nearest ten.

1. 74	2. 29	3. 15	4. 38	5. 93
6. 67	7. 42	8. 85	9. 56	10. 99
11. 539	12. 646	13. 475	14. 693	15. 868
16. 701	17. 382	18. 807	19. 918	20. 775.

Set 8 What does the red digit stand for?

1. 7382	2. 5482	3. 6428	4. 5906
5. 4591	6. 3617	7. 2375	8. 6374
9. 7538	10. 5432	11. 9610	12. 8526
13. 4291	14. 6750	15. 8534	16. 7783
17. 2355	18. 3069	19. 7184	20. 9195

Set 9 **In 534,621, what digit is in the**

1. hundreds place?

2. thousands place?

3. tens place?

4. ones place?

5. hundred thousands place?

6. ten thousands place?

Set 10 **< or >?**

1. 538 ⬤ 542

2. 674 ⬤ 647

3. 863 ⬤ 859

4. 5916 ⬤ 5961

5. 3827 ⬤ 2927

6. 7436 ⬤ 7099

7. 3218 ⬤ 3219

8. 8000 ⬤ 7999

9. 9301 ⬤ 9308

10. 82,164 ⬤ 59,738

11. 74,365 ⬤ 75,821

12. 521,683 ⬤ 520,317

13. 748,206 ⬤ 752,534

Set 11 **Round to the nearest thousand.**

1. 3462

2. 5578

3. 7843

4. 6803

5. 2718

6. 1605

7. 8455

8. 4500

9. 36,741

10. 52,833

11. 64,271

12. 75,672

13. 25,389

14. 76,811

15. 48,500

16. 73,999

17. 264,381

18. 502,736

19. 309,951

20. 699,821

Set 12 **In 528,364,159, what digit is in the**

1. hundreds place?

2. thousands place?

3. tens place?

4. millions place?

5. ten thousands place?

6. hundred millions place?

7. hundred thousands place?

8. ones place?

9. ten millions place?

Set 13

1. 42
   +25

2. 23
   +42

3. 53
   +30

4. 14
   +65

5. 34
   +51

6. 321
   +208

7. 235
   +302

8. 371
   +406

9. 418
   +240

10. 602
   +271

11. 502
   +341

12. 633
   +132

13. 300
   +574

14. 738
   +220

15. 521
   +400

Set 14

1. 64
   +28

2. 36
   +45

3. 79
   +18

4. 56
   +92

5. 83
   +60

6. 561
   +283

7. 728
   +149

8. 364
   +182

9. 593
   +140

10. 726
   +258

11. 426
   +490

12. 635
   +283

13. 529
   +216

14. 704
   +249

15. 652
   +281

Set 15

1. 58
   +69

2. 74
   +38

3. 87
   +56

4. 95
   +86

5. 86
   +59

6. 438
   +295

7. 753
   +189

8. 359
   +359

9. 658
   +242

10. 438
   +299

11. 555
   +376

12. 788
   +196

13. 297
   +479

14. 426
   +385

15. 385
   +426

Set 16

1. 5928
   +2813

2. 7426
   +1593

3. 5426
   +1387

4. 2964
   +1997

5. 38219
   +26543

6. 73691
   +28453

7. 91782
   +26538

8. 43027
   +15639

9. 371829
   +564283

10. 751208
   +349163

11. 271846
   +593742

12. 438296
   +341759

Set 17

1. 58
    26
    +34

2. 79
    38
    +55

3. 640
    373
    +296

4. 284
    375
    +917

5. 635
    883
    +426

6. 53
    61
    18
    +29

7. 47
    68
    95
    +36

8. 329
    474
    865
    +153

9. 278
    419
    706
    +388

10. 529
    636
    404
    +281

Set 18

1. 89
    − 23

2. 75
    − 13

3. 96
    − 42

4. 68
    − 30

5. 57
    − 25

6. 839
    − 230

7. 755
    − 142

8. 693
    − 221

9. 884
    − 354

10. 956
    − 213

11. 7829
    − 2304

12. 5384
    − 1052

13. 6977
    − 3406

14. 8594
    − 2041

15. 6385
    − 3142

Set 19

1. 60
    − 25

2. 81
    − 39

3. 73
    − 48

4. 65
    − 19

5. 93
    − 58

6. 483
    − 126

7. 562
    − 248

8. 748
    − 319

9. 391
    − 158

10. 825
    − 550

11. 926
    − 472

12. 746
    − 328

13. 839
    − 440

14. 728
    − 376

15. 950
    − 248

Set 20

1. 524
    − 158

2. 627
    − 259

3. 834
    − 258

4. 928
    − 379

5. 703
    − 265

6. 824
    − 346

7. 921
    − 586

8. 602
    − 375

9. 763
    − 498

10. 901
    − 625

11. 453
    − 289

12. 726
    − 478

13. 865
    − 689

14. 942
    − 758

15. 835
    − 599

Set 21

1. 7128
    − 3482

2. 4603
    − 2169

3. 9528
    − 3785

4. 8734
    − 5286

5. 69305
    − 43829

6. 78653
    − 26781

7. 83425
    − 42003

8. 74678
    − 58399

9. 391674
    − 176859

10. 538921
    − 252346

11. 635543
    − 382974

12. 782916
    − 634897

Set 22 Give the time.

1.

2.

3.

4.

5.

6.

7.

8.

Set 23 How many minutes from

1. 2:30 A.M. to 3:00 A.M.?

2. 4:15 P.M. to 4:30 P.M.?

3. 10:10 A.M. to 10:43 A.M.?

4. 9:15 A.M. to 10:00 A.M.?

5. 7:55 P.M. to 8:15 P.M.?

6. 6:45 P.M. to 7:35 P.M.?

7. 11:30 A.M. to 12:15 P.M.?

8. 11:55 P.M. to 12:35 A.M.?

Set 24 Give the total value in dollars.

1.

2.

3.

330

Set 25

1. 3×1 2. 3×2 3. 1×2 4. 5×2

5. 7×2 6. 7×0 7. 8×1 8. 8×0

9. 5×0 10. 6×1 11. 9×0 12. 8×2

13. 5×1 14. 4×1 15. 7×1 16. 2×2

17. 6×2 18. 6×0 19. 4×2 20. 9×2

Set 26

1. $\begin{array}{r} 3 \\ \times 9 \\ \hline \end{array}$ 2. $\begin{array}{r} 5 \\ \times 4 \\ \hline \end{array}$ 3. $\begin{array}{r} 3 \\ \times 3 \\ \hline \end{array}$ 4. $\begin{array}{r} 5 \\ \times 8 \\ \hline \end{array}$ 5. $\begin{array}{r} 4 \\ \times 8 \\ \hline \end{array}$ 6. $\begin{array}{r} 3 \\ \times 4 \\ \hline \end{array}$ 7. $\begin{array}{r} 4 \\ \times 7 \\ \hline \end{array}$

8. $\begin{array}{r} 5 \\ \times 3 \\ \hline \end{array}$ 9. $\begin{array}{r} 3 \\ \times 6 \\ \hline \end{array}$ 10. $\begin{array}{r} 4 \\ \times 4 \\ \hline \end{array}$ 11. $\begin{array}{r} 3 \\ \times 7 \\ \hline \end{array}$ 12. $\begin{array}{r} 4 \\ \times 6 \\ \hline \end{array}$ 13. $\begin{array}{r} 5 \\ \times 7 \\ \hline \end{array}$ 14. $\begin{array}{r} 3 \\ \times 8 \\ \hline \end{array}$

15. $\begin{array}{r} 4 \\ \times 5 \\ \hline \end{array}$ 16. $\begin{array}{r} 5 \\ \times 5 \\ \hline \end{array}$ 17. $\begin{array}{r} 5 \\ \times 2 \\ \hline \end{array}$ 18. $\begin{array}{r} 3 \\ \times 5 \\ \hline \end{array}$ 19. $\begin{array}{r} 5 \\ \times 6 \\ \hline \end{array}$ 20. $\begin{array}{r} 5 \\ \times 9 \\ \hline \end{array}$ 21. $\begin{array}{r} 4 \\ \times 9 \\ \hline \end{array}$

Set 27

1. $\begin{array}{r} 6 \\ \times 4 \\ \hline \end{array}$ 2. $\begin{array}{r} 7 \\ \times 1 \\ \hline \end{array}$ 3. $\begin{array}{r} 6 \\ \times 1 \\ \hline \end{array}$ 4. $\begin{array}{r} 7 \\ \times 5 \\ \hline \end{array}$ 5. $\begin{array}{r} 5 \\ \times 9 \\ \hline \end{array}$ 6. $\begin{array}{r} 7 \\ \times 7 \\ \hline \end{array}$

7. $\begin{array}{r} 7 \\ \times 3 \\ \hline \end{array}$ 8. $\begin{array}{r} 7 \\ \times 8 \\ \hline \end{array}$ 9. $\begin{array}{r} 4 \\ \times 8 \\ \hline \end{array}$ 10. $\begin{array}{r} 6 \\ \times 8 \\ \hline \end{array}$ 11. $\begin{array}{r} 7 \\ \times 2 \\ \hline \end{array}$ 12. $\begin{array}{r} 6 \\ \times 9 \\ \hline \end{array}$

13. $\begin{array}{r} 6 \\ \times 3 \\ \hline \end{array}$ 14. $\begin{array}{r} 6 \\ \times 7 \\ \hline \end{array}$ 15. $\begin{array}{r} 7 \\ \times 4 \\ \hline \end{array}$ 16. $\begin{array}{r} 7 \\ \times 9 \\ \hline \end{array}$ 17. $\begin{array}{r} 7 \\ \times 6 \\ \hline \end{array}$ 18. $\begin{array}{r} 4 \\ \times 7 \\ \hline \end{array}$

Set 28

1. $\begin{array}{r} 7 \\ \times 9 \\ \hline \end{array}$ 2. $\begin{array}{r} 8 \\ \times 7 \\ \hline \end{array}$ 3. $\begin{array}{r} 9 \\ \times 3 \\ \hline \end{array}$ 4. $\begin{array}{r} 8 \\ \times 1 \\ \hline \end{array}$ 5. $\begin{array}{r} 9 \\ \times 8 \\ \hline \end{array}$ 6. $\begin{array}{r} 9 \\ \times 6 \\ \hline \end{array}$

7. $\begin{array}{r} 8 \\ \times 8 \\ \hline \end{array}$ 8. $\begin{array}{r} 9 \\ \times 4 \\ \hline \end{array}$ 9. $\begin{array}{r} 8 \\ \times 6 \\ \hline \end{array}$ 10. $\begin{array}{r} 6 \\ \times 9 \\ \hline \end{array}$ 11. $\begin{array}{r} 9 \\ \times 7 \\ \hline \end{array}$ 12. $\begin{array}{r} 7 \\ \times 8 \\ \hline \end{array}$

13. $\begin{array}{r} 9 \\ \times 9 \\ \hline \end{array}$ 14. $\begin{array}{r} 8 \\ \times 4 \\ \hline \end{array}$ 15. $\begin{array}{r} 8 \\ \times 9 \\ \hline \end{array}$ 16. $\begin{array}{r} 9 \\ \times 5 \\ \hline \end{array}$ 17. $\begin{array}{r} 8 \\ \times 2 \\ \hline \end{array}$ 18. $\begin{array}{r} 9 \\ \times 1 \\ \hline \end{array}$

1. $3 \times \underline{?} = 24$ 2. $6 \times \underline{?} = 42$ 3. $6 \times \underline{?} = 54$ 4. $4 \times \underline{?} = 36$

5. $4 \times \underline{?} = 16$ 6. $7 \times \underline{?} = 63$ 7. $4 \times \underline{?} = 32$ 8. $9 \times \underline{?} = 81$

9. $7 \times \underline{?} = 56$ 10. $4 \times \underline{?} = 20$ 11. $8 \times \underline{?} = 48$ 12. $3 \times \underline{?} = 27$

13. $6 \times \underline{?} = 18$ 14. $5 \times \underline{?} = 40$ 15. $7 \times \underline{?} = 21$ 16. $9 \times \underline{?} = 45$

17. $7 \times \underline{?} = 49$ 18. $7 \times \underline{?} = 35$ 19. $8 \times \underline{?} = 72$ 20. $6 \times \underline{?} = 24$

Set 30

1. $15 \div 3$ 2. $24 \div 4$ 3. $24 \div 3$ 4. $35 \div 5$

5. $21 \div 3$ 6. $25 \div 5$ 7. $20 \div 4$ 8. $36 \div 4$

9. $30 \div 5$ 10. $15 \div 3$ 11. $12 \div 4$ 12. $28 \div 4$

13. $20 \div 5$ 14. $16 \div 4$ 15. $12 \div 3$ 16. $45 \div 5$

17. $18 \div 3$ 18. $40 \div 5$ 19. $32 \div 4$ 20. $27 \div 3$

Set 31

1. $6 \overline{)30}$ 2. $6 \overline{)48}$ 3. $7 \overline{)21}$ 4. $6 \overline{)6}$ 5. $7 \overline{)14}$

6. $5 \overline{)35}$ 7. $7 \overline{)28}$ 8. $6 \overline{)36}$ 9. $6 \overline{)12}$ 10. $7 \overline{)49}$

11. $7 \overline{)56}$ 12. $7 \overline{)35}$ 13. $7 \overline{)63}$ 14. $7 \overline{)42}$ 15. $6 \overline{)24}$

16. $6 \overline{)54}$ 17. $6 \overline{)18}$ 18. $4 \overline{)36}$ 19. $7 \overline{)7}$ 20. $6 \overline{)42}$

Set 32

1. $7 \overline{)56}$ 2. $9 \overline{)63}$ 3. $9 \overline{)18}$ 4. $8 \overline{)40}$ 5. $9 \overline{)72}$

6. $9 \overline{)9}$ 7. $8 \overline{)24}$ 8. $8 \overline{)16}$ 9. $9 \overline{)45}$ 10. $8 \overline{)72}$

11. $8 \overline{)48}$ 12. $7 \overline{)63}$ 13. $9 \overline{)81}$ 14. $8 \overline{)64}$ 15. $9 \overline{)27}$

16. $9 \overline{)36}$ 17. $8 \overline{)32}$ 18. $8 \overline{)56}$ 19. $9 \overline{)54}$ 20. $8 \overline{)8}$

Set 33

1. $4\overline{)23}$ 2. $5\overline{)39}$ 3. $6\overline{)37}$ 4. $8\overline{)38}$ 5. $5\overline{)41}$

6. $5\overline{)48}$ 7. $7\overline{)40}$ 8. $3\overline{)25}$ 9. $4\overline{)23}$ 10. $8\overline{)60}$

11. $7\overline{)50}$ 12. $4\overline{)18}$ 13. $9\overline{)75}$ 14. $6\overline{)41}$ 15. $3\overline{)20}$

16. $9\overline{)43}$ 17. $8\overline{)70}$ 18. $6\overline{)51}$ 19. $7\overline{)33}$ 20. $9\overline{)56}$

Set 34 What fraction is shaded?

1.   2. 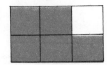   3.   4.

5.   6.   7. 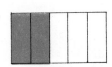   8.

Set 35 What fraction of the blocks are blue?

1.   2.   3.   4.

5.   6.   7.   8.

Set 36

1. $\frac{1}{2}$ of 8   2. $\frac{1}{3}$ of 3   3. $\frac{1}{4}$ of 12   4. $\frac{1}{2}$ of 18

5. $\frac{1}{6}$ of 24   6. $\frac{1}{2}$ of 6   7. $\frac{1}{3}$ of 6   8. $\frac{1}{4}$ of 20

9. $\frac{1}{3}$ of 21   10. $\frac{1}{6}$ of 30   11. $\frac{1}{2}$ of 10   12. $\frac{1}{5}$ of 30

13. $\frac{1}{8}$ of 16   14. $\frac{1}{4}$ of 16   15. $\frac{1}{8}$ of 24   16. $\frac{1}{3}$ of 12

17. $\frac{1}{2}$ of 12   18. $\frac{1}{3}$ of 9   19. $\frac{1}{5}$ of 20   20. $\frac{1}{4}$ of 8

Set 37

1. $\frac{2}{3}$ of 9
2. $\frac{2}{5}$ of 10
3. $\frac{3}{4}$ of 8
4. $\frac{3}{8}$ of 16

5. $\frac{4}{9}$ of 9
6. $\frac{4}{5}$ of 20
7. $\frac{2}{3}$ of 6
8. $\frac{5}{8}$ of 24

9. $\frac{2}{3}$ of 18
10. $\frac{2}{9}$ of 18
11. $\frac{5}{8}$ of 32
12. $\frac{3}{4}$ of 12

13. $\frac{3}{5}$ of 25
14. $\frac{2}{3}$ of 15
15. $\frac{2}{5}$ of 30
16. $\frac{5}{9}$ of 36

17. $\frac{3}{4}$ of 20
18. $\frac{3}{8}$ of 40
19. $\frac{5}{6}$ of 42
20. $\frac{2}{3}$ of 24

Set 38

1. $\frac{1}{2} = \frac{?}{4}$
2. $\frac{1}{3} = \frac{?}{6}$
3. $\frac{2}{3} = \frac{?}{6}$
4. $\frac{1}{2} = \frac{?}{8}$

5. $\frac{2}{3} = \frac{?}{12}$
6. $\frac{3}{4} = \frac{?}{8}$
7. $\frac{1}{2} = \frac{?}{6}$
8. $\frac{5}{6} = \frac{?}{12}$

9. $\frac{1}{4} = \frac{?}{12}$
10. $\frac{3}{8} = \frac{?}{16}$
11. $\frac{2}{3} = \frac{?}{9}$
12. $\frac{1}{3} = \frac{?}{12}$

13. $\frac{5}{8} = \frac{?}{16}$
14. $\frac{1}{3} = \frac{?}{9}$
15. $\frac{3}{4} = \frac{?}{12}$
16. $\frac{1}{4} = \frac{?}{12}$

Set 39 Reduce to lowest terms.

1. $\frac{2}{4}$
2. $\frac{2}{6}$
3. $\frac{6}{8}$
4. $\frac{2}{8}$
5. $\frac{4}{8}$
6. $\frac{4}{16}$
7. $\frac{3}{9}$

8. $\frac{4}{12}$
9. $\frac{5}{20}$
10. $\frac{3}{6}$
11. $\frac{8}{12}$
12. $\frac{4}{6}$
13. $\frac{6}{16}$
14. $\frac{15}{20}$

15. $\frac{10}{16}$
16. $\frac{6}{12}$
17. $\frac{6}{9}$
18. $\frac{3}{12}$
19. $\frac{5}{10}$
20. $\frac{9}{12}$
21. $\frac{5}{15}$

Set 40

1. $\frac{1}{3}$
$+\frac{1}{3}$

2. $\frac{1}{4}$
$+\frac{1}{4}$

3. $\frac{5}{9}$
$+\frac{1}{9}$

4. $\frac{3}{7}$
$+\frac{2}{7}$

5. $\frac{3}{8}$
$+\frac{2}{8}$

6. $\frac{5}{8}$
$+\frac{1}{8}$

7. $\frac{5}{6}$
$+\frac{2}{6}$

8. $\frac{3}{4}$
$+\frac{2}{4}$

9. $\frac{2}{6}$
$+\frac{1}{6}$

10. $\frac{1}{8}$
$+\frac{2}{8}$

11. $\frac{3}{10}$
$+\frac{4}{10}$

12. $\frac{3}{6}$
$+\frac{2}{6}$

13. $\frac{4}{5}$
$+\frac{1}{5}$

14. $\frac{4}{6}$
$+\frac{1}{6}$

Set 41

1. $\frac{1}{2} + \frac{1}{4}$ 2. $\frac{1}{3} + \frac{5}{6}$ 3. $\frac{5}{12} + \frac{1}{4}$ 4. $\frac{1}{4} + \frac{1}{8}$

5. $\frac{2}{3} + \frac{1}{6}$ 6. $\frac{1}{3} + \frac{2}{9}$ 7. $\frac{1}{2} + \frac{3}{8}$ 8. $\frac{4}{9} + \frac{2}{3}$

9. $\frac{2}{5} + \frac{3}{10}$ 10. $\frac{3}{4} + \frac{1}{2}$ 11. $\frac{3}{4} + \frac{1}{8}$ 12. $\frac{2}{3} + \frac{1}{6}$

13. $\frac{1}{12} + \frac{2}{3}$ 14. $\frac{2}{5} + \frac{1}{10}$ 15. $\frac{3}{8} + \frac{1}{4}$ 16. $\frac{5}{12} + \frac{1}{3}$

Set 42

1. $\frac{4}{9}$ 2. $\frac{2}{8}$ 3. $\frac{5}{8}$ 4. $\frac{4}{5}$ 5. $\frac{3}{8}$ 6. $\frac{4}{6}$ 7. $\frac{2}{6}$
$-\frac{1}{9}$ $-\frac{1}{8}$ $-\frac{1}{8}$ $-\frac{1}{5}$ $-\frac{2}{8}$ $-\frac{1}{6}$ $-\frac{1}{6}$

8. $\frac{3}{6}$ 9. $\frac{5}{6}$ 10. $\frac{5}{10}$ 11. $\frac{3}{7}$ 12. $\frac{4}{10}$ 13. $\frac{6}{10}$ 14. $\frac{3}{4}$
$-\frac{2}{6}$ $-\frac{2}{6}$ $-\frac{1}{10}$ $-\frac{2}{7}$ $-\frac{3}{10}$ $-\frac{4}{10}$ $-\frac{2}{4}$

Set 43

1. $\frac{5}{9} - \frac{1}{3}$ 2. $\frac{5}{8} - \frac{1}{2}$ 3. $\frac{5}{12} - \frac{1}{3}$ 4. $\frac{5}{6} - \frac{1}{3}$

5. $\frac{4}{5} - \frac{1}{10}$ 6. $\frac{1}{2} - \frac{1}{4}$ 7. $\frac{5}{8} - \frac{1}{4}$ 8. $\frac{3}{2} - \frac{3}{4}$

9. $\frac{3}{4} - \frac{3}{8}$ 10. $\frac{2}{3} - \frac{1}{6}$ 11. $\frac{8}{9} - \frac{2}{3}$ 12. $\frac{3}{5} - \frac{1}{10}$

13. $\frac{7}{8} - \frac{3}{4}$ 14. $\frac{5}{12} - \frac{1}{4}$ 15. $\frac{7}{12} - \frac{1}{2}$ 16. $\frac{7}{10} - \frac{1}{2}$

Set 44 Change to fractions.

1. $5\frac{1}{2}$ 2. $6\frac{1}{2}$ 3. $7\frac{1}{2}$ 4. $1\frac{1}{3}$ 5. $1\frac{2}{3}$ 6. $2\frac{1}{3}$

7. $2\frac{2}{3}$ 8. $2\frac{1}{4}$ 9. $2\frac{3}{4}$ 10. $3\frac{1}{4}$ 11. $3\frac{3}{4}$ 12. $5\frac{2}{3}$

13. $6\frac{1}{5}$ 14. $7\frac{3}{5}$ 15. $1\frac{1}{6}$ 16. $1\frac{5}{6}$ 17. $3\frac{3}{8}$ 18. $4\frac{7}{8}$

Set 45 Change to mixed form.

1. $\dfrac{7}{3}$ 2. $\dfrac{8}{3}$ 3. $\dfrac{9}{4}$ 4. $\dfrac{10}{3}$ 5. $\dfrac{9}{2}$ 6. $\dfrac{11}{2}$

7. $\dfrac{5}{4}$ 8. $\dfrac{7}{4}$ 9. $\dfrac{9}{5}$ 10. $\dfrac{11}{5}$ 11. $\dfrac{15}{4}$ 12. $\dfrac{17}{6}$

13. $\dfrac{18}{5}$ 14. $\dfrac{12}{7}$ 15. $\dfrac{14}{5}$ 16. $\dfrac{16}{3}$ 17. $\dfrac{17}{3}$ 18. $\dfrac{25}{6}$

Set 46

1. 23   2. 10   3. 20   4. 40   5. 32   6. 12
   ×2   ×6   ×3   ×2   ×2   ×3

7. 30   8. 30   9. 11   10. 44   11. 22   12. 12
   ×2   ×3   ×5   ×2   ×3   ×4

13. 12   14. 31   15. 11   16. 20   17. 11   18. 21
    ×4   ×3   ×8   ×4   ×6   ×4

Set 47

1. 52   2. 81   3. 51   4. 52   5. 72   6. 62
   ×4   ×5   ×6   ×3   ×4   ×3

7. 42   8. 60   9. 62   10. 61   11. 83   12. 74
   ×4   ×7   ×2   ×6   ×3   ×2

13. 43   14. 82   15. 91   16. 73   17. 50   18. 42
    ×3   ×4   ×8   ×2   ×6   ×3

Set 48

1. 35   2. 83   3. 97   4. 59   5. 73   6. 53
   ×4   ×5   ×3   ×2   ×6   ×8

7. 62   8. 95   9. 36   10. 47   11. 44   12. 82
   ×5   ×4   ×8   ×6   ×5   ×7

13. 84   14. 48   15. 75   16. 57   17. 29   18. 64
    ×5   ×6   ×4   ×3   ×8   ×7

Set 49

1. 258
   ×3

2. 147
   ×5

3. 248
   ×3

4. 274
   ×2

5. 128
   ×7

6. 156
   ×6

7. 276
   ×3

8. 147
   ×6

9. 168
   ×4

10. 248
    ×4

11. 364
    ×2

12. 195
    ×5

13. 187
    ×5

14. 296
    ×3

15. 426
    ×2

16. 238
    ×4

17. 259
    ×3

18. 483
    ×2

Set 50

1. 568
   ×4

2. 735
   ×5

3. 543
   ×6

4. 698
   ×7

5. 375
   ×6

6. 492
   ×8

7. 594
   ×8

8. 384
   ×3

9. 756
   ×6

10. 468
    ×7

11. 756
    ×5

12. 866
    ×7

13. 687
    ×5

14. 885
    ×7

15. 466
    ×4

16. 853
    ×9

17. 558
    ×8

18. 399
    ×9

Set 51

1. 2359
   ×3

2. 1948
   ×5

3. 2096
   ×8

4. 5736
   ×5

5. 7846
   ×7

6. 7492
   ×7

7. 3429
   ×4

8. 4524
   ×7

9. 4620
   ×6

10. 9528
    ×8

11. 6753
    ×5

12. 8786
    ×5

13. 3658
    ×4

14. 6738
    ×9

15. 5989
    ×6

Set 52

1. $3\overline{)39}$

2. $2\overline{)24}$

3. $3\overline{)30}$

4. $4\overline{)40}$

5. $3\overline{)63}$

6. $3\overline{)93}$

7. $3\overline{)60}$

8. $2\overline{)42}$

9. $4\overline{)84}$

10. $2\overline{)88}$

11. $6\overline{)66}$

12. $2\overline{)64}$

13. $5\overline{)55}$

14. $2\overline{)68}$

15. $2\overline{)28}$

16. $3\overline{)36}$

17. $7\overline{)70}$

18. $4\overline{)48}$

19. $3\overline{)90}$

20. $8\overline{)80}$

Set 53

1. $3\overline{)42}$ 2. $7\overline{)84}$ 3. $3\overline{)48}$ 4. $6\overline{)72}$ 5. $3\overline{)54}$

6. $4\overline{)56}$ 7. $4\overline{)52}$ 8. $5\overline{)75}$ 9. $6\overline{)78}$ 10. $4\overline{)92}$

11. $3\overline{)72}$ 12. $6\overline{)90}$ 13. $5\overline{)95}$ 14. $3\overline{)54}$ 15. $6\overline{)84}$

16. $5\overline{)65}$ 17. $3\overline{)81}$ 18. $4\overline{)64}$ 19. $8\overline{)96}$ 20. $4\overline{)96}$

Set 54

1. $5\overline{)63}$ 2. $3\overline{)59}$ 3. $4\overline{)67}$ 4. $8\overline{)90}$ 5. $6\overline{)77}$

6. $8\overline{)95}$ 7. $7\overline{)94}$ 8. $3\overline{)38}$ 9. $6\overline{)82}$ 10. $5\overline{)73}$

11. $4\overline{)57}$ 12. $7\overline{)85}$ 13. $8\overline{)99}$ 14. $8\overline{)94}$ 15. $7\overline{)90}$

16. $2\overline{)39}$ 17. $2\overline{)47}$ 18. $5\overline{)68}$ 19. $4\overline{)95}$ 20. $6\overline{)79}$

Set 55

1. $3\overline{)472}$ 2. $7\overline{)853}$ 3. $5\overline{)927}$ 4. $4\overline{)638}$ 5. $7\overline{)827}$

6. $3\overline{)457}$ 7. $6\overline{)946}$ 8. $4\overline{)827}$ 9. $7\overline{)904}$ 10. $3\overline{)947}$

11. $2\overline{)315}$ 12. $5\overline{)942}$ 13. $4\overline{)653}$ 14. $2\overline{)358}$ 15. $6\overline{)928}$

16. $6\overline{)708}$ 17. $3\overline{)721}$ 18. $5\overline{)850}$ 19. $8\overline{)965}$ 20. $8\overline{)942}$

Set 56

1. $7\overline{)156}$ 2. $8\overline{)414}$ 3. $6\overline{)193}$ 4. $7\overline{)584}$ 5. $4\overline{)304}$

6. $5\overline{)271}$ 7. $7\overline{)426}$ 8. $6\overline{)246}$ 9. $8\overline{)325}$ 10. $7\overline{)342}$

11. $8\overline{)608}$ 12. $6\overline{)208}$ 13. $6\overline{)528}$ 14. $5\overline{)476}$ 15. $9\overline{)627}$

16. $9\overline{)438}$ 17. $7\overline{)623}$ 18. $4\overline{)362}$ 19. $8\overline{)219}$ 20. $6\overline{)595}$

Set 57

1. $9\overline{)3628}$ 2. $8\overline{)4216}$ 3. $5\overline{)5374}$ 4. $6\overline{)3728}$

5. $2\overline{)5437}$ 6. $5\overline{)7928}$ 7. $4\overline{)6819}$ 8. $2\overline{)4609}$

9. $9\overline{)7034}$ 10. $3\overline{)2174}$ 11. $7\overline{)2738}$ 12. $5\overline{)8555}$

13. $9\overline{)3914}$ 14. $8\overline{)9174}$ 15. $4\overline{)8326}$ 16. $6\overline{)9266}$

Set 58

1. $\begin{array}{r}12\\ \times10\\ \hline\end{array}$ 2. $\begin{array}{r}23\\ \times10\\ \hline\end{array}$ 3. $\begin{array}{r}26\\ \times10\\ \hline\end{array}$ 4. $\begin{array}{r}34\\ \times10\\ \hline\end{array}$ 5. $\begin{array}{r}42\\ \times10\\ \hline\end{array}$

6. $\begin{array}{r}56\\ \times10\\ \hline\end{array}$ 7. $\begin{array}{r}74\\ \times10\\ \hline\end{array}$ 8. $\begin{array}{r}65\\ \times10\\ \hline\end{array}$ 9. $\begin{array}{r}86\\ \times10\\ \hline\end{array}$ 10. $\begin{array}{r}92\\ \times10\\ \hline\end{array}$

11. $\begin{array}{r}125\\ \times10\\ \hline\end{array}$ 12. $\begin{array}{r}136\\ \times10\\ \hline\end{array}$ 13. $\begin{array}{r}158\\ \times10\\ \hline\end{array}$ 14. $\begin{array}{r}232\\ \times10\\ \hline\end{array}$ 15. $\begin{array}{r}250\\ \times10\\ \hline\end{array}$

Set 59

1. $\begin{array}{r}24\\ \times20\\ \hline\end{array}$ 2. $\begin{array}{r}28\\ \times40\\ \hline\end{array}$ 3. $\begin{array}{r}36\\ \times60\\ \hline\end{array}$ 4. $\begin{array}{r}45\\ \times30\\ \hline\end{array}$ 5. $\begin{array}{r}56\\ \times70\\ \hline\end{array}$

6. $\begin{array}{r}78\\ \times50\\ \hline\end{array}$ 7. $\begin{array}{r}84\\ \times90\\ \hline\end{array}$ 8. $\begin{array}{r}65\\ \times80\\ \hline\end{array}$ 9. $\begin{array}{r}92\\ \times40\\ \hline\end{array}$ 10. $\begin{array}{r}68\\ \times60\\ \hline\end{array}$

11. $\begin{array}{r}120\\ \times30\\ \hline\end{array}$ 12. $\begin{array}{r}136\\ \times70\\ \hline\end{array}$ 13. $\begin{array}{r}245\\ \times20\\ \hline\end{array}$ 14. $\begin{array}{r}286\\ \times60\\ \hline\end{array}$ 15. $\begin{array}{r}316\\ \times50\\ \hline\end{array}$

16. $\begin{array}{r}426\\ \times80\\ \hline\end{array}$ 17. $\begin{array}{r}538\\ \times60\\ \hline\end{array}$ 18. $\begin{array}{r}673\\ \times70\\ \hline\end{array}$ 19. $\begin{array}{r}825\\ \times40\\ \hline\end{array}$ 20. $\begin{array}{r}926\\ \times70\\ \hline\end{array}$

Set 60

1. $\begin{array}{r}42\\ \times24\\ \hline\end{array}$ 2. $\begin{array}{r}53\\ \times32\\ \hline\end{array}$ 3. $\begin{array}{r}58\\ \times48\\ \hline\end{array}$ 4. $\begin{array}{r}65\\ \times52\\ \hline\end{array}$ 5. $\begin{array}{r}54\\ \times46\\ \hline\end{array}$

6. $\begin{array}{r}85\\ \times45\\ \hline\end{array}$ 7. $\begin{array}{r}78\\ \times34\\ \hline\end{array}$ 8. $\begin{array}{r}55\\ \times43\\ \hline\end{array}$ 9. $\begin{array}{r}75\\ \times53\\ \hline\end{array}$ 10. $\begin{array}{r}84\\ \times36\\ \hline\end{array}$

11. $\begin{array}{r}87\\ \times63\\ \hline\end{array}$ 12. $\begin{array}{r}39\\ \times28\\ \hline\end{array}$ 13. $\begin{array}{r}66\\ \times54\\ \hline\end{array}$ 14. $\begin{array}{r}95\\ \times82\\ \hline\end{array}$ 15. $\begin{array}{r}53\\ \times62\\ \hline\end{array}$

Set 61

1. 346 ×35	2. 354 ×27	3. 427 ×42	4. 529 ×57	5. 269 ×34
6. 635 ×58	7. 562 ×64	8. 257 ×28	9. 683 ×56	10. 294 ×43
11. 362 ×75	12. 283 ×36	13. 706 ×59	14. 316 ×29	15. 445 ×48

Set 62

23 ×0 0	23 ×1 23	23 ×2 46	23 ×3 69	23 ×4 92	23 ×5 115	23 ×6 138	23 ×7 161	23 ×8 184	23 ×9 207

1. 23)529   2. 23)942   3. 23)836   4. 23)375   5. 23)926

6. 23)784   7. 23)609   8. 23)721   9. 23)416   10. 23)835

11. 23)356   12. 23)471   13. 23)658   14. 23)592   15. 23)726

Set 63

1. 12)794   2. 33)960   3. 24)595   4. 14)673   5. 28)753

6. 35)573   7. 33)709   8. 32)673   9. 26)800   10. 16)960

11. 19)870   12. 13)863   13. 21)792   14. 31)642   15. 32)783

16. 25)658   17. 42)928   18. 36)859   19. 15)829   20. 43)952

Set 64 How much is shaded?
Give a decimal answer.

1.   2.   3.   4.

5.    6. 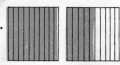   7.    8.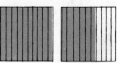

Set 65 How much is shaded?
Give a decimal answer.

1.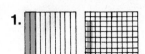

2.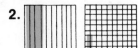

3.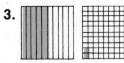

4.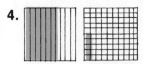

5.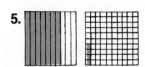

6.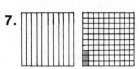

7.

8.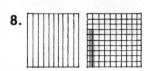

Set 66

1. 3.6 +2.2	2. 5.3 +2.4	3. 4.3 +3.5	4. 6.2 +3.4	5. 5.4 +2.3
6. 3.6 +2.8	7. 4.9 +3.6	8. 7.5 +1.6	9. .52 +.38	10. .74 +.18
11. 2.8 +2.8	12. 7.6 +3.9	13. .46 +.38	14. 8.3 +5.7	15. 4.7 +9.0

Set 67

1. 7.6 − 2.3	2. 5.9 − 1.4	3. 7.4 − 3.4	4. 6.4 − 2.1	5. 8.1 − 3.0
6. 6.3 − 2.8	7. .85 − .46	8. .72 − .59	9. 7.3 − 2.9	10. 7.0 − 4.8
11. .95 − .76	12. .82 − .75	13. 6.3 − 3.8	14. 9.8 − 4.9	15. .65 − .26

Set 68

1. .36 +.2	2. .46 +.9	3. .6 +.58	4. 1.3 +2	5. 6 +4.8
6. 5.4 +8	7. .76 +.2	8. .6 +.93	9. .75 +.5	10. .93 +.8
11. .8 − .23	12. 6.3 − 4	13. .5 − .36	14. .7 − .48	15. 6 − 3.4

341

Glossary

addend A number used in an addition problem.

$$9 \leftarrow \text{addend}$$
$$\underline{+4} \leftarrow \text{addend}$$
$$13 \leftarrow \text{sum}$$

angle A figure formed by two rays with the same endpoint.

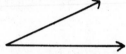

area The number of unit squares that cover a figure. The area of this figure is 5 square centimeters.

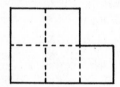

average The average of 4, 5, 5, 7, and 9 is 6. To find the average, add the numbers and divide by the number of numbers.

Celsius temperature (°C) The metric temperature scale in which 0°C is the freezing point of water and 100°C is the boiling point of water.

centimeter A metric unit of length. One centimeter is one hundredth of a meter.

circle A curved figure with all points a given distance from the center.

common multiple 30 is a common multiple of 5 and 6 because it is a multiple of 5 and a multiple of 6.

cone A solid figure shaped like this:

congruent figures Figures that have the same size and shape.

cube A rectangular solid ("box") with all edges the same length.

cylinder A solid figure shaped like this:

decimal In a decimal, a dot (decimal point) is written between the ones place and tenths place.

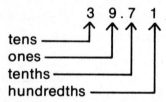

denominator In $\frac{2}{3}$, the denominator is 3.

diameter The distance across a circle through its center.

2 cm

difference The answer to a subtraction problem.

$$7$$
$$\underline{-3}$$
$$4 \leftarrow \text{difference}$$

digit Any one of the symbols 0, 1, 2, 3, 4, 5, 6, 7, 8, and 9.

equation A sentence with an equals sign, such as

$$3 \times 9 = 27$$

equivalent fractions Fractions for the same number. $\frac{1}{2}$, $\frac{2}{4}$, and $\frac{3}{6}$ are equivalent fractions.

even number A number that can be divided evenly by 2. The numbers 2, 4, 6, 8, 10, and 12 are even.

factors Numbers used in a multiplication problem.

$$\begin{array}{r} 8 \leftarrow \text{factor} \\ \times 6 \leftarrow \text{factor} \\ \hline 48 \leftarrow \text{product} \end{array}$$

Fahrenheit temperature (°F) The temperature scale in which 32°F is the freezing point of water and 212°F is the boiling point of water.

fraction A number such as $\frac{1}{2}$, $\frac{3}{4}$, and $\frac{4}{6}$.

gram A unit of weight (mass) in the metric system. One gram is one thousandth of a kilogram.

graph A picture used to show numerical information.

greater than A comparison of two numbers that are not the same. The symbol is >. For example, 7 > 2. (Another comparison is *less than*.)

kilogram A unit of weight (mass) in the metric system. A kilogram is 1000 grams.

kilometer A unit of length in the metric system. A kilometer is 1000 meters.

less than A comparison of two numbers that are not the same. The symbol is <. For example, 3 < 8. (Another comparison is *greater than*.)

line of symmetry If a figure can be folded along a line so the two parts of the figure match, the fold line is a line of symmetry.

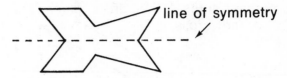
line of symmetry

liter A unit of volume in the metric system.

meter A unit of length in the metric system. A meter is 100 centimeters.

metric system An international system of measurement that uses meter, liter, gram, and Celsius temperature.

milliliter A unit of volume in the metric system. One milliliter is one thousandth of a liter.

mixed number A number that has a whole-number part and a fraction part. $2\frac{3}{4}$ is a mixed number.

multiple A product. 0, 4, 8, 12, 16, 20, and so on, are multiples of 4.

numerator In $\frac{2}{3}$, the numerator is 2.

odd number The whole numbers 1, 3, 5, 7, 9, 11, and so on, are odd numbers. An odd number cannot be divided evenly by 2.

order property of addition The order in which two numbers are added does not change the sum. Also called the commutative property of addition.

$$7 + 9 = 9 + 7$$

order property of multiplication The order in which two numbers are multiplied does not change the product. Also called the commutative property of multiplication.

$$7 \times 9 = 9 \times 7$$

ordinal number The numbers *first*, *second*, *third*, *fourth*, *fifth*, and so on, are ordinal numbers. They tell the order of objects.

parallel lines Lines in a plane that do not cross.

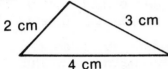

perimeter The distance around a figure. The sum of the lengths of the sides.

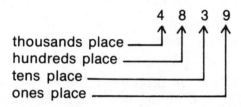

The perimeter is 9 cm.

place value The value given to the place, or position, of a digit in a numeral.

```
        4   8   3   9
thousands place ┘   │   │   │
hundreds place ─────┘   │   │
tens place ─────────────┘   │
ones place ─────────────────┘
```

prime number 2, 3, 5, 7, 11, 13, and so on, are prime numbers. They cannot be obtained by multiplying smaller whole numbers.

product The answer to a multiplication problem.

$$
\begin{array}{r}
7 \\
\times 8 \\
\hline
56 \leftarrow \text{product}
\end{array}
$$

pyramid A solid figure shaped like this:

quotient The answer to a division problem.

$$
\begin{array}{r}
7 \leftarrow \text{quotient} \\
8\overline{)56}
\end{array}
$$

radius The distance from the center of a circle to the circle.

ray A part of a line that has one endpoint. This is ray *AB*.

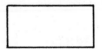

rectangle A figure with four sides and four square corners.

rectangular solid A box whose flat surfaces are all rectangles. A rectangular solid has length, width, and height.

remainder The number "left over" after a division.

$$
\begin{array}{r}
5 \\
3\overline{)16} \\
-15 \\
\hline
1 \leftarrow \text{remainder}
\end{array}
$$

right angle An angle that forms a square corner.

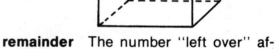

round To replace a number by another one that is easier to use. You round a number to the nearest ten by choosing the nearest multiple of ten. (5 is rounded up.)

$13 \rightarrow 10 \quad 27 \rightarrow 30 \quad 45 \rightarrow 50$

You round a number to the nearest hundred by choosing the nearest multiple of one hundred.

$487 \rightarrow 500 \quad 1238 \rightarrow 1200 \quad 550 \rightarrow 600$

segment Part of a line that has two endpoints. This is segment AB, segment BA, $\overline{AB}$, or $\overline{BA}$.

sphere The shape of a ball.

square A rectangle with four sides that are all the same length.

sum The answer to an addition problem.

$$\begin{array}{r} 23 \\ +58 \\ \hline 81 \end{array} \leftarrow \text{sum}$$

symmetry A figure has symmetry if it can be folded so the two parts of the figure match.

triangle A figure with three sides.

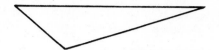

vertex The point at the "corner" of an angle, plane figure, or solid figure.

vertex   vertex   vertex

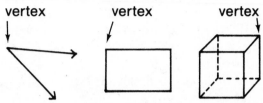

volume The number of unit cubes that fit inside an object.
The volume is 12 cubic centimeters.

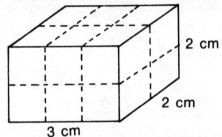

2 cm
2 cm
3 cm

whole number Any of the numbers 0, 1, 2, 3, 4, and so on.

Index